Pocket Guide
WILD
FLOWERS
OF BRITAIN AND NORTHERN EUROPE

DAVID SUTTON

LAROUSSE

Larousse plc
Elsley House, 24-30 Great Titchfield Street,
London W1P 7AD

This edition published by Larousse 1995
10 9 8 7 6 5 4 3 2

BRITISH LIBRARY CATALOGUING-IN-PUBLICATION DATA
A catalogue record for this book is available from
the British Library

ISBN 0 7523 0018 0

Senior Editor: Michèle Byam
Assistant Editor: Mandy Cleeve
Design: Smiljka Surla

Colour separations: Bright Arts, Hong Kong
Printed in Hong Kong

Contents

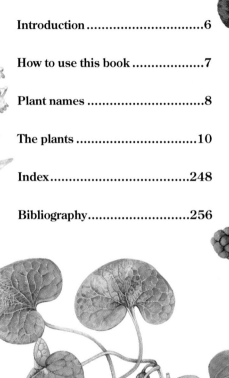

Introduction

This Pocket Guide is designed to be taken with you when you take a walk in the countryside or through parts of towns where plants are left to grow wild. Wherever possible, take the book to the plant and not *vice versa*. It is illegal to dig up wild plants in several countries, and the picking of wild flowers by 'flower lovers' has led to the virtual extinction of many attractive species.

In an illustrated Pocket Guide to plants, it is not possible to include all species for the area: a standard set of European floras and illustrations would take up one or two library shelves and would be far too costly and heavy to take into the countryside. A selection must be made. The main categories for exclusion are non-flowering plants, such as conifers, ferns and mosses; trees and shrubs, with the exception of plants such as Heathers and Roses which are usually thought of as 'flowers'; and grass-like plants including sedges and rushes – for all of these are identified using more technical detail and require specialist treatment. Preference has been given to the common and widespread plants. Many of the foreign species that have become naturalized are included; they are now often more common than the native plants.

The final selection of more than 800 species gives a reasonable coverage of at least the common plants of the British Isles, Ireland, northern France, Belgium, Luxembourg, Holland, West Germany and Denmark, and includes many plants of Norway and Sweden. Some plants have been included because they are highly distinctive and well known, despite their rarity (for example, Lady's-slipper: page 247).

Equipment

Finding and identifying wild flowers is an immensely satisfying hobby requiring a minimum of expense. A hand-lens with a magnification of about ten times is a useful purchase for examining the structure of flowers. It is possible to buy one with a small scale attached for making accurate measurements. A notebook is useful for recording details of the plant, particularly the colouring, number, relative size and extent of fusion of the petals; the arrangement and division of the leaves; and the sort of fruit, including any method by which it opens.

You may wish to record your 'find' with a photograph. A single-lens reflex camera is the most useful sort of camera for general photography of flowers. In order to see any detail of small flowers it is necessary to buy some sort of close-up lens, preferably giving about 1:1 reproduction. When taking a picture, bear in mind that the flower is usually much brighter than its background. It may be necessary to under-expose the film by one or even two f.-stops to avoid losing detail in the petals. Using an electronic flash can make it easier to obtain good depth of focus, sharpness and reliable exposures, but gives a less 'natural' result. Try and identify your plant in the field wherever possible, because identification from photographs can prove difficult.

HOW TO USE THIS BOOK

If you have a rough idea of the identity of the plant you have found, turn to the relevant part of the book (using the colour codes explained on page 8) and you will find similar species grouped on adjacent pages. Match the species against the illustrations, but always check through the description for confirmation. The description of the plant is mostly summarized in a fact panel, which contains the same elements for every species. This layout departs from

the practice in most Pocket Guides and floras, where the descriptions are often very brief and inconsistent.

The arrangement of species on a page is for a main species (of which several different elements are illustrated) and up to four further similar species. For the similar species, only the parts of the plant used for identification are shown, rather than a whole plant or flowering shoot. These similar species are often as common as the first.

The colour shows which group of plants each species belongs to. Use it to help you find the different groups as you flick through the book. The colour code is explained on page 8.

A text summarizes the overall look of the plant, drawing attention to its most important distinguishing features, and adds points of interest regarding its biology, history or significance to humankind.

Up to four similar species are illustrated on the same page, along with details of how they differ from the main species.

Labels pick out the best clues to identification.

Accurate illustrations of a whole plant or flowering shoot, with details of the flowers, fruits or other parts of the plant important for identification.

A fact panel provides a detailed summary of the type and size of the plant; where and when to look for it; the form of the stems, leaves and underground parts, flower-heads and flowers, fruits and seeds.

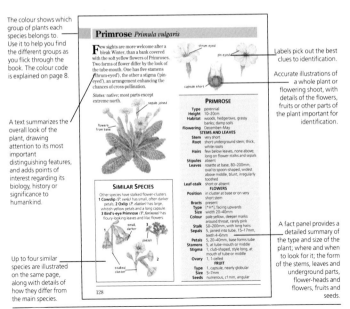

Primrose *Primula vulgaris*

Few sights are more welcome after a bleak Winter, than a bank covered with the soft yellow flowers of Primroses. Two forms of flower differ by the look of the tube-mouth. One has five stamens ('thrum-eyed'), the other a stigma ('pin-eyed'), an arrangement enhancing the chances of cross-pollination.

Status: native; most parts except extreme north.

thrum eyed

pin eyed

capsule short

sepals joined

flowers from base

SIMILAR SPECIES

Other species have stalked flower-clusters. **1 Cowslip** (*P. veris*) has small, often darker petals, **2 Oxlip** (*P. elatior*) has large, whitish-yellow petals and a long capsule. **3 Bird's-eye Primrose** (*P. farinosa*) has floury-looking leaves and lilac flowers.

small, darker

pinkish

stalked cluster

PRIMROSE	
Type	perennial
Height	10–20cm
Habitat	woods, hedgerows, grassy banks; damp soils
Flowering	December–May
STEMS AND LEAVES	
Stem	very short
Root	short underground stem; thick, white roots
Hairs	few below leaves, none above; long on flower-stalks and sepals
Stipules	absent
Leaves	rosette at base, 80–200mm, oval to spoon-shaped, widest above middle, blunt, irregularly toothed
Leaf-stalk	short or absent
FLOWERS	
Position	in cluster at base or on very short stem
Bracts	present
Type	[*H*], facing upwards
Colour	pale yellow, deeper marks around throat, rarely pink
Stalk	50–200mm, with long hairs
Sepals	5, joined into tube, 15–17mm, teeth 4–6mm
Petals	5, 20–40mm, base forms tube
Stamens	5, at tube-mouth or middle
Stigma	1, club-shaped, style long, at mouth of tube or middle
Ovary	1, 1-celled
FRUIT	
Type	1, capsule, nearly globular
Size	5–7mm
Seeds	numerous, c1mm, angular

128

Introduction

PLANT NAMES

Common names vary greatly and some species have over a hundred local names in a single country. As a simplification, English-language names have been standardized to the list published by the Botanical Society of the British Isles (Dony, Jury and Perring, 1986). Plants lacking a common name are usually recently naturalized, or grow only in certain countries covered by the book.

Scientific names are more stable and international in usage. Most are consistent with the standard European flora (Tutin *et al.* (Editors), 1964–1980) but some are updated using more recent British floras. Each scientific name is made up of a genus (plural: genera) name, with an initial capital letter, and a species name starting with a small letter. A third, subspecies (abbreviated subsp.) name is used to distinguish geographical variation within a species. A multiplication symbol (×) between the first two names indicates a hybrid between two species.

Order of plants

The plants in this book are arranged more or less in systematic order, those genera with similar construction of flowers and fruit being placed together in families and given a single name in the list below. Each group of families is given a colour reference marker. Use this coloured square at the corner of the pages to help you find the different groups of plants as you flick through the book.

Asarabacca and Mistletoe

Docks, Goosefoots, Hop and Nettles

Pink and Purslanes

Buttercups and Water-lilies

Cabbages, Poppies, Fumitories & Mignonettes

Stonecrops, Saxifrages and Sundews

Roses and Grass-of-Parnassus

Peas

Crane's-bills, Spurges, Wood-sorrels & Flaxes

St John's-worts, Milkworts and Balsams

Violets, Mallows, Rock-roses and Cucumbers

Willowherbs, Loosestrifes and Water-milfoils

Carrots and Ivy

Primroses, Heathers, Wintergreens and Thrift

Bedstraws, Gentians and Periwinkles

Bindweeds, Jacob's ladder & Water-starworts

Mints and Forget-me-nots

Figworts, Nightshades, Butterworts and Broomrapes

Plantains

Valerians, Teasels, Honeysuckles and Moschatel

Daisies and Bellflowers

Arrowhead, Frogbit and Flowering-rush

Lilies, Daffodils and Irises

Orchids, Lords-and Ladies and Duckweeds

Pocket Guide
WILD
FLOWERS
OF BRITAIN AND NORTHERN EUROPE

Asarabacca *Asarum europaeum*

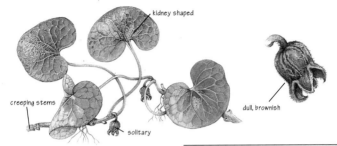

kidney shaped

creeping stems

solitary

dull, brownish

The lustrous, kidney-shaped leaves of this species are more noticeable than the curious 3-lobed flowers which are held close to the ground. Both the native Asarabacca and exotic relatives are popular as garden plants for their cyclamen-like foliage. Asarabacca was once used for respiratory ailments and complaints of the liver; it is used no longer because of harmful side effects.

Status: native or escaped from cultivation; widespread but rare in Britain, absent from Ireland.

SIMILAR SPECIES

Birthwort *Aristolochia clematitis* has more upright stems and clusters of tubular, yellow flowers.

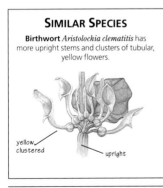

yellow clustered

upright

ASARABACCA

Type	perennial
Height	low-growing
Habitat	woods
Flowering	May–August
STEMS AND LEAVES	
Stem	5–10cm long, creeping, rooting
Root	branched, creeping stock
Hairs	short hairs on stems and flowers
Stipules	absent
Leaves	on alternate sides of stem, 25–100mm, kidney-shaped, glossy dark green, tip rounded, edge smooth, base heart-shaped
Leaf-stalk	longer than blade
FLOWERS	
Position	single, from tip of stem
Bracts	absent
Type	♂ inconspicuous
Size	11–15mm
Colour	dull purplish brown
Stalk	longer than flower
Perianth	3, triangular, equal, pointed, joined at base into short tube
Stamens	12
Stigmas	usually 6
Ovary	1, usually 6-celled
FRUIT	
Type	capsule, opening irregularly, globular, the perianth attached
Size	7–9mm
Seeds	numerous, 2–3mm, flattened

greenish flowers

white berries

forked

paired, leathery

B right, yellowish-green foliage springing from the branch of an otherwise bare tree in winter distinguishes the Mistletoe from a distance. Its special roots invade the tissues of the host tree and take nourishment, although the plant makes some of its own food using sunlight. Mistletoe grows on a large range of deciduous trees; it is especially common on Apple, although uncommon on Oak and found only rarely on conifers. Birds eating the berries wipe off sticky seeds from their beaks on to a branch, where the seeds grow into new plants. Mistletoe is familiar through the Christmas tradition of kissing under a sprig of the plant – magical properties have been attributed to the plant throughout the ages. In particular, the plants that grew on Oak featured much in ancient ceremonies of the Druids. Mistletoe has been used medicinally to treat heart disease and many different nervous disorders.

Status: native; most of area except for some northern parts and Ireland.

Similar species: none.

MISTLETOE

Type	perennial
Height	20–100cm
Habitat	parasite mainly on deciduous trees
Flowering	February–April

STEMS AND LEAVES

Stem	woody at base, repeatedly forking, green
Root	specially modified to invade wood of tree
Hairs	absent
Stipules	absent
Leaves	paired on opposite sides of stem, 50–80mm, narrow, sometimes curved, leathery, tip blunt, edge unbroken, base narrowed
Leaf-stalk	short

FLOWERS

Position	3–5 clustered at tip of stem, on ♂ or ♀ plants
Bracts	joined to flower-stalks
Type 1	♂ without sepals
Type 2	♀ with 4 sepals, 2–4mm
Size	4–6mm
Colour	greenish yellow
Stalk	short
Perianth	4, sepal-like, broadest at base, blunt
Stamens	4, joined to petals
Stigma	1
Ovary	1, 1-celled

FRUIT

Type	1, berry, white, mostly globe-shaped
Size	6–10mm
Seeds	1, sticky

Hop *Humulus lupulus*

A rather coarse, tough vine climbing by tendril-like tips to the twining stems. The backward-pointing, stiff hairs provide extra anchorage but can give a painful scratch. Cultivated plants are trained up strings supported by tall poles in fields. Tough fibres from the stems have been used in the manufacture of cloth and a form of paper has also been made from the stems. Tips of young shoots are edible and can be used fresh in salads or cooked like Asparagus, the latter method being favoured by the Romans. Hops produce the characteristic bitter taste of beer, a use extending at least back to the Middle Ages, and belong to the same family as the drug plant that yields marijuana. Extracts from the female flowers have a mild sedative action and have been used for insomnia and nervous ailments.

Status: native or often naturalized; common, most of area.

Similar species: none

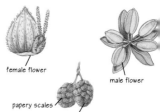

female flower

male flower

papery scales

cone-like fruit

♂

♀

lobed leaves

twining

HOP	
Type	perennial
Height	300–600cm
Habitat	hedges and bushes
Flowering	July–August
STEMS AND LEAVES	
Stem	climbing, twisting clockwise
Root	fibrous
Hairs	stiff, backward-pointing
Stipules	present
Leaves	paired on opposite sides of stem, mostly 100–150mm, 3–5 lobed, pointed, edge toothed, base heart-shaped
Leaf-stalk	about equal to blade
FLOWERS	
Position	numerous, in pendulous clusters, ♂ and ♀ flowers on different plants
Bracts	♀ up to 10mm, oval, becoming papery
Type 1	♂ in loose, branched cluster
Type 2	♀ in cone-like head, 15–20mm, yellowish green
Size	c5mm
Colour	green
Stalk	present only in ♂
Perianth	♂ 5-parted, ♀ undivided
Stamens	♂ with 5
Stigmas	♀ with 2
Ovary	1, 1-celled
FRUIT	
Type	cone of papery scales enclosing nut-like fruits
Size	cone 30–50mm
Seeds	not released

A species notorious on account of stinging hairs which cover most of the plant. Brushed lightly, the brittle tip of the stiff hair breaks off depositing a small drop of formic acid which causes the stinging sensation. Young shoots, rich in Vitamin C, can be eaten: the stinging action is destroyed by cooking. Some populations of the Common Nettle do not sting, but the reputation of the species ensures that those are rarely detected. Nettles provide the main food plant for many familiar butterflies.

Status: native; common in most of area.

♀ flower

♂ flower

nut-like fruit

female
paired
male
stinging

COMMON NETTLE

Type	perennial
Height	30–150cm
Habitat	hedgerows, woods, waste places; mainly rich soils
Flowering	June–August
STEMS AND LEAVES	
Stem	creeping or upright
Root	tough, yellow, fibrous
Hairs	stiff, mostly stinging
Stipules	present
Leaves	paired on opposite sides of stem, 40–80mm, oval, tip pointed, edge sharply toothed, base heart-shaped
Leaf-stalk	shorter than blade
FLOWERS	
Position	numerous, in branched, spike-like clusters from leaf-base, ♂ and ♀ flowers on different plants
Bracts	absent
Type 1	♂ with equal perianth-lobes
Type 2	♀ with unequal perianth-lobes, c1mm
Size	1.5–2mm
Colour	yellowish green
Stalk	absent
Perianth	4-parted
Stamens	4, springing open when ripe
Stigma	1, feathery
Ovary	1, 1-celled
FRUIT	
Type	single, nut-like, oval, enclosed by withered flower
Size	1–1.5mm
Seeds	not released

SIMILAR SPECIES

1 Small Nettle (*Urtica urens*) is an annual favouring lighter soils. **2 Pellitory-of-the-wall** (*Parietaria judaica*) has red stems and leaves with softer, stingless hairs.

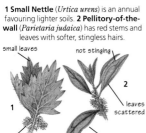

small leaves

not stinging

1

2

short

not toothed

leaves scattered

Amphibious Bistort *Polygonum amphibium*

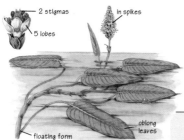

2 stigmas

5 lobes

in spikes

globular fruit

land form

tapered leaves

oblong leaves

floating form

An attractive plant with spikes of pink or red flowers, usually rising from the surface of a lake. There is a land form with more upright stems and tapered, hairy leaves. The common name refers to this amphibious nature, but 'bistort', meaning 'twice twisted', refers to the convoluted roots of Common Bistort.

Status: native, in suitable places through most of region.

SIMILAR SPECIES

1 Common Bistort (*Polygonum bistorta*) has slender, upright stems, smaller upper leaves and three stigmas. The nearly hairless **2 Redshank** (*Polygonum persicaria*) and hairy **3 Pale Persicaria** (*Polygonum lapathifolium*) are two weed species with smaller flowers.

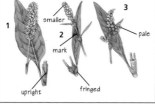

upright

smaller

mark

2

1

3

pale

fringed

AMPHIBIOUS BISTORT

Type	perennial
Height	floating form 30–75cm long; land form to 50cm
Habitat	lakes, canals, slow-moving rivers or by water
Flowering	July–September
STEMS AND LEAVES	
Stem	floating, rooting, sometimes upright
Root	creeping rhizome
Hairs	hairless or with short hairs
Stipules	joined forming tube
Leaves	spirally arranged on stem
Leaves 1	floating form 50–150mm, oblong, blunt, edge unbroken, base square or heart-shaped
Leaf-stalk	20–60mm
Leaves 2	land form pointed, base broader, rounded
Leaf-stalk	mostly short
FLOWERS	
Position	numerous, in blunt spike at tip of stem
Bracts	scale-like
Type	♂
Size	5–7mm
Colour	pink or red
Stalk	shorter than flower
Perianth	5-lobed, 3–5mm, lobes petal-like, equal
Stamens	5
Stigmas	2
Ovary	1, 1-celled
FRUIT	
Type	single, nut-like, enclosed by dried flower, globular, brown
Size	2–3mm
Seeds	not separate

small clusters of flowers

3-angled fruit

5 lobes

papery sheath

scattered leaves

Although very common, Knotgrass is often overlooked because of its rather insignificant flowers. The common name refers to the swelling where the leaf joins the stem in many species of Knotgrass.

Status: native; common through most of region.

SIMILAR SPECIES

1 Water-pepper (*P. hydropiper*), from damp places, has longer flower-heads, brown stipules. **2 Black-bindweed** (*Fallopia convolvulus*) is a climbing plant of cultivated and waste ground. Much larger at up to 2m tall. **3 Japanese Knotweed** (*Reynoutria japonica*) was introduced to gardens but is now widely naturalized.

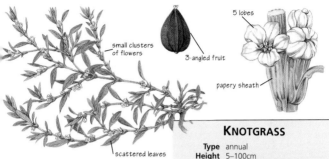

long head

1   2

3

climbing   much larger

KNOTGRASS

Type	annual
Height	5–100cm
Habitat	cultivated land, waste places, often near sea
Flowering	July–October
STEMS AND LEAVES	
Stem	upright or low-growing
Root	fibrous
Hairs	absent
Stipules	silvery, joined forming tube round stem
Leaves	spirally arranged around stem, 20–50mm, spear-shaped, tip pointed, edge unbroken, base narrowing into stalk
Leaf-stalk	about equal to stipules
FLOWERS	
Position	single or in loose clusters of 2–6 from base of leaf
Bracts	insignificant
Type	☿
Size	3–4.5mm
Colour	greenish with pink or white edges
Stalk	absent
Perianth	5-lobed, 2–3mm, joined at base into short tube
Stamens	5–8
Stigmas	2
Ovary	1, 1-celled
FRUIT	
Type	1, nut-like, 3-angled, enclosed by dried flower
Size	2.5–3.5mm
Seeds	not separate

Sheep's Sorrel *Rumex acetosella*

♂ flower

Perhaps the most distinctive feature of this plant is the foliage, which acquires a brilliant crimson hue late in the season and on poor soils. Pollen is carried by the wind from the male plants to the feathery stigmas of the female plants.

Status: native; common, most of area.

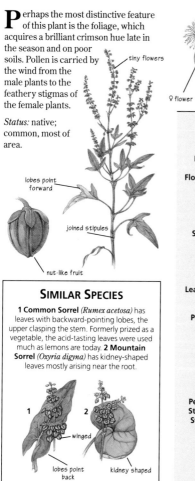

tiny flowers

♀ flower

lobes point forward

joined stipules

nut-like fruit

SIMILAR SPECIES

1 Common Sorrel (*Rumex acetosa*) has leaves with backward-pointing lobes, the upper clasping the stem. Formerly prized as a vegetable, the acid-tasting leaves were used much as lemons are today. **2 Mountain Sorrel** (*Oxyria digyna*) has kidney-shaped leaves mostly arising near the root.

winged

1 2

lobes point back

kidney shaped

SHEEP'S SORREL

Type	perennial
Height	up to 30cm
Habitat	heaths, grassland, waste ground; acid soils
Flowering	May–August
STEMS AND LEAVES	
Stem	upright or turning upright
Root	creeping, budding to make new stems
Hairs	absent
Stipules	joined forming tube
Leaves	on alternate sides of stem, up to 40mm, narrowly oval, often red-tinged, pointed, base usually with 2 forward-curving lobes
Leaf-stalk	longer than blade or absent above
FLOWERS	
Position	numerous, in branched clusters, ♂ and ♀ flowers on different plants
Bracts	absent
Type 1	♂ with stamens
Type 2	♀ 1.5–2mm, with ovary
Size	c2mm
Colour	green, becoming crimson
Stalk	nearly equal to flower
Perianth	6-lobed, 3 small, 3 larger
Stamens	6
Stigmas	3, feathery
Ovary	1, 1-celled
FRUIT	
Type	single, nut-like, 3-angled, enclosed by withered flower
Size	1.3–1.5mm
Seeds	not released

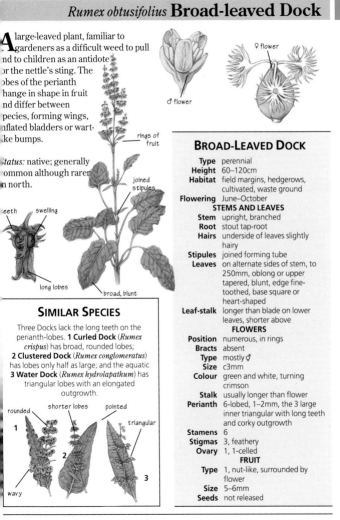

A large-leaved plant, familiar to gardeners as a difficult weed to pull and to children as an antidote for the nettle's sting. The lobes of the perianth change in shape in fruit and differ between species, forming wings, inflated bladders or wart-like bumps.

Status: native; generally common although rarer in north.

♂ flower

♀ flower

rings of fruit

joined stipules

teeth   swelling

long lobes

broad, blunt

BROAD-LEAVED DOCK

Type	perennial
Height	60–120cm
Habitat	field margins, hedgerows, cultivated, waste ground
Flowering	June–October

STEMS AND LEAVES

Stem	upright, branched
Root	stout tap-root
Hairs	underside of leaves slightly hairy
Stipules	joined forming tube
Leaves	on alternate sides of stem, to 250mm, oblong or upper tapered, blunt, edge fine-toothed, base square or heart-shaped
Leaf-stalk	longer than blade on lower leaves, shorter above

FLOWERS

Position	numerous, in rings
Bracts	absent
Type	mostly ♂
Size	c3mm
Colour	green and white, turning crimson
Stalk	usually longer than flower
Perianth	6-lobed, 1–2mm, the 3 large inner triangular with long teeth and corky outgrowth
Stamens	6
Stigmas	3, feathery
Ovary	1, 1-celled

FRUIT

Type	1, nut-like, surrounded by flower
Size	5–6mm
Seeds	not released

SIMILAR SPECIES

Three Docks lack the long teeth on the perianth-lobes. **1 Curled Dock** (*Rumex crispus*) has broad, rounded lobes; **2 Clustered Dock** (*Rumex conglomeratus*) has lobes only half as large; and the aquatic **3 Water Dock** (*Rumex hydrolapathum*) has triangular lobes with an elongated outgrowth.

rounded   shorter lobes   pointed

triangular

1

2

3

wavy

Fat-hen *Chenopodium album*

5-lobed

fruit

Perhaps the most common of a group of similar weed species with rather fleshy stems, Fat-hen is often striped with white or pink, and has angular leaves. It has been used as a vegetable and grain since the Stone Age, although largely abandoned in recent times.

Status: native; common throughout area.

tiny flowers

base tempered

striped stem

seed black

FAT-HEN

Type	annual
Height	10–150cm
Habitat	cultivated and waste ground; mostly rich soils
Flowering	July–October

STEMS AND LEAVES

Stem	upright, often striped with pink, slightly ridged
Root	fibrous
Hairs	small, swollen, giving a floury look
Stipules	absent
Leaves	spirally arranged, 12–82mm, diamond- to spear-shaped, tip pointed, edge unbroken or shallowly toothed, base wedge-shaped
Leaf-stalk	shorter than blade

FLOWERS

Position	numerous, in small clusters grouped in spikes
Bracts	present
Type	♂
Size	c1.5mm
Colour	pale green
Stalk	more or less stalkless
Perianth	5-lobed, each c1mm, oval, sepal-like
Stamens	5
Stigmas	2 on forked style
Ovary	1, 1-celled

FRUIT

Type	1, not opening, forming thin layer, enclosed by withered flower
Size	1.3–2mm
Seeds	1, 1.25–1.85mm, black, faintly grooved

SIMILAR SPECIES

1 Good-King-Henry (*Chenopodium bonus-henricus*) is perennial with triangular leaves, often lobed at the base. Orache species have separate male and female flowers, the latter enclosed by two bracts. **2 Spear-leaved Orache** (*Atriplex prostrata*) has leaves squarer-based than **3 Common Orache** (*Atriplex patula*).

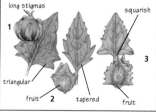

long stigmas

squarish

1

triangular

fruit 2

tapered

3

fruit

Found in salt-marshes, forming shrubby mounds with silvery leaves and tight clusters of tiny flowers, Sea-purslane tolerates flooding but prefers upper parts of the marsh, fringing the edges of channels.

Status: native; coasts, except for parts of north.

♂ flower

♀ flower

tiny flowers

mostly paired

silvery

fruit

woody

SEA-PURSLANE

Type	perennial
Height	45–150cm
Habitat	salt-marshes, usually on top edges of gulleys
Flowering	July–September
STEMS AND LEAVES	
Stem	woody below, turning upwards, often rooting
Root	short, creeping rhizome
Hairs	swollen, floury-looking
Stipules	absent
Leaves	paired on opposite sides of stem or alternate above, 10–40mm, elliptical, slightly fleshy, blunt, edge unbroken
Leaf-stalk	3–10mm
FLOWERS	
Position	numerous, spikes at stem-tip or leaf-base, ♂ and ♀ flowers on same plant
Bracts	2 3-lobed, bract-like parts cover ♀ flower
Type 1	♂ with perianth
Size	c2mm
Colour	mostly brownish yellow
Stalk	absent
Perianth	5-lobed
Stamens	5
Type 2	♀ without perianth, c1.5mm
Stigmas	2
Ovary	1, 1-celled
FRUIT	
Type	1, not opening, thin, hidden by 3-lobed bracts
Size	3–5mm
Seeds	1, c3mm, not released

SIMILAR SPECIES

Glossy-leaved **1 Sea Beet** (*Beta vulgaris* subsp. *maritima*), its fruits loosely clustered together, is the same species as cultivated Beetroot and Sugar Beet. **3 Frosted Orache** (*Atriplex laciniata*), from sandy shores, has diamond-shaped, toothed leaves and thick bracts, while **2 Grass-leaved** (*Atriplex littoralis*) or Shore Orache has narrow, scarcely toothed leaves and thin bracts.

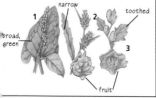

narrow

broad, green

1

2

3

toothed

fruit

Glasswort *Salicornia europaea*

A seemingly leafless succulent plant, at times so plentiful that acres of salt-marsh are covered by nothing else. The anomaly of an apparent desert-plant immersed in water is explained by the sea-water's salinity, which draws water from the plant.

Status: native; common around coasts except for parts of north.

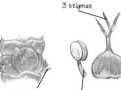

3 stigmas

tiny, sunken flowers   1 stamen

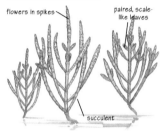

flowers in spikes   paired, scale-like leaves

succulent

SIMILAR SPECIES

1 Perennial Glasswort (*Arthrocnemum perenne*) has woody, rooting stems and flowers with two stamens. Related salt-marsh plants with more normal leaves include **2 Annual Sea-blite** (*Suaeda maritima*) with bluntish leaves, and **3 Prickly Saltwort** (*Salsola kali*) with spine-tipped leaves.

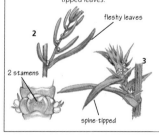

fleshy leaves

2

3

2 stamens

spine-tipped

GLASSWORT

Type	annual
Height	10–40cm
Habitat	salt-marshes; sandy mud
Flowering	August
STEMS AND LEAVES	
Stem	upright, often yellowish green, translucent
Root	fibrous
Hairs	absent
Stipules	absent
Leaves	paired on opposite sides of stem, joined except for tips into tube forming stem-segments, succulent, tip blunt, edge unbroken
Leaf-stalk	absent
FLOWERS	
Position	clusters of 3 on stem-segments towards stem-tip, forming tapered spike
Bracts	present
Type	♂, partly sunken into stem-segment
Size	c2.5mm
Colour	green
Stalk	absent
Perianth	indistinctly 3-lobed, roundish, succulent
Stamen	1, shortly stalked, scarcely projecting
Stigmas	3
Ovary	1, 1-celled
FRUIT	
Type	single, papery-walled
Size	c2mm
Seeds	1.2–1.8mm, covered with hairs

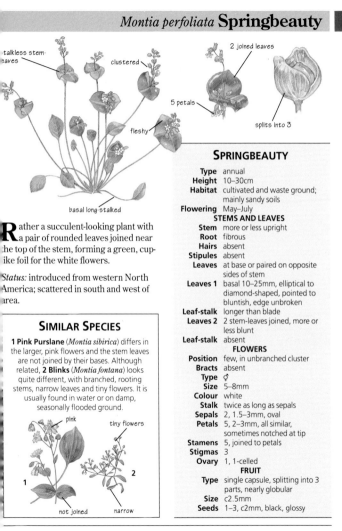

talkless stem-leaves

clustered

5 petals

fleshy

basal long-stalked

2 joined leaves

splits into 3

Rather a succulent-looking plant with a pair of rounded leaves joined near the top of the stem, forming a green, cup-like foil for the white flowers.

Status: introduced from western North America; scattered in south and west of area.

SIMILAR SPECIES

1 Pink Purslane (*Montia sibirica*) differs in the larger, pink flowers and the stem leaves are not joined by their bases. Although related, **2 Blinks** (*Montia fontana*) looks quite different, with branched, rooting stems, narrow leaves and tiny flowers. It is usually found in water or on damp, seasonally flooded ground.

pink

tiny flowers

1

2

not joined

narrow

SPRINGBEAUTY

Type	annual
Height	10–30cm
Habitat	cultivated and waste ground; mainly sandy soils
Flowering	May–July

STEMS AND LEAVES

Stem	more or less upright
Root	fibrous
Hairs	absent
Stipules	absent
Leaves	at base or paired on opposite sides of stem
Leaves 1	basal 10–25mm, elliptical to diamond-shaped, pointed to bluntish, edge unbroken
Leaf-stalk	longer than blade
Leaves 2	2 stem-leaves joined, more or less blunt
Leaf-stalk	absent

FLOWERS

Position	few, in unbranched cluster
Bracts	absent
Type	♂
Size	5–8mm
Colour	white
Stalk	twice as long as sepals
Sepals	2, 1.5–3mm, oval
Petals	5, 2–3mm, all similar, sometimes notched at tip
Stamens	5, joined to petals
Stigmas	3
Ovary	1, 1-celled

FRUIT

Type	single capsule, splitting into 3 parts, nearly globular
Size	c2.5mm
Seeds	1–3, c2mm, black, glossy

21

Greater Stitchwort *Stellaria holostea*

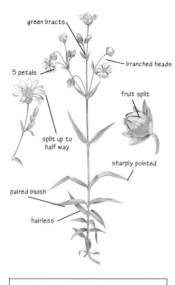

green bracts

5 petals

branched heads

fruit split

split up to half way

sharply pointed

paired bluish

hairless

The thread-like lower part of Stitchwort's stem looks impossibly thin and supports the plant only with the aid of its neighbours. Mixed with powdered acorns, the plant was used to treat a stitch or similar pains in the side.

Status: native, common throughout area

GREATER STITCHWORT

Type	perennial
Height	15–60cm
Habitat	woods or hedgerows
Flowering	April–June
STEMS AND LEAVES	
Stem	turning upwards, slender at base, sharply 4-angled
Root	slender, creeping stock
Hairs	hairless or hairy above
Stipules	absent
Leaves	paired on opposite sides of stem, 40–80mm, narrowly spear-shaped, bluish, finely pointed, edge rough, base rather broad
Leaf-stalk	absent
FLOWERS	
Position	few, in loose heads
Bracts	leaf-like
Type	♂
Size	20–30mm
Colour	white
Stalk	longer than flower
Sepals	5, 6–9mm, spear-shaped, with narrow, papery edge
Petals	5, 8–12mm, equal, split to about half-way
Stamens	10
Stigmas	3
Ovary	1, 1-celled
FRUIT	
Type	globular capsule, splitting into 6
Size	6–8mm
Seeds	numerous, 1.5–2mm, kidney-shaped, reddish-brown, rough with tiny outgrowths

SIMILAR SPECIES

Three other Stitchworts have whitish, papery bracts. **1 Lesser Stitchwort** (*Stellaria graminea*) has flowers 5–12mm long and green leaves; **2 Marsh Stitchwort** (*Stellaria. palustris*) has flowers 12–18mm across and bluish leaves; **3 Bog Stitchwort** (*Stellaria alsine*) has smaller flowers, with petals shorter than the sepals.

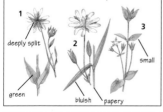

1

deeply split

green

2

bluish

papery

3

small

Stellaria media **Common Chickweed**

This ubiquitous weed flowers at almost any time of the year, as weather permits, with insignificant petals shorter than the sepals. The stems are rather fleshy but weak, so that the Chickweed flops over the ground or other plants. Poultry and cage birds are fond of the seed.

Status: native; very common throughout area.

shorter than sepals

fruit splits open

small flowers

turns upwards

5 stamens

petals deeply split

paired broad

COMMON CHICKWEED

Type	annual
Height	5–40cm
Habitat	cultivated and waste ground; mostly rich soils
Flowering	January–December
STEMS AND LEAVES	
Stem	much-branched, low-growing, turning upwards
Root	slender tap-root
Hairs	2 lines along stem, sepals stickily hairy
Stipules	absent
Leaves	paired on opposite sides of stem, 3–25mm, oval or elliptical, pointed, edge unbroken
Leaf-stalk	stalked or upper stalkless
FLOWERS	
Position	many, loose head at stem-tip
Bracts	present
Type	♂
Size	6–10mm
Colour	white
Stalk	lengthening in fruit
Sepals	5, narrow papery edge
Petals	5, mostly shorter than sepals, deeply 2-lobed
Stamens	usually 5, rarely up to 8
Stigmas	3
Ovary	1, 1-celled
FRUIT	
Type	single capsule, narrowly egg-shaped, splits into 6
Size	5–6mm
Seeds	many, 0.9–1.3mm, kidney-shaped, rough

SIMILAR SPECIES

Two related species differ in having stalked leaves and ten stamens. **1 Greater Chickweed** (*Stellaria neglecta*) has petals little longer than the sepals; and **2 Wood Stitchwort** (*Stellaria nemorum*) has petals about twice as long as the sepals. **3 Water Chickweed** (*Myosoton aquaticum*) has large petals and five stigmas.

10 stamens *longer than sepals*

large

most stalkless

23

Corn Spurrey *Spergula arvensis*

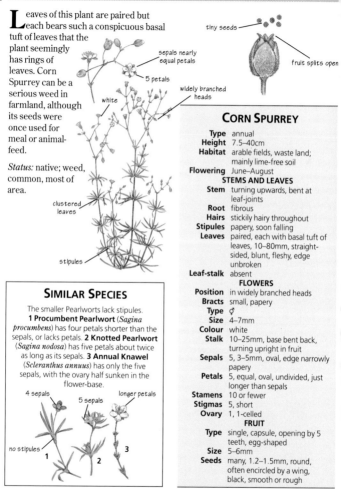

Leaves of this plant are paired but each bears such a conspicuous basal tuft of leaves that the plant seemingly has rings of leaves. Corn Spurrey can be a serious weed in farmland, although its seeds were once used for meal or animal-feed.

Status: native; weed, common, most of area.

tiny seeds

sepals nearly equal petals

5 petals

white

widely branched heads

clustered leaves

stipules

fruit splits open

CORN SPURREY

Type	annual
Height	7.5–40cm
Habitat	arable fields, waste land; mainly lime-free soil
Flowering	June–August
STEMS AND LEAVES	
Stem	turning upwards, bent at leaf-joints
Root	fibrous
Hairs	stickily hairy throughout
Stipules	papery, soon falling
Leaves	paired, each with basal tuft of leaves, 10–80mm, straight-sided, blunt, fleshy, edge unbroken
Leaf-stalk	absent
FLOWERS	
Position	in widely branched heads
Bracts	small, papery
Type	♂
Size	4–7mm
Colour	white
Stalk	10–25mm, base bent back, turning upright in fruit
Sepals	5, 3–5mm, oval, edge narrowly papery
Petals	5, equal, oval, undivided, just longer than sepals
Stamens	10 or fewer
Stigmas	5, short
Ovary	1, 1-celled
FRUIT	
Type	single, capsule, opening by 5 teeth, egg-shaped
Size	5–6mm
Seeds	many, 1.2–1.5mm, round, often encircled by a wing, black, smooth or rough

SIMILAR SPECIES

The smaller Pearlworts lack stipules. **1 Procumbent Pearlwort** (*Sagina procumbens*) has four petals shorter than the sepals, or lacks petals. **2 Knotted Pearlwort** (*Sagina nodosa*) has five petals about twice as long as its sepals. **3 Annual Knawel** (*Scleranthus annuus*) has only the five sepals, with the ovary half sunken in the flower-base.

4 sepals

5 sepals

longer petals

no stipules

1   2   3

Spergularia media **Greater Sea-spurrey**

The fleshy shoots and attractive pink flowers of Sea-spurreys may be found on the drier parts of a salt-marsh, where flooding is restricted to exceptional high tides.

Status: native; coasts throughout area.

5 petals
winged seeds
fruit splits
hairless

branched clusters
pink
silvery stipules
fleshy

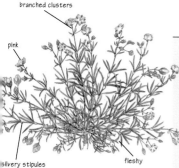

SIMILAR SPECIES

No other species has all the seeds winged.
1 Rock Sea-spurrey (*Spergularia rupicola*) has dense, sticky hairs and grows on cliffs or among rocks. **2 Lesser Sea-spurrey** (*Spergularia marina*) has smaller, deeper flowers and prefers drier parts of salt-marshes or salty places inland. **3 Sand Spurrey** (*Spergularia rubra*) has much smaller flowers and is often found on sandy soils inland.

1
sticky hairs
2
hairless
3
smaller
hairy

GREATER SEA-SPURREY

Type	perennial
Height	10–35cm
Habitat	salt-marshes; mud or sand
Flowering	June–September
STEMS AND LEAVES	
Stem	many, low-growing, turning or angled upwards
Root	stout, branched stock
Hairs	hairless or sepals sometimes stickily hairy
Stipules	triangular, papery, silvery
Leaves	paired on opposite sides of stem, 10–25mm, straight-sided, fleshy, tip hard, blunt to sharp, edge unbroken
Leaf-stalk	absent
FLOWERS	
Position	in widely branched head
Bracts	mostly small
Type	♂
Size	7.5–12mm
Colour	pink to whitish
Stalk	present
Sepals	5, 4–5mm, separate, blunt
Petals	5, 4.5–5.5mm, oval, blunt, edge not lobed
Stamens	usually 10
Stigmas	3
Ovary	1, 1-celled
FRUIT	
Type	single, capsule, splits into 3, withered sepals attached
Size	7–11mm
Seeds	c1.5mm, round, encircled by a pale wing

Red Campion *Silene dioica*

Typically a plant of the woodland margin, Red Campion is easily recognized by its rose-pink flowers and softly hairy leaves. This day-flowering Campion is usually pollinated by bees or hover-flies.

Status: native, common except for parts of south.

RED CAMPION

Type	perennial
Height	20–90cm
Habitat	woods, hedgerows, cliffs or limestone screes; mostly lime-rich soil
Flowering	May–June
STEMS AND LEAVES	
Stem	turning upright
Root	slender, creeping stock
Hairs	soft, may be sticky above
Stipules	absent
Leaves	paired on opposite sides of stem, 4–10mm, oval or oblong, pointed, edge unbroken
Leaf-stalk	winged or upper stalkless
FLOWERS	
Position	numerous, branched head at stem-tip, ♂ and ♀ flowers on different plants
Bracts	present
Type	open during day, scentless
Size	18–25mm
Colour	rose-pink, rarely white
Stalk	5–15mm
Sepals	5, 12–17.5mm, joined into tube with pointed teeth
Petals	5, deeply 2-lobed with stalk-like base
Stamens	♂ with 10
Stigmas	♀ with 5
Ovary	1, 1-celled
FRUIT	
Type	1, capsule, opening by 10 curled back teeth, oval
Size	10–15mm
Seeds	many, black, kidney-shaped, rough with tiny outgrowths

SIMILAR SPECIES

1 Moss Campion (*Silene acaulis*) is much smaller, with hairless leaves and grows on mountains. A plant of wet places, **2 Ragged-Robin** (*Lychnis flos-cuculi*) has deeply divided petals and hairless leaves. **3 Sticky Catchfly** (*Lychnis viscaria*) has sticky stems just beneath each leaf and, like the previous species, capsules with five teeth.

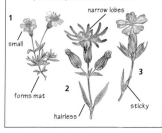

Large, creamy-white flowers that open in the evening make the White Campion seem to glow in the dusk. Moths, drawn by the scent, pollinate the flowers. White Campion forms pink-flowered hybrids where it grows with Red Campion.

Status: native or introduced to parts of west; common in most of the area.

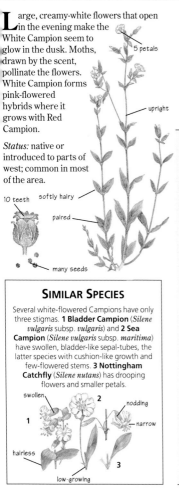

WHITE CAMPION

Type	perennial
Height	30–100cm
Habitat	cultivated and waste ground, hedgerows
Flowering	May–September
STEMS AND LEAVES	
Stem	upright, mostly branched
Root	thick, almost woody stock
Hairs	soft, stickily hairy above
Stipules	absent
Leaves	paired on opposite sides of stem, 30–100mm, elliptical or spear-shaped, pointed, edge unbroken, base narrowed
Leaf-stalk	only on lower leaves
FLOWERS	
Position	few, in branched heads, ♂ and ♀ on different plants
Bracts	present
Type	day-flowering, slight scent
Size	25–30mm
Colour	white
Stalk	elongating in fruit
Sepals	5, 23–30mm, joined into tube with narrow teeth
Petals	5, deeply 2-lobed
Stamens	♂ with 10
Stigmas	♀ with 5
Ovary	1, 1-celled
FRUIT	
Type	single, capsule, opens by 10 teeth, egg-shaped
Size	c15mm
Seeds	numerous, 1.3–1.5mm, kidney-shaped, grey, rough

SIMILAR SPECIES

Several white-flowered Campions have only three stigmas. **1 Bladder Campion** (*Silene vulgaris* subsp. *vulgaris*) and **2 Sea Campion** (*Silene vulgaris* subsp. *maritima*) have swollen, bladder-like sepal-tubes, the latter species with cushion-like growth and few-flowered stems. **3 Nottingham Catchfly** (*Silene nutans*) has drooping flowers and smaller petals.

Soapwort *Saponaria officinalis*

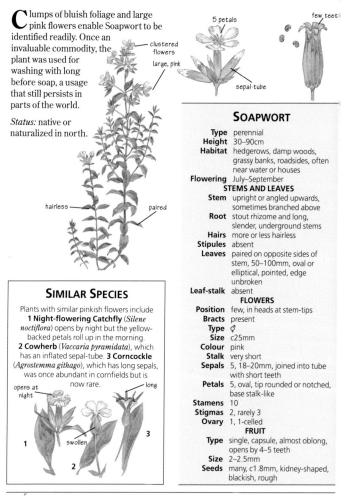

Clumps of bluish foliage and large pink flowers enable Soapwort to be identified readily. Once an invaluable commodity, the plant was used for washing with long before soap, a usage that still persists in parts of the world.

Status: native or naturalized in north.

5 petals

few teeth

clustered flowers

large, pink

sepal-tube

hairless

paired

SOAPWORT

Type	perennial
Height	30–90cm
Habitat	hedgerows, damp woods, grassy banks, roadsides, often near water or houses
Flowering	July–September
STEMS AND LEAVES	
Stem	upright or angled upwards, sometimes branched above
Root	stout rhizome and long, slender, underground stems
Hairs	more or less hairless
Stipules	absent
Leaves	paired on opposite sides of stem, 50–100mm, oval or elliptical, pointed, edge unbroken
Leaf-stalk	absent
FLOWERS	
Position	few, in heads at stem-tips
Bracts	present
Type	☿
Size	c25mm
Colour	pink
Stalk	very short
Sepals	5, 18–20mm, joined into tube with short teeth
Petals	5, oval, tip rounded or notched, base stalk-like
Stamens	10
Stigmas	2, rarely 3
Ovary	1, 1-celled
FRUIT	
Type	single, capsule, almost oblong, opens by 4–5 teeth
Size	2–2.5mm
Seeds	many, c1.8mm, kidney-shaped, blackish, rough

SIMILAR SPECIES

Plants with similar pinkish flowers include **1 Night-flowering Catchfly** (*Silene noctiflora*) opens by night but the yellow-backed petals roll up in the morning. **2 Cowherb** (*Vaccaria pyramidata*), which has an inflated sepal-tube. **3 Corncockle** (*Agrostemma githago*), which has long sepals, was once abundant in cornfields but is now rare.

opens at night

long

swollen

1

2

3

S lender stems and leaves make this
plant almost invisible in grassland,
until the opening flowers of intense pink
herald its presence. Pinks have long been
cultivated, and often differ greatly from
their wild progenitors.

Status: native; scattered localities in
lowland parts of area.

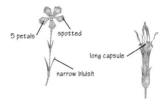

SIMILAR SPECIES

1 Childing Pink (*Petrorhagia nanteuilii*) has
small heads of flowers, opening singly,
enclosed by broad, papery scales.
2 Deptford Pink (*Dianthus armeria*) has
clustered flowers with slender bracts.
3 Cheddar Pink (*Dianthus
gratianopolitanus*), one of the rarest native
species in Britain and specially protected by
law, has larger, pale flowers.

MAIDEN PINK

Type	perennial
Height	15–45cm
Habitat	dry grassy places, fields, banks and hills
Flowering	June–September

STEMS AND LEAVES

Stem	forming low tufts, turning upright to flower
Root	slender, creeping stock
Hairs	rough hairs on leaf-edges
Stipules	absent
Leaves	paired, 10–25mm, narrowly spear-shaped, bluish, pointed or lowest blunt, edge unbroken
Leaf-stalk	absent

FLOWERS

Position	1–3, at stem-tips
Bracts	present
Type	⚥, scentless
Size	16–20mm
Colour	deep pink with pale spots or white, banded deep pink
Stalk	present
Sepals	5, 12–17mm, joined into tube, 2–4 scales at base
Petals	5, equal, broad, toothed, the base stalk-like
Stamens	10
Stigmas	2
Ovary	1, 1-celled

FRUIT

Type	single, capsule, opening by 4 teeth, cylindrical
Size	c15mm
Seeds	many, 2–2.5mm, oval, flattened, black

White Water-lily *Nymphaea alba*

nearly circular

floating leaves and flowers

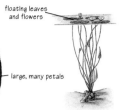

large, many petals

L arge, white, cup-shaped flowers and nearly circular leaves floating on the water's surface easily identify the White Water-lily. Plants in the north-west often have much smaller flowers than elsewhere.

Status: native; throughout area.

SIMILAR SPECIES

1 Yellow Water-lily (*Nuphar lutea*) has smaller flowers held above the water surface. The ripe fruit has an odd alcohol-like smell. **2 Least Water-lily** (*Nuphar pumila*) is even smaller and has non-overlapping petals. True to its name, **3 Fringed Water-lily** (*Nymphoides peltata*) has fringed petals but also elongated stems, short leaf-stalks, and is a relative of the Gentians.

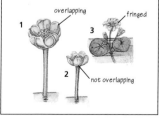

overlapping

fringed

1

3

2

not overlapping

WHITE WATER-LILY

Type	perennial
Height	underwater, up to 300cm
Habitat	lakes and ponds
Flowering	July–August
STEMS AND LEAVES	
Stem	short, forming a rhizome
Root	fleshy from rhizome
Hairs	absent
Stipules	present
Leaves	at base of plant, 100–300mm, nearly circular, floating, dark, glossy green above, often reddish below, rounded, edge unbroken, base forming deep cleft in circular outline
Leaf-stalk	up to 3m
FLOWERS	
Position	few
Type	☿, floating, scented
Size	50–200mm
Colour	white
Stalk	up to 3m
Sepals	4, spear-shaped, whitish
Petals	20–25, spirally arranged
Stamens	numerous
Stigmas	many, forming radiating lines on top of ovary
Ovary	1, many-celled
FRUIT	
Type	single, spongy capsule, opens underwater, oval to nearly globular
Size	16–40mm
Seeds	numerous, c3mm, floating

Ranunculus aquatilis **Common Water-crowfoot**

broad segments

fine segments

buttercup-like

clustered fruits

Dotted over the surface of a pond
sometimes in great profusion,
Water-crowfoot's white and yellow-
centred flowers contrast to perfection the
reflected blue of a summer's sky. This is a
true amphibious plant, having
mastered both land and water. Out of
the water the leaves are lobed like
those of Buttercups, but submerged
leaves are finely divided.

Status: native; most lowland areas.

COMMON WATER-CROWFOOT

Type	perennial or annual
Height	very variable
Habitat	ponds, slow streams or ditches
Flowering	May–June
STEMS AND LEAVES	
Stem	underwater or low-growing
Root	fibrous
Hairs	sparse
Stipules	present
Leaves	spirally arranged
Leaves 1	underwater, 30–60(–80)mm, with hair-like segments
Leaf-stalk	often shorter than blade
Leaves 2	floating, nearly circular, with 3–7 toothed lobes
Leaf-stalk	usually longer than blade
FLOWERS	
Position	1, opposite upper leaf
Type	⚥
Size	12–18mm
Colour	white with yellow base
Stalk	20–50mm
Sepals	usually 5
Petals	5, 5–10mm, equal
Stamens	13 or more
Stigmas	1 per ovary
Ovaries	numerous, 1-celled
FRUIT	
Type	numerous, short-beaked, hairy, in rounded head
Size	1.5–2mm
Seeds	1, not released

SIMILAR SPECIES

Species in flowing waters, like **1 River
Water-crowfoot** (*Ranunculus fluitans*) and
2 Thread-leaved Water-crowfoot
(*Ranunculus trichophyllus*), have only the
finely divided leaves; **3 Ivy-leaved
Crowfoot** (*Ranunculus hederaceus*) has only
the land form of leaf.

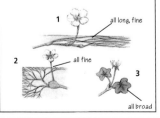

1 — all long, fine

2 — all fine

3 — all broad

Meadow Buttercup *Ranunculus acris*

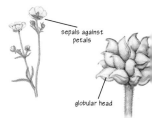

5 petals

smoothly rounded

hairy

sepals against petals

globular head

One of the most familiar summer flowers, Meadow Buttercup abounds in pastures everywhere. The rich yellow of the cup-shaped flowers is associated in folklore with the yellow butter from cattle that graze the pastures.

Status: native; common, most of area.

deeply lobed

middle lobe not stalked

SIMILAR SPECIES

Two other Buttercups have a stalked middle lobe to the leaves. **1 Bulbous Buttercup** (*Ranunculus acris bulbosus*) has a bulb-like base to the stem and sepals bent downwards, and **2 Creeping Buttercup** (*Ranunculus repens*) has creeping, rooting stems. **3 Goldilocks Buttercup** (*Ranunculus auricomus*) has basal leaves that are less divided, and often has petals missing.

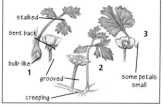

stalked

bent back

bulb-like

1

grooved

creeping

2

some petals small

3

MEADOW BUTTERCUP

Type	perennial
Height	15–100cm
Habitat	damp meadows, grassy places; lime-rich or neutral soils
Flowering	June–July
STEMS AND LEAVES	
Stem	upright, base hollow
Root	fibrous from stout stock
Hairs	pressed close on leaves, projecting on stem
Stipules	absent
Leaves	basal with 2–7 toothed lobes; stem-leaves scattered, upper narrowly lobed
Leaf-stalk	long or stalkless above
FLOWERS	
Position	numerous, in branched head from upper stem
Bracts	present
Type	mostly ♀, cup-shaped
Size	18–25mm
Colour	glossy yellow or whitish
Stalk	longer than flower
Sepals	usually 5, oval, hairy, pressed against petals
Petals	usually 5, 6–11mm, rounded
Stamens	numerous
Stigmas	1 per ovary
Ovaries	numerous, 1-celled
FRUIT	
Type	many in rounded head, nut-like, not opening, egg-shaped, hooked beak, smooth
Size	2.5–3mm
Seeds	1, not released

Ranunculus ficaria subsp. *ficaria* **Lesser Celandine**

The rich yellow flowers open with the Spring sunshine, often in such great numbers that they carpet with gold a woodland floor or hedge-bank. Some plants have tiny swollen buds called bulbils at the base of the leaves, and all plants have small tubers through which they are able to last the Winter.

Status: native, common throughout area.

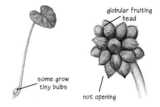

globular fruiting head

some grow tiny bulbs

not opening

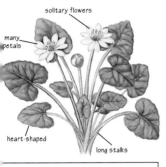

solitary flowers

many petals

heart-shaped

long stalks

SIMILAR SPECIES

Winter Aconite (*Eranthis hyemalis*) is similarly a Spring flower with numerous yellow petals, but differs in the collar-like bracts below the flower and the lobed leaves which grow only after flowering is finished.

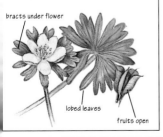

bracts under flower

lobed leaves

fruits open

LESSER CELANDINE

Type	perennial
Height	5–25cm
Habitat	woods, hedgerows, grassy places, stream-banks
Flowering	March–May
STEMS AND LEAVES	
Stem	angled upwards, base rooting
Root	fibrous, with many small, swollen tubers
Hairs	absent
Stipules	absent
Leaves	from base and spirally arranged around stem, 10–40mm, heart-shaped, blunt or rounded, edge shallowly toothed, base notched
Leaf-stalk	base broad, overlapping other stalks
FLOWERS	
Position	single, at tip of stem
Bracts	absent
Type	♂
Size	20–30mm
Colour	bright, glossy yellow, fading nearly white
Stalk	much longer than flower
Sepals	3, oval
Petals	8–12, narrowly oval
Stamens	numerous
Stigmas	1 per ovary
Ovaries	numerous, 1-celled
FRUIT	
Type	many in rounded head, not opening, egg-shaped to globular, short-beaked
Size	up to 2.5mm
Seeds	1, not released

Green Hellebore *Helleborus viridis*

green

deeply lobed

petals

broad sepals

An imposing plant with large, hand-shaped leaves but, unusually for such a large-flowered species, the flowers are green and easily overlooked. The sepals are large and showy, whereas the petals are reduced to tubular structures which produce nectar. This is a close relative of the white-flowered Christmas Rose of gardens.

Status: native or introduced in some places; scattered localities in southern half of the area.

SIMILAR SPECIES

Stinking Hellebore (*H. foetidus*) is easily distinguished by the smaller, more cup-shaped or almost globular flowers, edged with reddish purple.

reddish edge

cup-shaped

GREEN HELLEBORE

Type	perennial
Height	20–40cm
Habitat	woods and scrub; moist, lime-rich soils or scree
Flowering	March–April
STEMS AND LEAVES	
Stem	upright, little-branched
Root	stout, blackish stock
Hairs	absent or few above
Stipules	absent
Leaves	from base or scattered on stem basal leaves usually 2, with 7–13 elliptical, finger-like, pointed lobes, edge toothed
Leaf-stalk	long or absent on stem-leaves
FLOWERS	
Position	2–4, in widely branched head a tip of stem
Type	⚥
Size	30–50mm
Colour	yellowish green
Stalk	slightly nodding
Sepals	5, equal, elliptical or oval, petal-like
Petals	9–12, much smaller than sepals, tubular, green
Stamens	numerous
Stigmas	1 per ovary
Ovaries	3–8, 1-celled
FRUIT	
Type	3–8, pod-like, splits down inner edge to release seeds
Size	c20mm
Seeds	numerous, with fleshy white ridge on one side

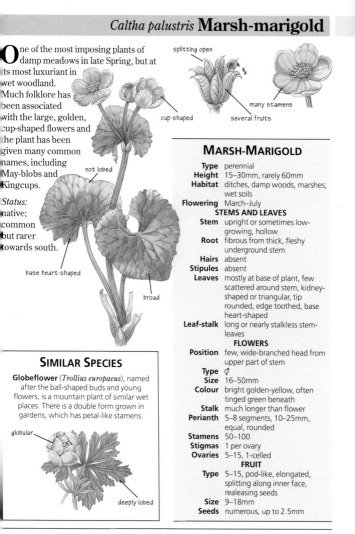

One of the most imposing plants of damp meadows in late Spring, but at its most luxuriant in wet woodland. Much folklore has been associated with the large, golden, cup-shaped flowers and the plant has been given many common names, including May-blobs and Kingcups.

Status: native; common but rarer towards south.

splitting open

cup-shaped

many stamens

several fruits

not lobed

base heart-shaped

broad

MARSH-MARIGOLD

Type	perennial
Height	15–30mm, rarely 60mm
Habitat	ditches, damp woods, marshes; wet soils
Flowering	March–July

STEMS AND LEAVES

Stem	upright or sometimes low-growing, hollow
Root	fibrous from thick, fleshy underground stem
Hairs	absent
Stipules	absent
Leaves	mostly at base of plant, few scattered around stem, kidney-shaped or triangular, tip rounded, edge toothed, base heart-shaped
Leaf-stalk	long or nearly stalkless stem-leaves

FLOWERS

Position	few, wide-branched head from upper part of stem
Type	☿
Size	16–50mm
Colour	bright golden-yellow, often tinged green beneath
Stalk	much longer than flower
Perianth	5–8 segments, 10–25mm, equal, rounded
Stamens	50–100
Stigmas	1 per ovary
Ovaries	5–15, 1-celled

FRUIT

Type	5–15, pod-like, elongated, splitting along inner face, realeasing seeds
Size	9–18mm
Seeds	numerous, up to 2.5mm

SIMILAR SPECIES

Globeflower (*Trollius europaeus*), named after the ball-shaped buds and young flowers, is a mountain plant of similar wet places. There is a double form grown in gardens, which has petal-like stamens.

globular

deeply lobed

Wood Anemone *Anemone nemorosa*

A Spring flower which often grows in such great profusion that it carpets the floor of woodland with delicate, many-petalled flowers of white, tinged and veined with purple. The main leaves arise from the ground only after flowering is completed.

Status: native; often very common, throughout area.

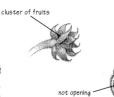

cluster of fruits

not opening

3 stem leaves

usually 6 petals

solitary

many stamens

lower leaf long-stalked

WOOD ANEMONE

Type	perennial
Height	6–30cm
Habitat	deciduous woods; all but most acid or wet soils
Flowering	March–May
STEMS AND LEAVES	
Stem	upright, unbranched
Root	fibrous from thin, creeping underground stem
Hairs	absent or sparse on leaves
Stipules	absent
Leaves	3 around stem, 1–2 from base after flowering, 3-parted, with pointed, toothed lobes
Leaf-stalk	long or stem-leaves short
FLOWERS	
Position	single, from tip of stem
Bracts	absent
Type	♂
Size	20–40mm
Colour	white, tinged and veined with purplish pink, rarely reddish purple
Stalk	long, upright or nodding
Perianth	5–9 segments, usually 6–7, equal, oblong-elliptical
Stamens	50–70
Stigmas	1 per ovary
Ovaries	10–30, 1-celled
FRUIT	
Type	10–30, nut-like, not opening, in pendulous, globular clusters, egg-shaped, beaked, downy
Size	4–4.5mm
Seeds	1 per fruit, not released

SIMILAR SPECIES

1 Blue Anemone (*Anemone apennina*) is grown for its beautiful blue flowers and often becomes naturalized. The native, summer-flowering **2 Pasqueflower** (*Pulsatilla vulgaris*) has larger, purple flowers and heads of long-plumed fruits. **3 Pale Pasqueflower** (*Pulsatilla vernalis*) grows in mountains only in the east of the area.

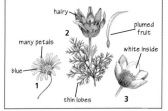

hairy

many petals

plumed fruit

white inside

blue

thin lobes

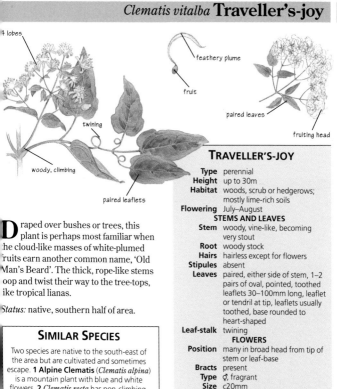

4 lobes

feathery plume

fruit

paired leaves

fruiting head

twining

woody, climbing

paired leaflets

D raped over bushes or trees, this plant is perhaps most familiar when the cloud-like masses of white-plumed fruits earn another common name, 'Old Man's Beard'. The thick, rope-like stems loop and twist their way to the tree-tops, like tropical lianas.

Status: native, southern half of area.

SIMILAR SPECIES

Two species are native to the south-east of the area but are cultivated and sometimes escape. **1 Alpine Clematis** (*Clematis alpina*) is a mountain plant with blue and white flowers. **2 *Clematis recta*** has non-climbing, annual stems and large heads of tiny, white, hawthorn-scented flowers.

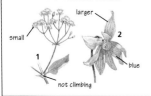

small

larger

2

1

blue

not climbing

TRAVELLER'S-JOY

Type	perennial
Height	up to 30m
Habitat	woods, scrub or hedgerows; mostly lime-rich soils
Flowering	July–August
STEMS AND LEAVES	
Stem	woody, vine-like, becoming very stout
Root	woody stock
Hairs	hairless except for flowers
Stipules	absent
Leaves	paired, either side of stem, 1–2 pairs of oval, pointed, toothed leaflets 30–100mm long, leaflet or tendril at tip, leaflets usually toothed, base rounded to heart-shaped
Leaf-stalk	twining
FLOWERS	
Position	many in broad head from tip of stem or leaf-base
Bracts	present
Type	⚥, fragrant
Size	c20mm
Colour	greenish white
Stalk	about equalling flower
Perianth	usually 4, hairy beneath
Stamens	numerous
Stigmas	1 per ovary
Ovaries	numerous, 1-celled
FRUIT	
Type	numerous, nut-like with long, whitish, feathery plume, not opening, in a rounded cluster
Size	c25mm
Seeds	1, not released

Columbine *Aquilegia vulgaris*

Columbine has unusual nodding flowers: all five of the petals are horn-shaped, each tip drawn out and curved over into a hollow spur. The spur contains a drop of sweet nectar, and it is this that attracts pollinating insects to the plant.

Status: native but cultivated and often escaping.

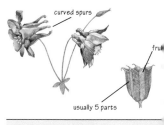

curved spurs

fruit

usually 5 parts

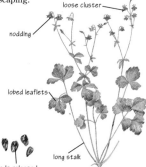

loose cluster

nodding

lobed leaflets

long stalk

seeds released

COLUMBINE

Type	perennial
Height	40–100cm
Habitat	damp places on lime-rich soils, woods, fens
Flowering	May–June
STEMS AND LEAVES	
Stem	upright, branched above
Root	short, thick, stock
Hairs	hairless or softly hairy
Stipules	absent
Leaves	basal or scattered around stem, divided into blunt, irregularly 3-lobed, toothed, leaflets, bluish green above
Leaf-stalk	long, broad-based to absent on stem-leaves
FLOWERS	
Position	few, in loose cluster towards top of stem
Type	♂
Size	30–50mm
Colour	blue, white or pink
Stalk	nodding
Sepals	5, 15–30mm, oval, pointed, coloured like petals
Petals	5, c30mm, oblong, with curved, spur-like base
Stamens	c50
Stigmas	1 per ovary
Ovaries	5, rarely 10, 1-celled
FRUIT	
Type	5, rarely 10, pod-like, opening along inner edge, upright
Size	15–25mm
Seeds	numerous, 2–2.5mm, globular, black, glossy

SIMILAR SPECIES

1 Forking Larkspur (*Consolida regalis*) differs in the wider branching, divided lower bracts and shorter fruit. **2 Larkspur** (*Consolida ambigua*) has only one spur and one pod-like fruit. The hooded or helmet-shaped purple flowers of **3 Monk's-hood** (*Aconitum napellus*) conceal the extremely poisonous nature of the plant.

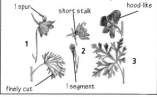

1 spur

short stalk

hood-like

1

2

3

finely cut

1 segment

Thalictrum flavum **Common Meadow-rue**

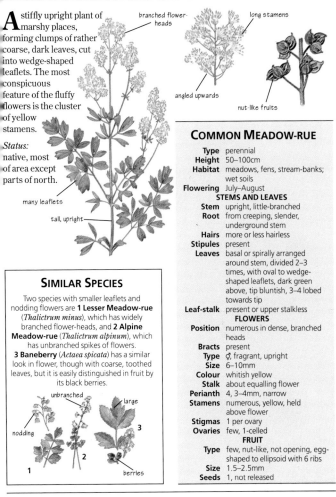

A stiffly upright plant of marshy places, forming clumps of rather coarse, dark leaves, cut into wedge-shaped leaflets. The most conspicuous feature of the fluffy flowers is the cluster of yellow stamens.

Status: native, most of area except parts of north.

branched flower-heads

long stamens

angled upwards

nut-like fruits

many leaflets

tall, upright

SIMILAR SPECIES

Two species with smaller leaflets and nodding flowers are **1 Lesser Meadow-rue** (*Thalictrum minus*), which has widely branched flower-heads, and **2 Alpine Meadow-rue** (*Thalictrum alpinum*), which has unbranched spikes of flowers.
3 Baneberry (*Actaea spicata*) has a similar look in flower, though with coarse, toothed leaves, but it is easily distinguished in fruit by its black berries.

unbranched

large

nodding

berries

1   2   3

COMMON MEADOW-RUE

Type	perennial
Height	50–100cm
Habitat	meadows, fens, stream-banks; wet soils
Flowering	July–August
STEMS AND LEAVES	
Stem	upright, little-branched
Root	from creeping, slender, underground stem
Hairs	more or less hairless
Stipules	present
Leaves	basal or spirally arranged around stem, divided 2–3 times, with oval to wedge-shaped leaflets, dark green above, tip bluntish, 3–4 lobed towards tip
Leaf-stalk	present or upper stalkless
FLOWERS	
Position	numerous in dense, branched heads
Bracts	present
Type	☿, fragrant, upright
Size	6–10mm
Colour	whitish yellow
Stalk	about equalling flower
Perianth	4, 3–4mm, narrow
Stamens	numerous, yellow, held above flower
Stigmas	1 per ovary
Ovaries	few, 1-celled
FRUIT	
Type	few, nut-like, not opening, egg-shaped to ellipsoid with 6 ribs
Size	1.5–2.5mm
Seeds	1, not released

Common Poppy *Papaver rhoeas*

Poppies paint a new road verge or embankment a brilliant hue in their first year, but rapidly decline and after a few years exist only as seeds in the soil, waiting until the land is turned again. Once a common sight in cornfields, more effective seed cleaning and use of selective herbicides have made Poppies much rarer.

Status: native; often very common, rare in parts of north.

4 petals

nodding buds

over-lapping

COMMON POPPY

Type	annual
Height	20–60cm
Habitat	newly dug and waste ground, arable fields
Flowering	June–August
STEMS AND LEAVES	
Stem	upright, milky sap
Root	slender taproot
Hairs	stiff, outward-pointing
Stipules	absent
Leaves	at base or spirally around stem, 30–150mm, cut into narrow lobes or leaflets, upper leaves mostly 3-lobed, pointed, toothed
Leaf-stalk	present or upper stalkless
FLOWERS	
Position	single, from base of leaf
Bracts	absent
Type	♂
Size	70–100mm
Colour	scarlet, rarely pink or white, usually with blackish blotch at base
Stalk	longer than flower
Sepals	2, bristly, soon falling
Petals	4, 20–40mm, rounded, crumpled, soon falling
Stamens	numerous, anthers bluish
Stigmas	8–12, forming radiating bands on top of ovary
Ovary	1, with 8–12 cells
FRUIT	
Type	1, capsule, opens by ring of pores at top, nearly globular, smooth
Size	10–20mm
Seeds	many, c1mm, blackish

broad capsule

leaflets

SIMILAR SPECIES

Two Poppies have elongated fruits: the **1 Long-headed Poppy** (*Papaver dubium*) with a smooth fruit, and the **2 Prickly Poppy** (*Papaver argemone*) with a spiny fruit. **3 Opium Poppy** (*Papaver somniferum*) has purplish flowers and much larger capsules.

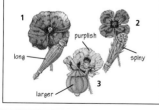

long

purplish

spiny

larger

Glaucium flavum **Yellow Horned-poppy**

A striking plant of coastal dunes and shingle banks, with large yellow flowers held above blue-green foliage. Its curved, horn-like fruits, unlike those of the cornfield Poppies, split open lengthways leaving the seeds embedded in a middle wall.

Status: native, most coasts.

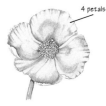

4 petals

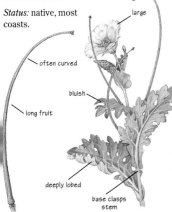

large

often curved

long fruit

bluish

deeply lobed

base clasps stem

SIMILAR SPECIES

Welsh Poppy (*Meconopsis cambrica*), a plant of inland, mostly mountainous, areas, has leaves that are more divided, and much shorter fruits which open by pores like common Poppies. This species is related to the magnificent blue Himalayan Poppy, which is cultivated in gardens.

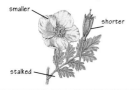

smaller

shorter

stalked

YELLOW HORNED-POPPY

Type	perennial or biennial
Height	30–90cm
Habitat	mainly dunes or shingle banks by sea
Flowering	June–September
STEMS AND LEAVES	
Stem	upright, branched, with yellow sap when cut
Root	thick tap-root
Hairs	rather sparse, rough
Stipules	absent
Leaves	from base or scattered around stem, 150–350mm, bluish green, tip blunt, edge lobed and toothed, often wavy
Leaf-stalk	present or absent on upper leaves
FLOWERS	
Position	single, from base of leaf
Bracts	absent
Type	♂
Size	60–90mm
Colour	yellow
Stalk	short
Sepals	2, separate, soon falling
Petals	4, almost equal, nearly circular
Stamens	numerous, yellow
Stigmas	2, nearly stalkless
Ovary	1, 2-celled
FRUIT	
Type	1, capsule, 2 sides splitting almost to base, long, thin, usually curved
Size	150–300mm
Seeds	numerous, minutely pitted

Greater Celandine *Chelidonium majus*

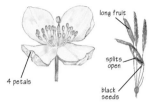

sepals fall

4 petals

long fruit

splits open

black seeds

yellow sap

toothed leaflets

The flowers of Greater Celandine look like tiny yellow Poppies, but its fruits appear more like those of the Cresses and Cabbages. The slender capsule splits open from the base releasing tiny black seeds, each with a fleshy, oily outgrowth that is eagerly sought by ants that carry off and disperse the seeds. The plant was formerly widely used for the treatment of sore or cloudy eyes, although the bright orange sap is acrid and poisonous. External application of the sap was used to treat warts, corns and ringworm, although it will equally damage any skin that it touches. In Russia, the plant has been used as an anti-cancer drug. The native distribution of Greater Celandine has been obscured by innumerable escapes from cultivation; it is now found in gardens mostly as a weed.

Status: native or introduced in some localities; common, throughout area.

Similar species: none.

GREATER CELANDINE

Type	perennial
Height	30–90cm
Habitat	banks and walls, often near houses
Flowering	May–August
STEMS AND LEAVES	
Stem	upright, branched, with orange sap
Root	woody stock, covered with fibres from old leaf-bases
Hairs	sparse
Stipules	absent
Leaves	at base of plant or scattered around stem, cut into 2–3 pairs of leaflets with leaflet at tip, blunt, edge with rounded teeth
Leaf-stalk	long below, absent above
FLOWERS	
Position	2–6, from tip of stem
Bracts	present
Type	♂
Size	20–25mm
Colour	bright yellow
Stalk	about equalling flower
Sepals	2, separate, soon falling, hairy
Petals	4, up to 10mm, oval, broadest above middle
Stamens	numerous, yellow
Stigma	1, 2 lobes on short style
Ovary	1, 1-celled
FRUIT	
Type	1, capsule, splitting from bottom, narrow
Size	30–50mm
Seeds	many, 1.5–2mm, black with fleshy, white outgrowth

This plant's name suggests a smoky nature, inspired partly by the look of finely divided, greyish leaves on widely branched stems and the tiny, dull purple flowers. Fumitory also has an acrid smell to the root and the sap makes eyes weep.

Status: native; common throughout most of area.

greyish green

many small leaflets

usually upright

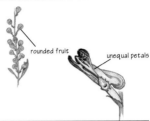

rounded fruit

unequal petals

SIMILAR SPECIES

1 White Ramping-fumitory (*F. capreolata*); has climbing stems, broader leaf-segments and larger, white flowers, tipped with purple. Corydalis species have many-seeded pods. **2 Yellow Corydalis** (*Corydalis lutea*); has bright yellow flowers, and **3 Climbing Corydalis** (*C. claviculata*) climbs and has small, creamy-white flowers.

paler base

yellow

white

1

2

3

larger

long pods

COMMON FUMITORY

Type	annual
Height	12–40cm
Habitat	cultivated ground; mostly light soils
Flowering	May–October
STEMS AND LEAVES	
Stem	nearly upright or climbing
Root	slender tap-root
Hairs	hairless
Stipules	absent
Leaves	spirally arranged, 20–100mm, many spear-shaped or oblong, bluish lobes
Leaf-stalk	present, lower broad-based
FLOWERS	
Position	10–40, in crowded spike from opposite leaf-base
Bracts	narrow, pointed, shorter than flower-stalk
Type	♂
Size	7–9mm
Colour	pink with blackish-purple tips to inner petals
Stalk	shorter than flowers
Sepals	2, 2–3.5mm, oval, toothed at base, soon falling
Petals	4, unequal, inner pair joined, hidden by larger, outer pair
Stamens	2
Stigma	1, 2-lobed
Ovary	1, 1-celled
FRUIT	
Type	1, nut-like, not opening, globular, blunt or notched
Size	2–2.5mm
Seeds	1, not released

Garlic Mustard *Alliaria petiolata*

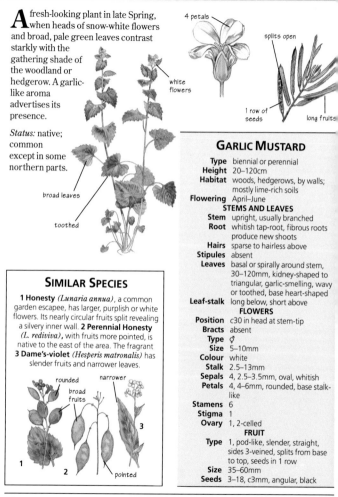

A fresh-looking plant in late Spring, when heads of snow-white flowers and broad, pale green leaves contrast starkly with the gathering shade of the woodland or hedgerow. A garlic-like aroma advertises its presence.

Status: native; common except in some northern parts.

broad leaves

toothed

4 petals

splits open

white flowers

1 row of seeds

long fruits

SIMILAR SPECIES

1 Honesty *(Lunaria annua)*, a common garden escapee, has larger, purplish or white flowers. Its nearly circular fruits split revealing a silvery inner wall. **2 Perennial Honesty** *(L. rediviva)*, with fruits more pointed, is native to the east of the area. The fragrant **3 Dame's-violet** *(Hesperis matronalis)* has slender fruits and narrower leaves.

rounded

broad fruits

narrower

pointed

GARLIC MUSTARD

Type	biennial or perennial
Height	20–120cm
Habitat	woods, hedgerows, by walls; mostly lime-rich soils
Flowering	April–June
STEMS AND LEAVES	
Stem	upright, usually branched
Root	whitish tap-root, fibrous roots produce new shoots
Hairs	sparse to hairless above
Stipules	absent
Leaves	basal or spirally around stem, 30–120mm, kidney-shaped to triangular, garlic-smelling, wavy or toothed, base heart-shaped
Leaf-stalk	long below, short above
FLOWERS	
Position	c30 in head at stem-tip
Bracts	absent
Type	♂
Size	5–10mm
Colour	white
Stalk	2.5–13mm
Sepals	4, 2.5–3.5mm, oval, whitish
Petals	4, 4–6mm, rounded, base stalk-like
Stamens	6
Stigma	1
Ovary	1, 2-celled
FRUIT	
Type	1, pod-like, slender, straight, sides 3-veined, splits from base to top, seeds in 1 row
Size	35–60mm
Seeds	3–18, c3mm, angular, black

4 petals

broad lobes

usually in water

2 rows of seeds

B est known as a salad plant or garnish with hot-tasting leaves, Water-cress is a species of the Cabbage family which normally grows in shallow water. Fleshy, hollow stems bear dark green leaves, paired leaflets and spikes of white, four-petalled flowers. Plants from stagnant water or where sheep graze should not be eaten because of the parasitic liver-fluke, which also attacks humans.

Status: native; lowland, throughout area.

SIMILAR SPECIES

Narrow-fruited Water-cress
(*N. microphyllum*) often has leaves tinged with purple, especially in Autumn, and narrow fruits with a single row of seeds.

thin

1 row of seeds

WATER-CRESS

Type	perennial
Height	10–60cm
Habitat	ditches, streams, rivers; wet soil or shallow water
Flowering	May–October

STEMS AND LEAVES

Stem	low-growing, turning upright, rooting, often floating, hollow
Root	branched, creeping stock
Hairs	absent
Stipules	absent
Leaves	spirally arranged, 1–4 pairs of leaflets, each elliptical to circular, blunt, edge unbroken or partly toothed
Leaf-stalk	present or absent above

FLOWERS

Position	many, in spike-like heads
Bracts	absent
Type	♂
Size	4–6mm
Colour	white
Stalk	8–12mm
Sepals	4, alternating with petals
Petals	4, equal, rounded with stalk-like base
Stamens	6
Stigma	1, sometimes 2-lobed
Ovary	1, 2-celled

FRUIT

Type	1, pod-like, level or curving upwards, sides swollen with faint mid-vein, seeds in 2 rows
Size	13–18mm
Seeds	many, c2mm, egg-shaped, shallowly pitted

Cuckooflower *Cardamine pratensis*

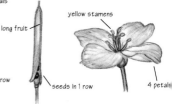

large equal petals

long fruit

upper narrow

toothed leaflets

yellow stamens

seeds in 1 row

4 petals

Attractive lavender flowers, opening at a time of the year when the cuckoo starts to call, mark out the clumps of Cuckooflower in a meadow or by a stream. The seeds are effectively dispersed by the pod, which splits open suddenly, hurling the seeds from the plant.

Status: native; throughout region.

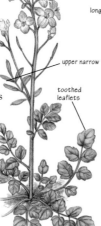

CUCKOOFLOWER

Type	perennial
Height	15–60cm
Habitat	meadows or streams; damp soil or shallow water
Flowering	April–June

STEMS AND LEAVES

Stem	upright, usually unbranched
Root	short, nearly horizontal stock, many fibrous roots
Hairs	sparse, on leaves
Stipules	absent
Leaves	basal or spirally arranged, lower with broad, toothed leaflets, upper leaves with narrow, unbroken leaflets
Leaf-stalk	present

FLOWERS

Position	7–20, in rounded heads which elongate in fruit
Bracts	absent
Type	♂
Size	12–18mm
Colour	lilac, rarely white
Stalk	8–25mm
Sepals	4, 3–4mm, papery edges, tip violet
Petals	4, 8–13mm, equal, oval, often notched, base stalk-like
Stamens	4–6
Stigma	1, sometimes 2-lobed
Ovary	1, 2-celled

FRUIT

Type	1, pod-like, suddenly coils open, slender, seeds in 1 row
Size	25–40mm
Seeds	numerous, c2mm, oblong

SIMILAR SPECIES

1 Large Bitter-cress (*C. amara*) has purple anthers. Explosive fruits are also found in two small-flowered species, making them troublesome in gardens. The annual **2 Hairy Bitter-cress** (*C. hirsuta*) mostly has four stamens, whereas **3 Wavy Bitter-cress** (*C. flexuosa*) has six and is usually perennial.

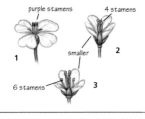

purple stamens

4 stamens

smaller

6 stamens

1

2

3

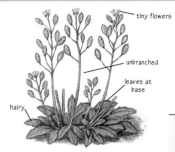

tiny flowers

unbranched

leaves at base

hairy

4 notched petals

broad fruit

forked hairs

2 rows of seeds

A diminutive plant of dry, often shallow or sandy soil, that has a rosette of leaves densely covered with odd Y-shaped or branched hairs. The short, flattened fruits quickly ripen and split open, revealing a silvery inner wall and two rows of seeds.

Status: native, most of area except for parts of north.

SIMILAR SPECIES

Several species from dry places lack the notch in the petals. **1 Wall Whitlowgrass** (*Draba muralis*) has taller, leafy stems. Much longer fruits are a feature of **2 Thale Cress** (*Arabidopsis thaliana*), which has cylindrical fruits, and **3 Hairy Rock-cress** (*Arabis hirsuta*), which has flattened fruits and winged seeds.

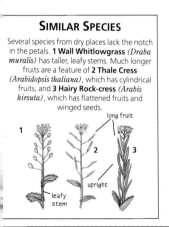

long fruit

1

2

3

upright

leafy stem

COMMON WHITLOWGRASS

Type	annual
Height	2–20cm
Habitat	dry places, often among rocks or on walls
Flowering	March–June
STEMS AND LEAVES	
Stem	straight or base branched
Root	fibrous
Hairs	dense, forked or star-shaped
Stipules	absent
Leaves	in rosette at base, 10–15mm, elliptical or spear-shaped, pointed, edge unbroken or 1–2 teeth
Leaf-stalk	broad
FLOWERS	
Position	in a rounded head, elongating in fruit
Bracts	absent
Type	♀
Size	3–6mm
Colour	white, some tinged red
Stalk	1.5–6mm
Sepals	4, 1.5–2.5mm
Petals	4, 1.5–6mm, equal, deeply notched, base stalk-like
Stamens	6, 4 long, 2 short
Stigma	1
Ovary	1, 2-celled
FRUIT	
Type	1, pod-like, oval, usually broadest above middle, flattened, sides split leaving broad inner wall, seeds in 2 rows
Size	3–9mm
Seeds	40–60, 0.3–0.4mm, flattened

Shepherd's-purse *Capsella bursa-pastoris*

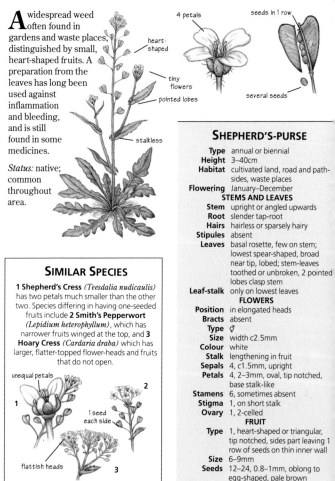

A widespread weed often found in gardens and waste places, distinguished by small, heart-shaped fruits. A preparation from the leaves has long been used against inflammation and bleeding, and is still found in some medicines.

Status: native; common throughout area.

4 petals

heart-shaped

tiny flowers

pointed lobes

stalkless

seeds in 1 row

several seeds

SIMILAR SPECIES

1 Shepherd's Cress *(Teesdalia nudicaulis)* has two petals much smaller than the other two. Species differing in having one-seeded fruits include **2 Smith's Pepperwort** *(Lepidium heterophyllum)*, which has narrower fruits winged at the top, and **3 Hoary Cress** *(Cardaria draba)* which has larger, flatter-topped flower-heads and fruits that do not open.

unequal petals

1

2

1 seed each side

flattish heads

3

SHEPHERD'S-PURSE

Type	annual or biennial
Height	3–40cm
Habitat	cultivated land, road and path-sides, waste places
Flowering	January–December
STEMS AND LEAVES	
Stem	upright or angled upwards
Root	slender tap-root
Hairs	hairless or sparsely hairy
Stipules	absent
Leaves	basal rosette, few on stem; lowest spear-shaped, broad near tip, lobed; stem-leaves toothed or unbroken, 2 pointed lobes clasp stem
Leaf-stalk	only on lowest leaves
FLOWERS	
Position	in elongated heads
Bracts	absent
Type	♂
Size	width c2.5mm
Colour	white
Stalk	lengthening in fruit
Sepals	4, c1.5mm, upright
Petals	4, 2–3mm, oval, tip notched, base stalk-like
Stamens	6, sometimes absent
Stigma	1, on short stalk
Ovary	1, 2-celled
FRUIT	
Type	1, heart-shaped or triangular, tip notched, sides part leaving 1 row of seeds on thin inner wall
Size	6–9mm
Seeds	12–24, 0.8–1mm, oblong to egg-shaped, pale brown

Thlaspi arvense **Field Penny-cress**

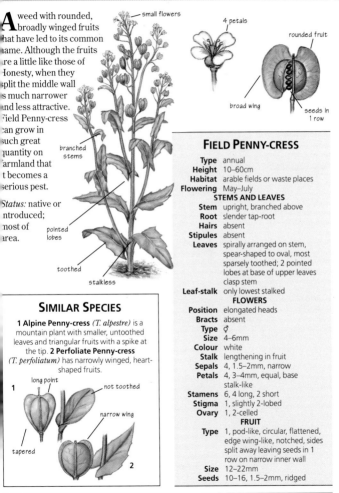

A weed with rounded, broadly winged fruits that have led to its common name. Although the fruits are a little like those of Honesty, when they split the middle wall is much narrower and less attractive. Field Penny-cress can grow in such great quantity on farmland that it becomes a serious pest.

Status: native or introduced; most of area.

small flowers

branched stems

pointed lobes

toothed

stalkless

4 petals

rounded fruit

broad wing

seeds in 1 row

FIELD PENNY-CRESS

Type	annual
Height	10–60cm
Habitat	arable fields or waste places
Flowering	May–July
STEMS AND LEAVES	
Stem	upright, branched above
Root	slender tap-root
Hairs	absent
Stipules	absent
Leaves	spirally arranged on stem, spear-shaped to oval, most sparsely toothed; 2 pointed lobes at base of upper leaves clasp stem
Leaf-stalk	only lowest stalked
FLOWERS	
Position	elongated heads
Bracts	absent
Type	♂
Size	4–6mm
Colour	white
Stalk	lengthening in fruit
Sepals	4, 1.5–2mm, narrow
Petals	4, 3–4mm, equal, base stalk-like
Stamens	6, 4 long, 2 short
Stigma	1, slightly 2-lobed
Ovary	1, 2-celled
FRUIT	
Type	1, pod-like, circular, flattened, edge wing-like, notched, sides split away leaving seeds in 1 row on narrow inner wall
Size	12–22mm
Seeds	10–16, 1.5–2mm, ridged

SIMILAR SPECIES

1 Alpine Penny-cress *(T. alpestre)* is a mountain plant with smaller, untoothed leaves and triangular fruits with a spike at the tip. **2 Perfoliate Penny-cress** *(T. perfoliatum)* has narrowly winged, heart-shaped fruits.

long point

not toothed

narrow wing

tapered

1

2

Black Mustard *Brassica nigra*

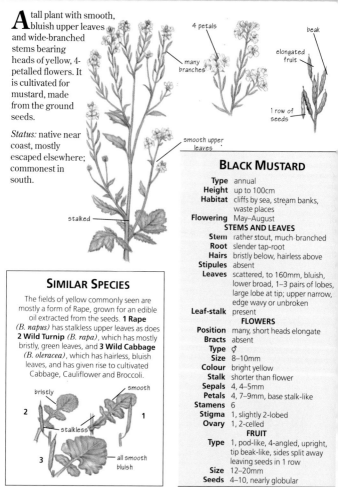

A tall plant with smooth, bluish upper leaves and wide-branched stems bearing heads of yellow, 4-petalled flowers. It is cultivated for mustard, made from the ground seeds.

Status: native near coast, mostly escaped elsewhere; commonest in south.

4 petals

many branches

beak

elongated fruit

1 row of seeds

smooth upper leaves

stalked

SIMILAR SPECIES

The fields of yellow commonly seen are mostly a form of Rape, grown for an edible oil extracted from the seeds. **1 Rape** (*B. napus*) has stalkless upper leaves as does **2 Wild Turnip** (*B. rapa*), which has mostly bristly, green leaves, and **3 Wild Cabbage** (*B. oleracea*), which has hairless, bluish leaves, and has given rise to cultivated Cabbage, Cauliflower and Broccoli.

bristly

smooth

stalkless

all smooth bluish

2

1

3

BLACK MUSTARD

Type	annual
Height	up to 100cm
Habitat	cliffs by sea, stream banks, waste places
Flowering	May–August
STEMS AND LEAVES	
Stem	rather stout, much-branched
Root	slender tap-root
Hairs	bristly below; hairless above
Stipules	absent
Leaves	scattered, to 160mm, bluish, lower broad, 1–3 pairs of lobes, large lobe at tip; upper narrow, edge wavy or unbroken
Leaf-stalk	present
FLOWERS	
Position	many, short heads elongate
Bracts	absent
Type	☿
Size	8–10mm
Colour	bright yellow
Stalk	shorter than flower
Sepals	4, 4–5mm
Petals	4, 7–9mm, base stalk-like
Stamens	6
Stigma	1, slightly 2-lobed
Ovary	1, 2-celled
FRUIT	
Type	1, pod-like, 4-angled, upright, tip beak-like, sides split away leaving seeds in 1 row
Size	12–20mm
Seeds	4–10, nearly globular

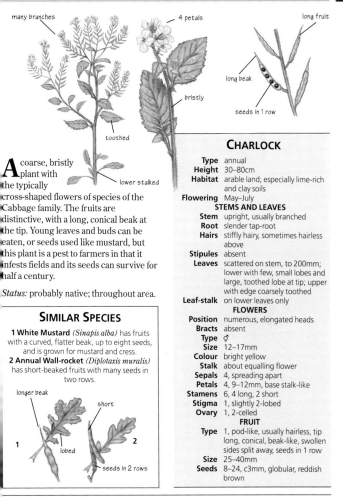

many branches

4 petals

long fruit

long beak

seeds in 1 row

bristly

toothed

lower stalked

Acoarse, bristly plant with the typically cross-shaped flowers of species of the Cabbage family. The fruits are distinctive, with a long, conical beak at the tip. Young leaves and buds can be eaten, or seeds used like mustard, but this plant is a pest to farmers in that it infests fields and its seeds can survive for half a century.

Status: probably native; throughout area.

SIMILAR SPECIES

1 White Mustard (*Sinapis alba*) has fruits with a curved, flatter beak, up to eight seeds, and is grown for mustard and cress.
2 Annual Wall-rocket (*Diplotaxis muralis*) has short-beaked fruits with many seeds in two rows.

longer beak

short

lobed

seeds in 2 rows

1

2

CHARLOCK

Type	annual
Height	30–80cm
Habitat	arable land; especially lime-rich and clay soils
Flowering	May–July

STEMS AND LEAVES

Stem	upright, usually branched
Root	slender tap-root
Hairs	stiffly hairy, sometimes hairless above
Stipules	absent
Leaves	scattered on stem, to 200mm; lower with few, small lobes and large, toothed lobe at tip; upper with edge coarsely toothed
Leaf-stalk	on lower leaves only

FLOWERS

Position	numerous, elongated heads
Bracts	absent
Type	♂
Size	12–17mm
Colour	bright yellow
Stalk	about equalling flower
Sepals	4, spreading apart
Petals	4, 9–12mm, base stalk-like
Stamens	6, 4 long, 2 short
Stigma	1, slightly 2-lobed
Ovary	1, 2-celled

FRUIT

Type	1, pod-like, usually hairless, tip long, conical, beak-like, swollen sides split away, seeds in 1 row
Size	25–40mm
Seeds	8–24, c3mm, globular, reddish brown

Sea Rocket *Cakile maritima*

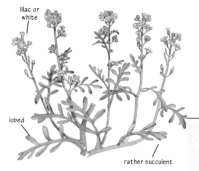

A common and distinctive plant of the drift-line of sandy or shingle sea-shores, usually with succulent, lobed leaves and lilac flowers. At the top of each short fruit is a corky-walled segment which breaks away with its single seed, to float in the sea while wind and tide carry it to some distant shore.

Status: native; all round coasts.

SIMILAR SPECIES

Several other species of the Cabbage family grow on the shore. **1 Sea Stock** *(Matthiola sinuata)* has greyish, hairy, scarcely lobed leaves and slender fruits. **2 Sea-kale** *(Crambe maritima)* has large, wavy-edged leaves and branched heads of pale flowers.

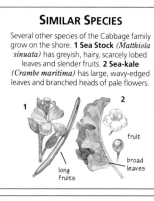

SEA ROCKET

Type	annual
Height	15–45cm
Habitat	drift-lines of sand and shingle beaches
Flowering	June–August
STEMS AND LEAVES	
Stem	low-growing or angled upwards, branched
Root	slender tap-root
Hairs	absent
Stipules	absent
Leaves	spirally arranged, 30–60mm, lower mostly with oblong, rarely toothed lobes; upper with few or no lobes
Leaf-stalk	only on lower leaves
FLOWERS	
Position	numerous, crowded in short spike at branch-tip
Bracts	absent
Type	♂
Size	8–12mm
Colour	purple, lilac or white
Stalk	about equalling flower
Sepals	4, 3–5mm, upright
Petals	4, 6–10mm, base stalk-like
Stamens	6
Stigma	1
Ovary	1, 2-celled
FRUIT	
Type	1, pod-like, not opening, upper part pointed, corky-walled, breaking off when ripe; lower part remains on plant
Size	10–25mm
Seeds	1–2, 4–5mm, smooth

Raphanus raphanistrum **Wild Radish**

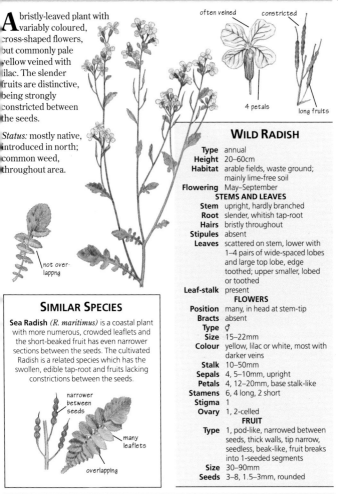

A bristly-leaved plant with variably coloured, cross-shaped flowers, but commonly pale yellow veined with lilac. The slender fruits are distinctive, being strongly constricted between the seeds.

Status: mostly native, introduced in north; common weed, throughout area.

often veined   constricted

4 petals   long fruits

not over-lapping

SIMILAR SPECIES

Sea Radish *(R. maritimus)* is a coastal plant with more numerous, crowded leaflets and the short-beaked fruit has even narrower sections between the seeds. The cultivated Radish is a related species which has the swollen, edible tap-root and fruits lacking constrictions between the seeds.

narrower between seeds

many leaflets

overlapping

WILD RADISH

Type	annual
Height	20–60cm
Habitat	arable fields, waste ground; mainly lime-free soil
Flowering	May–September
STEMS AND LEAVES	
Stem	upright, hardly branched
Root	slender, whitish tap-root
Hairs	bristly throughout
Stipules	absent
Leaves	scattered on stem, lower with 1–4 pairs of wide-spaced lobes and large top lobe, edge toothed; upper smaller, lobed or toothed
Leaf-stalk	present
FLOWERS	
Position	many, in head at stem-tip
Bracts	absent
Type	♂
Size	15–22mm
Colour	yellow, lilac or white, most with darker veins
Stalk	10–50mm
Sepals	4, 5–10mm, upright
Petals	4, 12–20mm, base stalk-like
Stamens	6, 4 long, 2 short
Stigma	1
Ovary	1, 2-celled
FRUIT	
Type	1, pod-like, narrowed between seeds, thick walls, tip narrow, seedless, beak-like, fruit breaks into 1-seeded segments
Size	30–90mm
Seeds	3–8, 1.5–3mm, rounded

Weld *Reseda luteola*

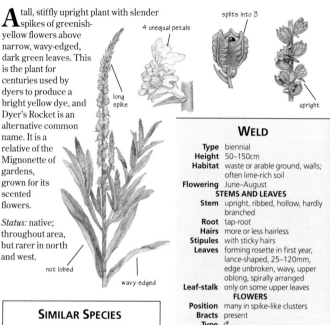

splits into 3

4 unequal petals

long spike

upright

A tall, stiffly upright plant with slender spikes of greenish-yellow flowers above narrow, wavy-edged, dark green leaves. This is the plant for centuries used by dyers to produce a bright yellow dye, and Dyer's Rocket is an alternative common name. It is a relative of the Mignonette of gardens, grown for its scented flowers.

Status: native; throughout area, but rarer in north and west.

not lobed

wavy-edged

WELD

Type	biennial
Height	50–150cm
Habitat	waste or arable ground, walls; often lime-rich soil
Flowering	June–August
STEMS AND LEAVES	
Stem	upright, ribbed, hollow, hardly branched
Root	tap-root
Hairs	more or less hairless
Stipules	with sticky hairs
Leaves	forming rosette in first year, lance-shaped, 25–120mm, edge unbroken, wavy, upper oblong, spirally arranged
Leaf-stalk	only on some upper leaves
FLOWERS	
Position	many in spike-like clusters
Bracts	present
Type	♂
Size	4–5mm
Colour	yellowish-green
Stalk	c1mm
Sepals	4, remaining in fruit
Petals	3–5, mostly 4, front petal slender, others cut into 3 or more lobes
Stamens	20–25
Stigmas	3
Ovary	1, 1-celled
FRUIT	
Type	1, capsule, nearly globular, tip opens by 3 teeth
Size	5–6mm
Seeds	numerous, 0.8–1mm, black, smooth, glossy

SIMILAR SPECIES

1 Wild Mignonette *(R. lutea)* is a smaller, branched plant with deeply lobed leaves.
2 Corn Mignonette *(R. phyteuma)* is similar but has white flowers and ripe fruits that hang down.

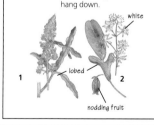

white

lobed

nodding fruit

Drosera rotundifolia **Round-leaved Sundew**

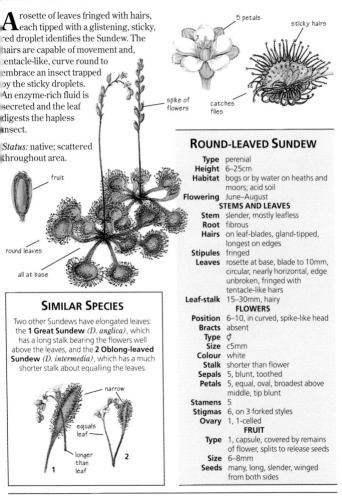

A rosette of leaves fringed with hairs, each tipped with a glistening, sticky, red droplet identifies the Sundew. The hairs are capable of movement and, tentacle-like, curve round to embrace an insect trapped by the sticky droplets. An enzyme-rich fluid is secreted and the leaf digests the hapless insect.

Status: native; scattered throughout area.

5 petals

sticky hairs

spike of flowers

catches flies

fruit

round leaves

all at base

SIMILAR SPECIES

Two other Sundews have elongated leaves: the **1 Great Sundew** *(D. anglica)*, which has a long stalk bearing the flowers well above the leaves, and the **2 Oblong-leaved Sundew** *(D. intermedia)*, which has a much shorter stalk about equalling the leaves.

narrow

equals leaf

longer than leaf

1

2

ROUND-LEAVED SUNDEW

Type	perenial
Height	6–25cm
Habitat	bogs or by water on heaths and moors; acid soil
Flowering	June–August
STEMS AND LEAVES	
Stem	slender, mostly leafless
Root	fibrous
Hairs	on leaf-blades, gland-tipped, longest on edges
Stipules	fringed
Leaves	rosette at base, blade to 10mm, circular, nearly horizontal, edge unbroken, fringed with tentacle-like hairs
Leaf-stalk	15–30mm, hairy
FLOWERS	
Position	6–10, in curved, spike-like head
Bracts	absent
Type	⚥
Size	c5mm
Colour	white
Stalk	shorter than flower
Sepals	5, blunt, toothed
Petals	5, equal, oval, broadest above middle, tip blunt
Stamens	5
Stigmas	6, on 3 forked styles
Ovary	1, 1-celled
FRUIT	
Type	1, capsule, covered by remains of flower, splits to release seeds
Size	6–8mm
Seeds	many, long, slender, winged from both sides

Orpine *Sedum telephium*

5 petals

flattish heads

fleshy

toothed

A broad-leaved, succulent plant with rounded, dense heads of purple flowers. It is related to the 'Ice Plant' of gardens, and is similarly popular with bees.

Status: native; scattered over much of area but rarer in the north.

ORPINE

Type	perennial
Height	20–60cm
Habitat	woods and hedgerows
Flowering	July–September
STEMS AND LEAVES	
Stem	upright, hardly branched, usually several
Root	stout, carrot-like tubers
Hairs	absent
Stipules	absent
Leaves	spirally placed on stem, 20–80mm, oval or oblong, bluish, often red-tinged, fleshy, blunt, toothed, base wedge-shaped or rounded
Leaf-stalk	mostly stalkless
FLOWERS	
Position	many, crowded in rounded head at tips of stems
Bracts	present
Type	☿
Size	9–12mm
Colour	reddish purple
Stalk	shorter than flower
Sepals	5, shorter than petals, spear-shaped, pointed
Petals	5, 3–5mm, spear-shaped, pointed
Stamens	10
Stigmas	1 to each ovary
Ovaries	5, 1-celled
FRUIT	
Type	5, pod-like, upright, slender, splitting to release seeds
Size	5–7mm
Seeds	numerous, small, elongated

SIMILAR SPECIES

1 Roseroot *(Rhodiola rosea)* is a mountain plant with similar foliage but yellowish, 4-petalled flowers on male or female plants. Though with a very different shape of leaf, **2 Navelwort** *(Umbilicus rupestris)* has flowers and fruits of similar structure but with petals joined into a tube. It is common on walls and banks in the west.

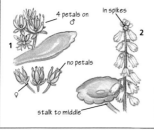

4 petals on ♂

in spikes

no petals

♀

2

stalk to middle

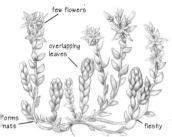

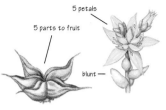

T his dwarf, succulent plant of dry,
 sunny places, has small, overlapping
leaves and short stems forming mats. It
is common on walls, rocks, cindery
edges of railway tracks, or even old roofs.
The leaves are hot-tasting, hence the
common name.

Status: native; most of area except parts
of north.

SIMILAR SPECIES

1 Reflexed Stonecrop *(S. reflexum)* is
larger with longer, pointed leaves and flattish
heads of yellow flowers. Two white-flowered
species are **2 English Stonecrop**
(S. anglicum), which has tiny leaves and few
flowers, and **3 White Stonecrop** *(S. album)*,
which has oblong leaves and broad heads of
tiny flowers.

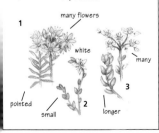

BITING STONECROP

Type	perennial
Height	2–10cm
Habitat	dunes, shingle, dry grassy places, walls
Flowering	June–July
STEMS AND LEAVES	
Stem	creeping, numerous, forms mats, turning upwards
Root	fibrous
Hairs	absent
Stipules	absent
Leaves	spirally around stem, 3–5mm, nearly triangular, broad-based, thick, succulent, mostly overlapping, blunt, edge unbroken
Leaf-stalk	absent
FLOWERS	
Position	2–4 per branch, few branches near stem-tip
Bracts	present
Type	⚥
Size	c12mm
Colour	bright yellow
Stalk	nearly stalkless
Sepals	5, oval, blunt-tipped
Petals	5, 8–9mm, spear-shaped, pointed, spreading apart
Stamens	10
Stigmas	1 per ovary
Ovaries	5, 1-celled
FRUIT	
Type	5, pod-like, pointed, spread apart, top splits
Size	5–6mm
Seeds	many, c1mm, egg-shaped

Meadow Saxifrage *Saxifraga granulata*

fruit tip splits

5 petals rounded

A delightful meadow plant with snow-white flowers and lobed, kidney-shaped leaves. At the base are tiny bulb-like buds, which serve to propagate the plant. A double form is sometimes grown in gardens.

Status: native; scattered localities, mainly east of area.

rounded, lobed

bulb-like

SIMILAR SPECIES

Two mountain species are **1 Starry Saxifrage** *(S. stellaris)*, its rosettes of leaves found especially where water seeps over rocks, and **2 Mossy Saxifrage** *(S. hypnoides)*, which forms moss-like cushions on rocks. **3 Rue-leaved Saxifrage** *(S. tridactylites)* is a small annual plant of dry, mainly lowland places, its leaves often tinged with red.

1

spotted

at base

leafy stem

thin lobes

3

small

2

forms mat

MEADOW SAXIFRAGE

Type	perennial
Height	10–50cm
Habitat	dryish grassland; all but acid soils
Flowering	April–June
STEMS AND LEAVES	
Stem	single, upright
Root	fibrous, bulb-like buds from base of lowest leaves
Hairs	scattered, long, white, stickily hairy above
Stipules	absent
Leaves	rosette at base, few on stem, blade 5–30mm, most kidney-shaped, lobed; upper sharply toothed, base wedge-shaped
Leaf-stalk	longer than blade or short on stem-leaves
FLOWERS	
Position	2–12, in widely branched head at tip of stem
Bracts	small, slender
Type	♂
Size	10–15mm
Colour	white
Stalk	4–20mm, stickily hairy
Sepals	5, oval, tip blunt
Petals	5, 10–17mm, oval
Stamens	10
Stigmas	2, on long styles
Ovary	1, 2-celled
FRUIT	
Type	1, capsule, egg-shaped, splits along upper edge
Size	6–8mm
Seeds	many, egg-shaped, rough

Opposite-leaved Golden-saxifrage
Chrysoplenium oppositifolium

A plant of shady banks, among tree-roots or beneath boulders, brightening the gloom with a yellowish colour to the entire top of the plant. The rounded leaves are rather succulent, and are sometimes eaten in the mountains of north-eastern France.

Status: native; common, most of area.

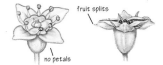
fruit splits

no petals

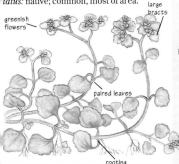

greenish flowers

large bracts

paired leaves

rooting

OPPOSITE-LEAVED GOLDEN-SAXIFRAGE

Type	perennial
Height	5–15cm
Habitat	wet, shady places, often by streams or springs
Flowering	April–July
STEMS AND LEAVES	
Stem	low-growing, rooting, forming large patches, turning upwards to flower
Root	fibrous
Hairs	scattered, pressed close to lower leaves, upper leaves hairless
Stipules	absent
Leaves	paired on opposite sides of stem, 10–20mm, circular, blunt, edge unbroken or with shallow, rounded teeth, base square or broadly wedge-shaped
Leaf-stalk	about equalling blade, upper shorter
FLOWERS	
Position	few, in flattish heads
Bracts	leaf-like, greenish yellow
Type	♂
Size	3–4mm
Colour	greenish yellow
Stalk	absent
Sepals	4–5, oval to triangular
Petals	absent
Stamens	8
Stigmas	2, on separate styles
Ovary	1, 1-celled
FRUIT	
Type	1, capsule, splits down centre
Size	5–6mm
Seeds	many, blackish, rough

SIMILAR SPECIES

Alternate-leaved Golden-saxifrage
(*C. alternifolium*) differs in its creeping, underground, scaly stems, from which most of the kidney-shaped leaves arise. Most flowering stems have only a single leaf, but if there are more they are not paired.

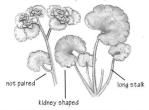

not paired

kidney shaped

long stalk

Grass-of-Parnassus *Parnassia palustris*

fruit opens

5 petals

long stalk

fringed

heart-shaped

This beautiful, honey-scented, moorland flower is not at all grass-like but has long-stemmed, white, cup-shaped flowers, delicately veined with green, and a tuft of heart-shaped leaves. It was formerly found more widely on marshy ground, but its range has been restricted by drainage and 'improvement' of land. Five of the stamens have been transformed into special structures, fringed with glistening drops, which attract insects with the false promise of abundant nectar. These structures distinguish the species from those of the Saxifrage family, which otherwise have a rather similar structure to the flowers. Grass-of-Parnassus has been used in the past to treat liver and nervous complaints.

most at base

Status: native; widespread but rather scattered, rarer in south.

Similar species: none.

GRASS-OF-PARNASSUS

Type	perennial
Height	10–30cm
Habitat	marshes and moors; wet ground
Flowering	July–October

STEMS AND LEAVES

Stem	upright, straight
Root	short, upright stock
Hairs	hairless
Stipules	absent
Leaves	most basal, 10–50mm, heart-shaped, bluish green, often red-spotted beneath, sharpish, edge unbroken; 1 stem-leaf near base of flowering stem
Leaf-stalk	longer than blade, absent on stem-leaf

FLOWERS

Position	single, on long stalk from base of single stem-leaf
Bracts	absent
Type	♂
Size	15–30mm
Colour	white, grey-green veins
Stalk	much longer than flower
Sepals	5, spear-shaped
Petals	5, 7–12mm, equal, oval, tip notched
Stamens	5, with 5 modified stamens fringed with sticky drops
Stigmas	4, not stalked
Ovary	1, 1-celled except at base

FRUIT

Type	1, capsule, egg-shaped, 4 grooves, splits into 4
Size	15–20mm
Seeds	many, 1.5–2mm, oblong

60

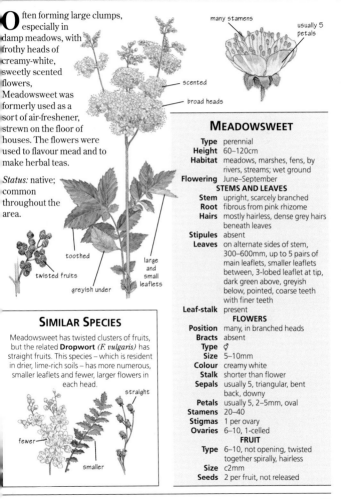

Filipendula ulmaria **Meadowsweet**

Often forming large clumps, especially in damp meadows, with frothy heads of creamy-white, sweetly scented flowers, Meadowsweet was formerly used as a sort of air-freshener, strewn on the floor of houses. The flowers were used to flavour mead and to make herbal teas.

Status: native; common throughout the area.

many stamens

usually 5 petals

scented

broad heads

toothed

twisted fruits

greyish under

large and small leaflets

SIMILAR SPECIES

Meadowsweet has twisted clusters of fruits, but the related **Dropwort** (*F. vulgaris*) has straight fruits. This species – which is resident in drier, lime-rich soils – has more numerous, smaller leaflets and fewer, larger flowers in each head.

straight

fewer

smaller

MEADOWSWEET

Type	perennial
Height	60–120cm
Habitat	meadows, marshes, fens, by rivers, streams; wet ground
Flowering	June–September

STEMS AND LEAVES

Stem	upright, scarcely branched
Root	fibrous from pink rhizome
Hairs	mostly hairless, dense grey hairs beneath leaves
Stipules	absent
Leaves	on alternate sides of stem, 300–600mm, up to 5 pairs of main leaflets, smaller leaflets between, 3-lobed leaflet at tip, dark green above, greyish below, pointed, coarse teeth with finer teeth
Leaf-stalk	present

FLOWERS

Position	many, in branched heads
Bracts	absent
Type	♂
Size	5–10mm
Colour	creamy white
Stalk	shorter than flower
Sepals	usually 5, triangular, bent back, downy
Petals	usually 5, 2–5mm, oval
Stamens	20–40
Stigmas	1 per ovary
Ovaries	6–10, 1-celled

FRUIT

Type	6–10, not opening, twisted together spirally, hairless
Size	c2mm
Seeds	2 per fruit, not released

Cloudberry *Rubus chamaemorus*

Cloudberry is a rather surprising plant, producing its succulent, raspberry-like fruits on short, herb-like stems near ground level instead of the shrubby growth normally associated with such fruits. The leaves are also unusual in that they have radiating lobes and a rather crinkly texture.

Status: native; common in some mountain areas, absent from much of the south.

turns orange

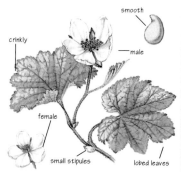

smooth

crinkly

male

female

small stipules

lobed leaves

SIMILAR SPECIES

Stone Bramble *(Rubus saxatilis)* is a plant of rocky places, usually in woodland shade, and differs from Cloudberry in having leaves divided into three leaflets and scarlet ripe fruits.

3 leaflets

few segments

CLOUDBERRY

Type	perennial
Height	5–20cm
Habitat	mountains, moors and bogs; damp ground
Flowering	June–August

STEMS AND LEAVES

Stem	flowering stems upright, replaced each year
Root	long, creeping rhizome
Hairs	short
Stipules	oval, papery
Leaves	on alternate sides of stem, 15–80mm, few, rounded, with 5–7 triangular, blunt, toothed lobes, base heart-shaped
Leaf-stalk	10–70

FLOWERS

Position	single, at stem-tip, ♂ and ♀ flowers on separate plants
Bracts	absent
Type 1	♂ with numerous stamens
Type 2	♀ with 1 stigma per ovary
Size	18–30mm
Colour	white
Stalk	present
Sepals	5, shorter than petals, oval, pointed
Petals	5, 8–15mm, oval, blunt
Ovaries	few, 1-celled

FRUIT

Type	few, berry-like segments in a rounded cluster with middle attached when shed, turns red, then orange
Size	cluster 15–20mm
Seeds	1 per fruit, not released

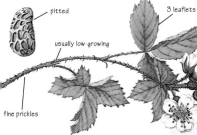

pitted

3 leaflets

usually low-growing

bluish

fine prickles

Commonly an understorey plant of woodland, it has low, arching, spiny stems, rooting at the tip, making hoop-like obstacles to trip up the unwary. This is one of the smaller Brambles, with few fruit-segments developing from each flower.

Status: native; widespread, commonest in south.

SIMILAR SPECIES

1 Bramble *(Rubus fruticosus agg.)* is a name given to many species, differing in details of stem-angles, prickles, hairs or leaf-shape, and requiring considerable expertise for accurate identification. **2 Raspberry** *(Rubus idaeus)* differs by its paired leaflets and red fruits of which the centre usually stays on the plant.

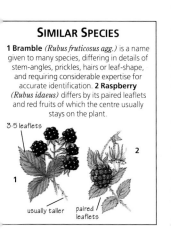

3-5 leaflets

usually taller

paired leaflets

DEWBERRY

Type	perennial
Height	up to 45cm
Habitat	scrub, woodland, grassland; mostly lime-rich soil
Flowering	June–September
STEMS AND LEAVES	
Stem	arching, tip roots, not angled, sparsely prickly, waxy, lasts 2 years, flowers in second
Root	fibrous
Hairs	sparse, mainly above
Stipules	spear-shaped, on leaf-stalk
Leaves	scattered around stem, 3 oval or diamond-shaped, toothed or lobed leaflets
Leaf-stalk	present
FLOWERS	
Position	few, in branched head from stem-tip or leaf-base
Bracts	absent
Type	♂
Size	20–25mm
Colour	white or pink-tinged
Stalk	slender, sparsely prickly
Sepals	5, long-pointed, white-edged
Petals	5, nearly circular, equal
Stamens	numerous
Stigmas	1 per ovary
Ovaries	2–5, rarely to 20, 1-celled
FRUIT	
Type	2–5, rarely to 20, berry-like parts, black, whitish, waxy covering; base stays with segments when shed
Size	8–18mm
Seeds	single, not released

Dog-rose *Rosa canina*

O ne of the most familiar of all wild flowers, abounding in hedgerows and adorning them with its delicately scented, shell-pink flowers. In the autumn, red, berry-like fruits or hips are attractive. Children are still given rose-hip syrup, which is rich in Vitamin C.

Status: native; common through most of area but rarer in parts of north.

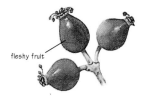

fleshy fruit

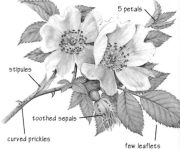

5 petals

stipules

toothed sepals

curved prickles

few leaflets

SIMILAR SPECIES

There are many forms and species of wild Rose. **1 Harsh Downy-rose** (*R. tomentosa*), which has hairy leaves and fruits, has straight prickles. **2 Sweet-briar** (*R. rubiginosa*) has sticky, apple-scented hairs beneath the leaves and the sepals stay on the ripening fruit.

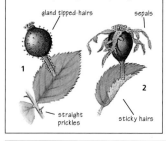

gland tipped hairs

sepals

1

2

straight prickles

sticky hairs

DOG-ROSE

Type	perennial
Height	100–300cm
Habitat	woods, scrub, hedges
Flowering	June–July

STEMS AND LEAVES

Stem	arching, with strongly curved or hooked prickles
Root	woody stock
Hairs	absent or sometimes short hairs beneath leaves
Stipules	long, broad, on leaf-stalk
Leaves	on alternate sides of stem, with 2–3 pairs of oval or elliptical, toothed leaflets, each 15–40mm
Leaf-stalk	present

FLOWERS

Position	1–4, at ends of stems
Bracts	broad
Type	♂
Size	15–25mm, rarely 50mm
Colour	pink or white
Stalk	5–20mm
Sepals	5, lobed, bent back, falling in fruit
Petals	5, 20–25mm
Stamens	numerous
Stigmas	many in conical head
Ovaries	numerous, 1-celled

FRUIT

Type	1, berry-like, egg-shaped or ellipsoidal, outer layer formed from flower-base, contains nut-like fruits, scarlet, smooth
Size	10–20mm
Seeds	1 to each nut-like fruit, not released

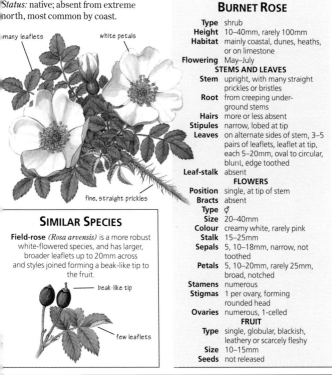

This dainty little Rose is most common near the sea, spreading by suckers to cover large areas on old dunes and heaths. The plant is easily recognized: the fruits are almost black, instead of the red of other species. The leaves have small, toothed leaflets and resemble those of Salad Burnet or Burnet Saxifrage.

Status: native; absent from extreme north, most common by coast.

sepals attached

blackish

many leaflets

white petals

fine, straight prickles

SIMILAR SPECIES

Field-rose *(Rosa arvensis)* is a more robust white-flowered species, and has larger, broader leaflets up to 20mm across and styles joined forming a beak-like tip to the fruit.

beak-like tip

few leaflets

BURNET ROSE

Type	shrub
Height	10–40mm, rarely 100mm
Habitat	mainly coastal, dunes, heaths, or on limestone
Flowering	May–July
STEMS AND LEAVES	
Stem	upright, with many straight prickles or bristles
Root	from creeping underground stems
Hairs	more or less absent
Stipules	narrow, lobed at tip
Leaves	on alternate sides of stem, 3–5 pairs of leaflets, leaflet at tip, each 5–20mm, oval to circular, blunt, edge toothed
Leaf-stalk	absent
FLOWERS	
Position	single, at tip of stem
Bracts	absent
Type	♂
Size	20–40mm
Colour	creamy white, rarely pink
Stalk	15–25mm
Sepals	5, 10–18mm, narrow, not toothed
Petals	5, 10–20mm, rarely 25mm, broad, notched
Stamens	numerous
Stigmas	1 per ovary, forming rounded head
Ovaries	numerous, 1-celled
FRUIT	
Type	single, globular, blackish, leathery or scarcely fleshy
Size	10–15mm
Seeds	not released

Agrimony *Agrimonia eupatoria*

A stiffly upright plant, with slender spikes of yellow flowers and rather coarse leaves with leaflets of varying size. The nodding fruits have a ring of hooked spines, which may catch in an animal's fur, thus effecting dispersal. Agrimony once had many uses, including as an antidote for snake-bite and to give relief from colds, in the form of a wine with oranges, lemons, and ginger.

Status: native; most of area except parts of north.

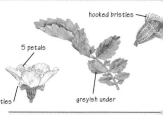

hooked bristles

5 petals

bristles

greyish under

long spikes

many leaflets

AGRIMONY

Type	perennial
Height	30–60cm
Habitat	grassy places, hedgebanks, fields and road-verges
Flowering	June–August

STEMS AND LEAVES

Stem	upright, mostly unbranched
Root	rhizome
Hairs	gland-tipped on stems, grey-woolly beneath leaves
Stipules	leaf-like
Leaves	on alternate sides of stem, most near base, 3–6 main pairs of elliptical, coarse-toothed leaflets, 20–60mm long, small leaflets between, leaflet at tip; upper leaves with few leaflets
Leaf-stalk	short

FLOWERS

Position	many, in spike at stem-tip
Bracts	present, lower 3-lobed
Type	♂
Size	5–8mm
Colour	golden yellow
Stalk	1–3mm, shorter than flower
Sepals	5, oval, pointed
Petals	5, oval
Stamens	10–20
Stigmas	1 per ovary
Ovaries	1–2, 1-celled

FRUIT

Type	single, conical, hard wall encloses 1–2 nut-like fruits, grooved, ring of hooked spines near top
Size	6–7mm
Seeds	not released

SIMILAR SPECIES

Fragrant Agrimony (*Agrimonia procera*) is rarer, more robust, and has sweetly scented flowers; the lowest spines of the fruit are bent backwards.

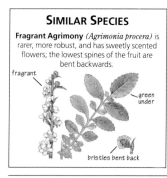

fragrant

green under

bristles bent back

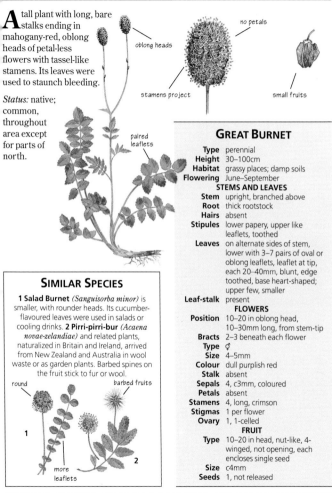

A tall plant with long, bare stalks ending in mahogany-red, oblong heads of petal-less flowers with tassel-like stamens. Its leaves were used to staunch bleeding.

Status: native; common, throughout area except for parts of north.

oblong heads

no petals

stamens project

small fruits

paired leaflets

GREAT BURNET

Type	perennial
Height	30–100cm
Habitat	grassy places; damp soils
Flowering	June–September
STEMS AND LEAVES	
Stem	upright, branched above
Root	thick rootstock
Hairs	absent
Stipules	lower papery, upper like leaflets, toothed
Leaves	on alternate sides of stem, lower with 3–7 pairs of oval or oblong leaflets, leaflet at tip, each 20–40mm, blunt, edge toothed, base heart-shaped; upper few, smaller
Leaf-stalk	present
FLOWERS	
Position	10–20 in oblong head, 10–30mm long, from stem-tip
Bracts	2–3 beneath each flower
Type	♂
Size	4–5mm
Colour	dull purplish red
Stalk	absent
Sepals	4, c3mm, coloured
Petals	absent
Stamens	4, long, crimson
Stigmas	1 per flower
Ovary	1, 1-celled
FRUIT	
Type	10–20 in head, nut-like, 4-winged, not opening, each encloses single seed
Size	c4mm
Seeds	1, not released

SIMILAR SPECIES

1 Salad Burnet *(Sanguisorba minor)* is smaller, with rounder heads. Its cucumber-flavoured leaves were used in salads or cooling drinks. **2 Pirri-pirri-bur** *(Acaena novae-zelandiae)* and related plants, naturalized in Britain and Ireland, arrived from New Zealand and Australia in wool waste or as garden plants. Barbed spines on the fruit stick to fur or wool.

round

barbed fruits

more leaflets

1

2

67

Mountain Avens *Dryas octopetala*

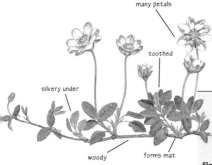

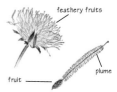

many petals

toothed

feathery fruits

silvery under

woody

forms mat

fruit

plume

W iry stems of Mountain Avens support a tough mat of dark green foliage which carpets rocky places or hangs down cliffs. In Summer it is dotted with anemone-like flowers of white petals encircling a boss of golden stamens. Later, it has feathery, plumed fruits like those of the distantly related Pasqueflower and Traveller's Joy. A mountain plant in the south of the area, it is found by the Atlantic shore in the north-west. This is mainly an Arctic plant, elsewhere being a relict from the last Ice Age when it covered large expanses south of the ice-sheet. Mountain Avens is often cultivated as a rockery plant in gardens, and is propagated by layering young shoots or from seed. Uses for the plant include infusion as a stomach tonic and a gargle to treat infections of the mouth and throat.

Status: native; mountains towards south, more common at low altitudes towards Arctic.

Similar species: none.

MOUNTAIN AVENS

Type	perennial
Height	low-growing
Habitat	rock crevices, mountain ledges, sometimes near sea-level; base-rich rocks
Flowering	June–July
STEMS AND LEAVES	
Stem	up to 50cm long, woody, twisted, much-branched
Root	creeping
Hairs	dense, white beneath leaves, hairless above, flower-stalks and sepals with gland-tipped hairs
Stipules	papery, brownish
Leaves	on alternate sides of stem, 5–40mm, oblong or oval, evergreen, blunt, toothed, base squarish
Leaf-stalk	present
FLOWERS	
Position	single, from base of leaf
Bracts	absent
Type	♂
Size	25–40mm
Colour	white
Stalk	20–80mm, upright
Sepals	7–10, oblong
Petals	8–16, 7–17mm, oblong
Stamens	numerous
Stigmas	1 per ovary
Ovaries	numerous
FRUIT	
Type	numerous in cluster, nut-like at base, with long, feathery, whitish plume
Size	20–30mm
Seeds	not released

S hady places are home to the small yellow, upturned flowers and hooked, animal-dispersed fruits of Wood Avens. In gardens it is awkward to remove because the brittle stems snap, leaving the roots. Faintly clove-scented, the roots were once used to flavour ale or as an insect-repellent.

Status: native; most of area except parts of north.

turns upwards

bristly

hooked fruits

brittle

stipules

paired leaflets

WOOD AVENS

Type	perennial
Height	20–60cm
Habitat	shady places, woods, hedges; damp, rich soils
Flowering	June–August
STEMS AND LEAVES	
Stem	mostly upright, brittle
Root	fibrous from short stock
Hairs	short, rather bristly
Stipules	lower as row of bristles; upper toothed, leaflet-like
Leaves	basal or on alternate sides of stem; lower with 2–4 unequal pairs of leaflets, leaflet at tip, each 5–80mm, blunt, toothed, base wedge-shaped; upper with 3 leaflets or lobes
Leaf-stalk	present
FLOWERS	
Position	2–5, in wide-branched heads
Bracts	present
Type	♂
Size	10–15mm
Colour	yellow
Stalk	longer than flower, upright
Sepals	5, oval, pointed
Petals	5, 5–9mm, oval, blunt
Stamens	numerous
Stigmas	1 per ovary
Ovaries	numerous, 1-celled
FRUIT	
Type	numerous in small head, nut-like, egg-shaped, tip hooked
Size	3–6mm
Seeds	not released

SIMILAR SPECIES

1 Water Avens (*G. rivale*), in wet places, has larger, nodding, orange-pink flowers. **2 Hybrid Avens** (*G. x intermedium*) grows near Wood Avens, with intermediate but often very variable flowers. **3 Marsh Cinquefoil** (*Potentilla palustris*) has reddish sepals and slender, purple petals.

nodding

pinkish

reddish

1

2

3

usually level

spreading leaflets

Tormentil *Potentilla erecta*

nut-like fruits

4 petals

Four-petalled, buttercup-like flowers of Tormentil are a common sight on heaths or other grassy places. Its dried roots have many uses including treating mouth infections or sunburn, and provide a red dye. Tormentil is a larval food of the Grizzled Skipper butterfly.

2 stipules

3 leaflets

Status: native; common, throughout area.

SIMILAR SPECIES

Stems of **1 Creeping Cinquefoil** *(P. reptans)* run along the ground, regularly sending up long-stalked leaves and single flowers.
2 Silverweed *(P. anserina)* grows in the same way but its numerous, paired leaflets are silvery beneath. The silvery leaves of **3 Hoary Cinquefoil** *(P. argentea)* look more like those of Tormentil.

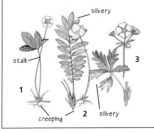

silvery

stalk

silvery

creeping

1

2

3

TORMENTIL

Type	perennial
Height	10–30cm, rarely 50cm
Habitat	grassland, heaths, wood clearing; mainly acid soil
Flowering	June–September
STEMS AND LEAVES	
Stem	low-growing to nearly upright, slender, branched
Root	thick, woody stock
Hairs	short, pressed to surface
Stipules	like leaflets, lobed
Leaves	basal or on alternate sides of stem, with 3 or rarely 5 leaflets; lower 5–10mm, blunt, toothed; upper 10–20mm, narrower, lobed or toothed above
Leaf-stalk	long below, absent above
FLOWERS	
Position	numerous in branched head
Bracts	leaf-like, upper undivided
Type	♂
Size	7–15mm
Colour	yellow
Stalk	much longer than flower
Sepals	4, 3–5mm, spear-shaped, pointed, surrounded by bract-like structures
Petals	4, 3–6mm, tip notched
Stamens	14–20
Stigmas	1 per ovary
Ovaries	4–8, rarely to 20, 1-celled
FRUIT	
Type	mostly 4–8 in rounded head, nut-like, egg-shaped, rough
Size	c2mm
Seeds	not released

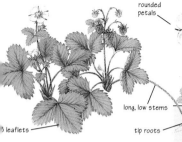

rounded petals

fleshy

pip-like fruit

long, low stems

tip roots

3 leaflets

Like a diminutive version of the Garden Strawberry, the fruits of the Wild Strawberry are less succulent but full of flavour. Plants spread by low, arching stems called runners. The fleshy part of a Strawberry is derived from the swollen base of the flower, the fruits proper being the yellowish pips on the surface.

Status: native; common throughout area.

SIMILAR SPECIES

1 Hautbois Strawberry *(F. moschata)*, mainly from the east of the area, is larger and has fruits devoid of pips at the base. **2 Garden Strawberry** *(F. x ananassa)* is commonly naturalized. **3 Barren Strawberry** *(Potentilla sterilis)* lacks the fleshy base to the nut-like fruits.

overlapping petals

no pips at base

1

notched petals

3

dry fruit

2

WILD STRAWBERRY

Type	perennial
Height	5–30cm
Habitat	shady places, woods, hedgerows, grassland; mainly lime-rich soils
Flowering	April–July

STEMS AND LEAVES

Stem	nearly upright or low, arching and rooting
Root	thick, woody stock
Hairs	spreading out on stem, silky under leaves
Stipules	papery, often purplish
Leaves	basal or on alternate sides of stem, with 3 leaflets, each 10–60mm, oval, blunt, toothed
Leaf-stalk	long

FLOWERS

Position	few, in branched head
Bracts	leaf-like, upper undivided
Type	♂
Size	12–18mm
Colour	white
Stalk	longer than flower
Sepals	5, 3–6mm, oval, pointed, bent back in fruit, 5 extra bract-like parts
Petals	5, 5–7mm, oval, blunt
Stamens	c20
Stigmas	1 per ovary
Ovaries	numerous, 1-celled

FRUIT

Type	egg-shaped or spherical, red, juicy base, mainly tiny, nut-like fruits on surface
Size	10–20mm
Seeds	1 per fruit, not released

Hairy Lady's-mantle
Alchemilla filicaulis subsp. vestita

no petals

fruit enclosed

small bracts

4 sepals

Although its flowers are inconspicuous, the broad leaves of this plant are lobed with fan-like folds, for which it is often grown in gardens. Water-droplets are exuded by the leaves when the air humidity is high, usually before the morning sun touches them.

small clusters

Status: native; most of area but rarer in south.

toothed

radiating lobes

folded

SIMILAR SPECIES

One of the more distinct of many related species is **1 Alpine Lady's-mantle** *(A. alpina)*, its narrowly lobed leaves silvery beneath. **2 Parsley-piert** *(Aphanes arvensis)* is a much smaller, annual plant of waste or cultivated ground. **3 Sibbaldia** *(Sibbaldia procumbens)* has leaves cut into leaflets and usually has narrow, yellow petals.

narrow

1

silvery under

tiny flowers

2

small petals

leaflets

3

HAIRY LADY'S-MANTLE

Type	perennial
Height	5–45cm
Habitat	open woods, rock-ledges, grassland; damp lime-rich or neutral soil
Flowering	June–September
STEMS AND LEAVES	
Stem	turning or angled upwards
Root	thick, woody stock
Hairs	rather dense, projecting
Stipules	papery, often purple-tinged
Leaves	basal or few on alternate sides of stem; lower 10–150mm, circular or kidney-shaped with 7–9 toothed lobes, notch between lobes wide; upper smaller, with fewer lobes
Leaf-stalk	long below, short above
FLOWERS	
Position	in small clusters on near stem-tips
Bracts	leaf-like, toothed
Type	♂
Size	3–4mm
Colour	green
Stalk	shorter than flower
Sepals	4, oval, broad-based
Petals	absent
Stamens	4, between sepals
Stigma	1, club-shaped
Ovary	1, 1-celled
FRUIT	
Type	1, nut-like, enclosed by base of flower, not opening
Size	2–3mm
Seeds	1, not released

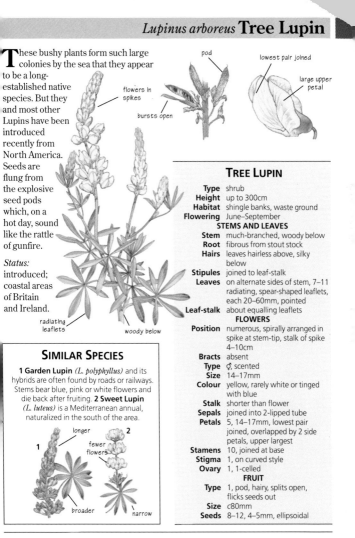

These bushy plants form such large colonies by the sea that they appear to be a long-established native species. But they and most other Lupins have been introduced recently from North America. Seeds are flung from the explosive seed pods which, on a hot day, sound like the rattle of gunfire.

Status: introduced; coastal areas of Britain and Ireland.

pod

bursts open

flowers in spikes

lowest pair joined

large upper petal

radiating leaflets

woody below

SIMILAR SPECIES

1 Garden Lupin *(L. polyphyllus)* and its hybrids are often found by roads or railways. Stems bear blue, pink or white flowers and die back after fruiting. **2 Sweet Lupin** *(L. luteus)* is a Mediterranean annual, naturalized in the south of the area.

longer

fewer flowers

1

2

broader

narrow

TREE LUPIN

Type	shrub
Height	up to 300cm
Habitat	shingle banks, waste ground
Flowering	June–September
STEMS AND LEAVES	
Stem	much-branched, woody below
Root	fibrous from stout stock
Hairs	leaves hairless above, silky below
Stipules	joined to leaf-stalk
Leaves	on alternate sides of stem, 7–11 radiating, spear-shaped leaflets, each 20–60mm, pointed
Leaf-stalk	about equalling leaflets
FLOWERS	
Position	numerous, spirally arranged in spike at stem-tip, stalk of spike 4–10cm
Bracts	absent
Type	♂, scented
Size	14–17mm
Colour	yellow, rarely white or tinged with blue
Stalk	shorter than flower
Sepals	joined into 2-lipped tube
Petals	5, 14–17mm, lowest pair joined, overlapped by 2 side petals, upper largest
Stamens	10, joined at base
Stigma	1, on curved style
Ovary	1, 1-celled
FRUIT	
Type	1, pod, hairy, splits open, flicks seeds out
Size	c80mm
Seeds	8–12, 4–5mm, ellipsoidal

73

Tufted Vetch *Vicia cracca*

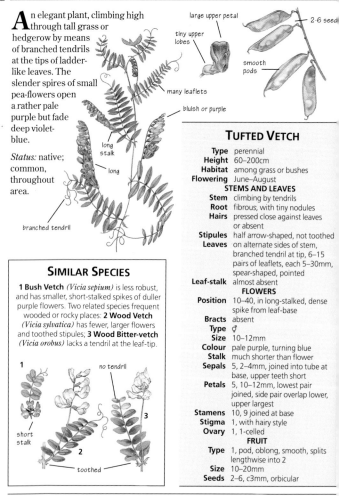

An elegant plant, climbing high through tall grass or hedgerow by means of branched tendrils at the tips of ladder-like leaves. The slender spires of small pea-flowers open a rather pale purple but fade deep violet-blue.

Status: native; common, throughout area.

large upper petal

tiny upper lobes

2–6 seed

smooth pods

many leaflets

blush or purple

long stalk

long

branched tendril

SIMILAR SPECIES

1 Bush Vetch (*Vicia sepium*) is less robust, and has smaller, short-stalked spikes of duller purple flowers. Two related species frequent wooded or rocky places: **2 Wood Vetch** (*Vicia sylvatica*) has fewer, larger flowers and toothed stipules; **3 Wood Bitter-vetch** (*Vicia orobus*) lacks a tendril at the leaf-tip.

short stalk

no tendril

1

2

3

toothed

TUFTED VETCH

Type	perennial
Height	60–200cm
Habitat	among grass or bushes
Flowering	June–August
STEMS AND LEAVES	
Stem	climbing by tendrils
Root	fibrous, with tiny nodules
Hairs	pressed close against leaves or absent
Stipules	half arrow-shaped, not toothed
Leaves	on alternate sides of stem, branched tendril at tip, 6–15 pairs of leaflets, each 5–30mm, spear-shaped, pointed
Leaf-stalk	almost absent
FLOWERS	
Position	10–40, in long-stalked, dense spike from leaf-base
Bracts	absent
Type	♂
Size	10–12mm
Colour	pale purple, turning blue
Stalk	much shorter than flower
Sepals	5, 2–4mm, joined into tube at base, upper teeth short
Petals	5, 10–12mm, lowest pair joined, side pair overlap lower, upper largest
Stamens	10, 9 joined at base
Stigma	1, with hairy style
Ovary	1, 1-celled
FRUIT	
Type	1, pod, oblong, smooth, splits lengthwise into 2
Size	10–20mm
Seeds	2–6, c3mm, orbicular

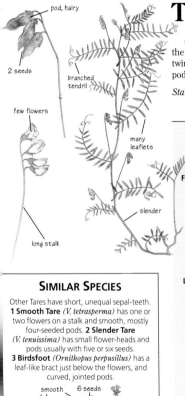

pod, hairy

2 seeds

branched tendril

few flowers

many leaflets

slender

long stalk

Tares have caused farmers problems for thousands of years, reducing yields and making harvesting difficult, and are mentioned as such in the Bible. Slender stems climb with twining tendrils, to bear tiny flowers and pods amidst fields of grain.

Status: native, throughout area.

HAIRY TARE

Type	annual
Height	20–30cm, rarely 70cm
Habitat	cultivated ground, grassy places
Flowering	May–August
STEMS AND LEAVES	
Stem	climbing, slender
Root	fibrous, with tiny nodules
Hairs	nearly hairless
Stipules	often lobed
Leaves	on alternate sides of stem, branched tendril at tip, 4–10 pairs of leaflets, each 5–12mm, narrowly oblong, tip squarish or notched
Leaf-stalk	mostly absent
FLOWERS	
Position	1–9, in short spike from leaf-base, stalk 10–30mm
Bracts	absent
Type	⚥
Size	2–4mm, rarely 5mm
Colour	dull white or purplish
Stalk	shorter than flower
Sepals	5, c2mm, bases joined, teeth equal, longer than tube
Petals	5, 4–5mm, lowest 2 joined, 2 side petals overlap lower
Stamens	10, 9 joined at base
Stigma	1, style hairless or hairy
Ovary	1, 1-celled
FRUIT	
Type	1, pod, splits lengthwise, oblong, hairy, black
Size	6–11 x 3–5mm
Seeds	usually 2, c1mm, round

SIMILAR SPECIES

Other Tares have short, unequal sepal-teeth.
1 Smooth Tare *(V. tetrasperma)* has one or two flowers on a stalk and smooth, mostly four-seeded pods. **2 Slender Tare** *(V. tenuissima)* has small flower-heads and pods usually with five or six seeds.
3 Birdsfoot *(Ornithopus perpusillus)* has a leaf-like bract just below the flowers, and curved, jointed pods.

smooth
6 seeds
4 seeds
bract
1
2
3

Common Vetch *Vicia sativa*

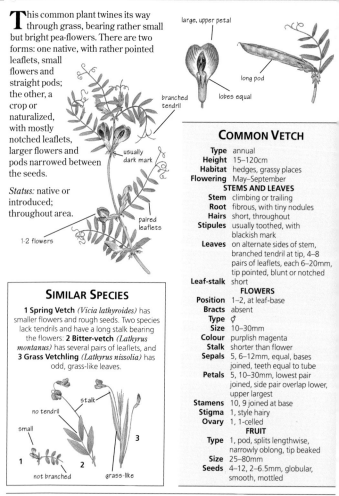

This common plant twines its way through grass, bearing rather small but bright pea-flowers. There are two forms: one native, with rather pointed leaflets, small flowers and straight pods; the other, a crop or naturalized, with mostly notched leaflets, larger flowers and pods narrowed between the seeds.

Status: native or introduced; throughout area.

large, upper petal

long pod

lobes equal

branched tendril

usually dark mark

paired leaflets

1-2 flowers

COMMON VETCH

Type	annual
Height	15–120cm
Habitat	hedges, grassy places
Flowering	May–September
STEMS AND LEAVES	
Stem	climbing or trailing
Root	fibrous, with tiny nodules
Hairs	short, throughout
Stipules	usually toothed, with blackish mark
Leaves	on alternate sides of stem, branched tendril at tip, 4–8 pairs of leaflets, each 6–20mm, tip pointed, blunt or notched
Leaf-stalk	short
FLOWERS	
Position	1–2, at leaf-base
Bracts	absent
Type	♂
Size	10–30mm
Colour	purplish magenta
Stalk	shorter than flower
Sepals	5, 6–12mm, equal, bases joined, teeth equal to tube
Petals	5, 10–30mm, lowest pair joined, side pair overlap lower, upper largest
Stamens	10, 9 joined at base
Stigma	1, style hairy
Ovary	1, 1-celled
FRUIT	
Type	1, pod, splits lengthwise, narrowly oblong, tip beaked
Size	25–80mm
Seeds	4–12, 2–6.5mm, globular, smooth, mottled

SIMILAR SPECIES

1 Spring Vetch *(Vicia lathyroides)* has smaller flowers and rough seeds. Two species lack tendrils and have a long stalk bearing the flowers: **2 Bitter-vetch** *(Lathyrus montanus)* has several pairs of leaflets, and **3 Grass Vetchling** *(Lathyrus nissolia)* has odd, grass-like leaves.

no tendril

stalk

small

not branched

1

2

3

grass-like

Ononis repens **Common Restharrow**

Restharrow's pretty pink pea-flowers are found in dry grassy places, especially chalk-grassland. Tough, matted, underground stems of restharrow literally arrested the harrow of ox-drawn ploughs. Farmers disliked the plant also because it gave an unpleasant taint to cow's milk, yet the underground stems were sometimes cut for chewing like Wild Liquorice.

Status: native; most of area, rarer in north.

or 3
aflets

hairy all round stem

stipules

curves upwards

large upper petal

short pod

COMMON RESTHARROW

Type	perennial
Height	30–60cm
Habitat	grassy places; dry, often lime-rich soils
Flowering	June–September
STEMS AND LEAVES	
Stem	low-growing or angled upwards, woody, rooting below
Root	creeping underground stem
Hairs	long or short and sticky, hairy all round stems
Stipules	toothed, bases clasp stem
Leaves	on alternate sides of stem, each up to 20mm, with 1–3 leaflets, tip blunt, edge toothed
Leaf-stalk	3–5mm, shorter than leaf
FLOWERS	
Position	1–2 at leaf-base
Bracts	leaf-like
Type	♂
Size	10–20mm
Colour	pink or purple
Stalk	much shorter than flower
Sepals	5, bases joined, teeth equal, longer than tube, enlarged in fruit
Petals	5, 7–20mm, lowest pair joined, side pair overlap lower, upper largest, broad
Stamens	10, bases joined
Stigma	1, style long, hairless
Ovary	1, 1-celled
FRUIT	
Type	1, pod, splits lengthwise, shorter than sepals, oblong
Size	5–7mm
Seeds	1–4, 2–3mm, globular, rough

SIMILAR SPECIES

1 Spiny Restharrow (*O. spinosa*) has spine-tipped stems, with two lines of hairs. **2 Large Yellow-restharrow** (*O. natrix*), from the south of the area, is a much stickier plant, its yellow flowers pencilled red.

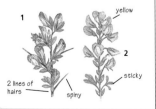

1

2

yellow

2 lines of hairs

spiny

sticky

Meadow Vetchling *Lathyrus pratensis*

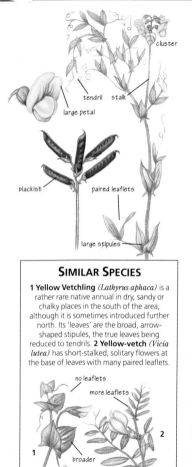

cluster

tendril stalk

large petal

blackish

paired leaflets

large stipules

A common plant of meadows and grassy edges of roads or paths, it has clusters of rich yellow pea-flowers. Specialized nodules on its roots turn nitrogen from the air into a form which enriches the pasture.

Status: native; throughout area.

MEADOW VETCHLING

Type	perennial
Height	30–120cm
Habitat	grassland, scrub
Flowering	May–August
STEMS AND LEAVES	
Stem	climbs or trails, angled
Root	fibrous, with tiny nodules
Hairs	short, throughout plant
Stipules	10–25mm, arrow-shaped
Leaves	on alternate sides of stem, tendril at tip sometimes branched, 1 pair of leaflets, each 10–30mm, spear-shaped, pointed
Leaf-stalk	about equalling leaflets
FLOWERS	
Position	5–12, in long-stalked head from leaf-base
Bracts	minute
Type	♂
Size	15–18mm
Colour	yellow, greenish veins
Stalk	shorter than flower
Sepals	5, bases joined, teeth equalling tube
Petals	5, 11–18mm, lowest pair joined, side pair overlap lower, upper largest
Stamens	10, 9 joined at base
Stigma	1, hairy on one side
Ovary	1, 1-celled
FRUIT	
Type	1, pod, splits lengthwise, oblong, blackish
Size	25–35mm
Seeds	5–10, 3–4mm, globular, smooth

SIMILAR SPECIES

1 Yellow Vetchling (*Lathyrus aphaca*) is a rather rare native annual in dry, sandy or chalky places in the south of the area, although it is sometimes introduced further north. Its 'leaves' are the broad, arrow-shaped stipules, the true leaves being reduced to tendrils. **2 Yellow-vetch** (*Vicia lutea*) has short-stalked, solitary flowers at the base of leaves with many paired leaflets.

no leaflets

more leaflets

1   broader   2

Lathyrus sylvestris

This exotic-looking plant has long-stalked heads of pink pea-flowers, similar to the cultivated Sweet Pea. Its leaves have two narrow leaflets and a tendril enabling the plant to scramble over surrounding vegetation.

Status: native; scattered through area except extreme north.

narrow wing-like edge

rough seeds

long

2 leaflets

narrow

branched tendril

winged

stipules

NARROW-LEAVED EVERLASTING-PEA

Type	perennial
Height	100–200cm
Habitat	woods, scrub, hedges, railway embankments
Flowering	June–August

STEMS AND LEAVES

Stem	climbing, broadly winged
Root	fibrous, with tiny nodules
Hairs	absent
Stipules	up to 20mm, slender, pointed, narrow basal lobe
Leaves	on alternate sides of stem, branched tendril at tip, 2 leaflets, each 70–150mm, narrowly elliptical or spear-shaped, bluish, pointed
Leaf-stalk	shorter than leaflets

FLOWERS

Position	3–12 in head on stalk 100–200mm long, from leaf-base
Bracts	small, pointed
Type	♂
Size	15–17mm
Colour	rosy pink
Stalk	shorter than flower
Sepals	5, unequal, bases joined, teeth shorter than tube
Petals	5, 12–17mm, lowest pair joined, side pair overlap lower
Stamens	10, 9 joined at base
Stigma	1, style curved, hairy
Ovary	1, 1-celled

FRUIT

Type	1, pod, splits lengthwise, oblong, top edge winged
Size	50–70mm
Seeds	8–14, 5–6mm, globular, rough

SIMILAR SPECIES

Two southern species are sometimes naturalized further north. **1 Broad-leaved Everlasting-pea** *(L. latifolius)* has broader leaves and stipules. **2 Tuberous Pea** *(L. tuberosus)* has narrow, angled stems, swollen tubers and crimson flowers. The low-growing **3 Sea Pea** *(L. japonicus)* has several pairs of broad leaflets and grows on dunes, shingle beaches or, rarely, lake-shores.

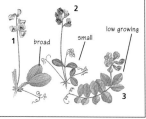

1   broad

2

small

low growing

3

Lucerne *Medicago sativa*

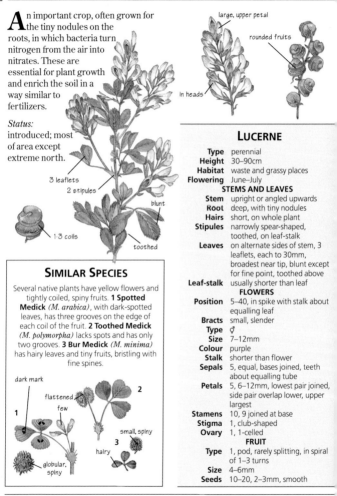

An important crop, often grown for the tiny nodules on the roots, in which bacteria turn nitrogen from the air into nitrates. These are essential for plant growth and enrich the soil in a way similar to fertilizers.

Status: introduced; most of area except extreme north.

large, upper petal

rounded fruits

in heads

3 leaflets
2 stipules
blunt
1-3 coils
toothed

SIMILAR SPECIES

Several native plants have yellow flowers and tightly coiled, spiny fruits. **1 Spotted Medick** (*M. arabica*), with dark-spotted leaves, has three grooves on the edge of each coil of the fruit. **2 Toothed Medick** (*M. polymorpha*) lacks spots and has only two grooves. **3 Bur Medick** (*M. minima*) has hairy leaves and tiny fruits, bristling with fine spines.

dark mark
flattened
few
1
2
small, spiny
3
hairy
globular, spiny

LUCERNE

Type	perennial
Height	30–90cm
Habitat	waste and grassy places
Flowering	June–July
STEMS AND LEAVES	
Stem	upright or angled upwards
Root	deep, with tiny nodules
Hairs	short, on whole plant
Stipules	narrowly spear-shaped, toothed, on leaf-stalk
Leaves	on alternate sides of stem, 3 leaflets, each to 30mm, broadest near tip, blunt except for fine point, toothed above
Leaf-stalk	usually shorter than leaf
FLOWERS	
Position	5–40, in spike with stalk about equalling leaf
Bracts	small, slender
Type	♂
Size	7–12mm
Colour	purple
Stalk	shorter than flower
Sepals	5, equal, bases joined, teeth about equalling tube
Petals	5, 6–12mm, lowest pair joined, side pair overlap lower, upper largest
Stamens	10, 9 joined at base
Stigma	1, club-shaped
Ovary	1, 1-celled
FRUIT	
Type	1, pod, rarely splitting, in spiral of 1–3 turns
Size	4–6mm
Seeds	10–20, 2–3mm, smooth

Hop Trefoil is a small, clover-like plant with tiny yellow flower-heads, and is common in short grass. The fruiting heads look like diminutive hops, owing to the dry petals which remain attached.

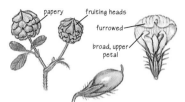

papery · fruiting heads · furrowed · broad, upper petal

Status: native; very common, most of area.

small heads

3 leaflets

stipules

stalked middle leaflet

HOP TREFOIL

Type	annual
Height	5–35cm, rarely to 50cm
Habitat	grassy places; dryish soil
Flowering	June–September

STEMS AND LEAVES

Stem	upright or angled upwards
Root	fibrous, with tiny nodules
Hairs	over whole plant
Stipules	oval, joined to leaf-stalk, not toothed
Leaves	on alternate sides of stem, with 3 leaflets, the end one stalked, each 6–10mm, tip blunt or notched, edge toothed
Leaf-stalk	shorter than leaflets

FLOWERS

Position	20–30, in head from leaf-base, stalk about equals leaf
Bracts	absent
Type	♂
Size	4–6mm
Colour	yellow, turning pale brown
Stalk	very short
Sepals	5, unequal, bases joined, teeth about equal tube
Petals	5, 3–6mm, remaining in fruit, lowest pair joined, side pair overlap lower, upper broad, becomes grooved
Stamens	10, 9 joined at base
Stigma	1, with curved style
Ovary	1, 1-celled

FRUIT

Type	1, egg-shaped pod, not opening
Size	2–2.5mm
Seeds	1, 1–1.5mm, yellow

SIMILAR SPECIES

1 Lesser Trefoil *(T. dubium)* has smaller fruiting heads, the dark brown upper petals lacking grooves but folded over the pod.
2 Slender Trefoil *(T. micranthum)* has stalkless middle leaflets and very few flowers in a head. In flower, **3 Black Medick** *(Medicago lupulina)* is often mistaken for Hop Trefoil but has coiled black pods without remains of flowers.

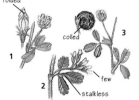

folded · coiled · 3 · 1 · 2 · few · stalkless

Hare's-foot Clover *Trifolium arvense*

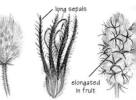

pink · long sepals · soft hairs · elongated in fruit

A slender, short-lived annual, often covering large areas on sand-dunes in early Summer. Attractive, pink, softly hairy flower-heads give the plant its common name. In fruit, the reddish, bristle-like sepal-teeth project from the head like a miniature bottle-brush.

Status: native; scattered, most common in south and east.

hairy

3 leaflets

stipules

SIMILAR SPECIES

The cultivated **1 Crimson Clover** (*T. incarnatum*) is more robust, and has crimson petals, although a rarer pale form on cliff-tops is native. Two low-growing species are **2 Knotted Clover** (*T. striatum*), which has stalkless flower-heads, and **3 Strawberry Clover** (*T. fragiferum*), which has an inflated, reddish sepal-tube in fruit.

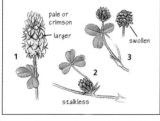

pale or crimson · larger · swollen · stalkless

1 · 2 · 3

HARE'S-FOOT CLOVER

Type	annual or biennial
Height	5–40cm
Habitat	arable fields, pastures, dunes; dry, sandy soil
Flowering	June–September
STEMS AND LEAVES	
Stem	upright or angled upwards
Root	fibrous, with tiny nodules
Hairs	soft, downy, white or pink, dense on sepals
Stipules	oval, bristle-like tip
Leaves	on alternate sides of stem, with 3 leaflets, each 10–15, oblong, blunt or sharpish
Leaf-stalk	to 10mm, upper stalkless
FLOWERS	
Position	numerous, in stalked, cylindrical heads to 25mm, from stem-tip or leaf-base
Bracts	absent
Type	♂
Size	3.5–7mm
Colour	white or pink
Stalk	almost absent
Sepals	5, about equal, bases joined, bristle-like teeth, reddish, longer than tube and petals
Petals	5, remaining in fruit, 2.5–7mm, lower 2 joined, side 2 overlapping, upper largest
Stamens	10, 9 joined at base
Stigma	1, style-tip curved
Ovary	1, 1-celled
FRUIT	
Type	1, pod, egg-shaped
Size	1–1.5mm
Seeds	1, c0.8mm, egg-shaped

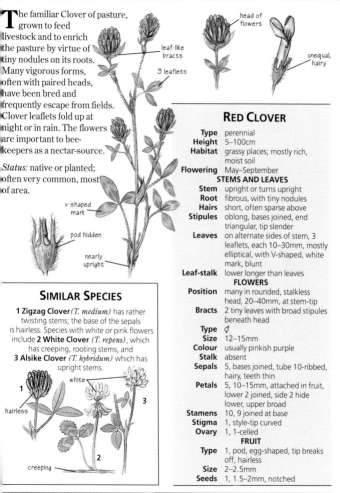

Trifolium pratense **Red Clover**

The familiar Clover of pasture, grown to feed livestock and to enrich the pasture by virtue of tiny nodules on its roots. Many vigorous forms, often with paired heads, have been bred and frequently escape from fields. Clover leaflets fold up at night or in rain. The flowers are important to bee-keepers as a nectar-source.

Status: native or planted; often very common, most of area.

Labels on illustration: head of flowers; leaf-like bracts; 3 leaflets; unequal, hairy; v-shaped mark; pod hidden; nearly upright

SIMILAR SPECIES

1 Zigzag Clover *(T. medium)* has rather twisting stems; the base of the sepals is hairless. Species with white or pink flowers include **2 White Clover** *(T. repens)*, which has creeping, rooting stems, and **3 Alsike Clover** *(T. hybridum)* which has upright stems.

Labels: hairless; white; 1; 2; 3; creeping

RED CLOVER

Type	perennial
Height	5–100cm
Habitat	grassy places; mostly rich, moist soil
Flowering	May–September

STEMS AND LEAVES

Stem	upright or turns upright
Root	fibrous, with tiny nodules
Hairs	short, often sparse above
Stipules	oblong, bases joined, end triangular, tip slender
Leaves	on alternate sides of stem, 3 leaflets, each 10–30mm, mostly elliptical, with V-shaped, white mark, blunt
Leaf-stalk	lower longer than leaves

FLOWERS

Position	many in rounded, stalkless head, 20–40mm, at stem-tip
Bracts	2 tiny leaves with broad stipules beneath head
Type	♂
Size	12–15mm
Colour	usually pinkish purple
Stalk	absent
Sepals	5, bases joined, tube 10-ribbed, hairy, teeth thin
Petals	5, 10–15mm, attached in fruit, lower 2 joined, side 2 hide lower, upper broad
Stamens	10, 9 joined at base
Stigma	1, style-tip curved
Ovary	1, 1-celled

FRUIT

Type	1, pod, egg-shaped, tip breaks off, hairless
Size	2–2.5mm
Seeds	1, 1.5–2mm, notched

Tall Melilot *Melilotus altissima*

A tall, bushy plant with many branched stems bearing slender, spiky flower-heads. The whole plant has an aroma of new-mown hay, especially when dried. Melilots were once used to treat blisters, swellings and sore eyes.

Status: native or introduced in west; most of area.

flowers in spikes

stipules

3 leaflets

net-like pattern

petals about equal

blackish

short hairs

TALL MELILOT

Type	biennial or perennial
Height	60–150cm
Habitat	grassland, wood clearings; damp, sometimes salty soil
Flowering	June–August
STEMS AND LEAVES	
Stem	upright, branched
Root	fibrous, with tiny nodules
Hairs	under leaves, on sepals
Stipules	slender, bristle-like
Leaves	on alternate sides of stem, with 3 leaflets, each 15–30mm, oblong or oval, blunt, edge toothed
Leaf-stalk	shorter than leaflets
FLOWERS	
Position	many, in stalked head, 20–50mm, from leaf-base
Bracts	hair-like
Type	♂
Size	5–6mm
Colour	yellow
Stalk	shorter than flower
Sepals	5, bases joined, teeth longer than tube
Petals	5, 5–6mm, about equal, lower 2 joined, side 2 overlap, upper broad
Stamens	10, 9 joined
Stigma	1, style long, curved
Ovary	1, 1-celled
FRUIT	
Type	1, egg-shaped pod, most not opening, net-like pattern, hairy, pointed, black
Size	5–6mm
Seeds	2, 2–2.5mm, notched

SIMILAR SPECIES

Other Melilots have hairless fruits. **1 White Melilot** *(M. alba)* is easily identified by the white petals. **2 Ribbed Melilot** *(M. officinalis)* has short lower petals and blunt, ridged, brown ripe pods. **3 Small Melilot** *(M. indica)* has tiny flowers and smaller, olive-green ripe pods.

3

smaller

short lower

white

1

hairless

2

A plant of sunny, grassy places, with wiry stems bearing yellow pea-flowers tipped or streaked with red. Of its many common names, 'Eggs and bacon' recalls the yellow and red flowers. The leaves are food to the larvae of the Silver-studded Blue butterfly and the Six-spot Burnet moth.

Status: native; throughout area.

often reddish

clustered flowers

straight pods

curves upwards

3 leaflets

2 stipules

COMMON BIRD'S-FOOT-TREFOIL

Type	perennial
Height	10–40cm
Habitat	grassy places
Flowering	June–September

STEMS AND LEAVES

Stem	low-growing, tips turn up
Root	stout, woody stock
Hairs	hairless or rarely hairy
Stipules	minute
Leaves	on alternate sides of stem, 5 leaflets, lower 2 stipule-like, each 3–10mm, oval, blunt, edge unbroken
Leaf-stalk	very short

FLOWERS

Position	2–8 in short head, stalk up to 80mm, from leaf-base
Bracts	divided into 3
Type	♂
Size	10–16mm
Colour	yellow, often tinged or veined with red
Stalk	shorter than flowers
Sepals	5, equal, bases joined, teeth about equal tube
Petals	9–16mm, lower 2 joined, side 2 overlap, upper largest
Stamens	10, 9 joined at base
Stigma	1, style long, straight
Ovary	1, 1-celled

FRUIT

Type	1, pod, splits lengthwise, cylindrical, straight; partitions between seeds
Size	15–30mm
Seeds	many, 1–1.5mm, kidney-shaped

SIMILAR SPECIES

1 Greater Bird's-foot-trefoil *(L. uliginosus)*, of wetter places, has tall, upright, hollow stems and creeping underground stems. **2 Horseshoe Vetch** *(Hippocrepis comosa)* has many leaflets and wavy pods that break into horseshoe-shaped segments. **3 Dragon's-teeth** *(Tetragonolobus maritimus)* has larger flowers and pods with 4, wing-like angles.

wavy

2

single angled

1

paired leaflets

3

upright, hollow

Kidney Vetch *Anthyllis vulneraria*

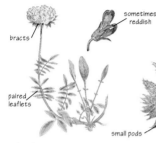

sometimes reddish

bracts

woolly

short head

paired leaflets

small pods

A plant of sunny, grassy places, especially the short turf around tops of sea-cliffs. The flower-heads often have a dual nature, one half in flower, the other in bud or fruit.

Status: native; widespread, most of area, most common by coast.

SIMILAR SPECIES

Several pea-flowered species have more elongated flower-heads. **1 Wild Liquorice** (*Astragalus glycyphyllos*) has cream-coloured flowers and long, curved, hairless pods. Two yellow-flowered species that have swollen, hairy pods are **2 Yellow Alpine Milk-vetch** (*A. frigidus*) with tiny sepal-teeth and ellipsoidal pods and **3 Wild Lentil** (*A. cicer*) with oval, membranous pods and sepal-teeth about half as long as the tube.

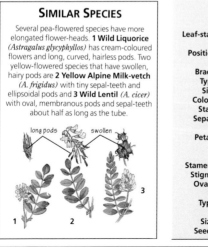

long pods

swollen

1   2   3

KIDNEY VETCH

Type	perennial, rarely annual
Height	5–60cm
Habitat	grassy places; dry, often lime-rich soils
Flowering	June–September
STEMS AND LEAVES	
Stem	upright or turns upright
Root	fibrous, with tiny nodules
Hairs	short, silky
Stipules	small, soon fall
Leaves	on alternate sides of stem, to 140mm, mostly 5–15 oval to oblong leaflets, that at tip often largest, lower scattered, upper paired
Leaf-stalk	short or absent
FLOWERS	
Position	numerous, in dense, mostly paired, long-stalked heads
Bracts	2, leafy, several leaflets
Type	⚥
Size	12–15mm
Colour	yellow, rarely tinged red
Stalk	mostly absent
Sepals	5, bases joined, inflated, woolly, teeth short, unequal
Petals	5, 10–15mm, lowest pair joined, side pair overlap lower, upper largest
Stamens	10, 9 joined at base
Stigma	1, club-shaped
Ovary	1, 1-celled
FRUIT	
Type	1 nearly globular pod, not opening, sepals persist
Size	c3mm
Seeds	1–2, 2–2.5mm, notched

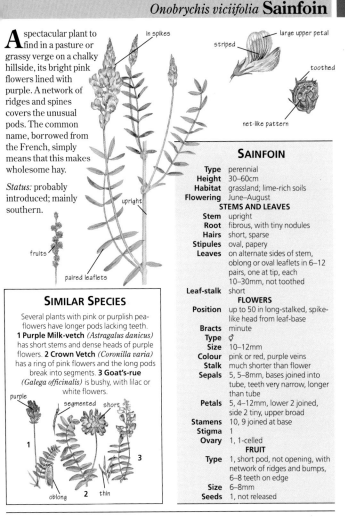

Onobrychis viciifolia **Sainfoin**

A spectacular plant to find in a pasture or grassy verge on a chalky hillside, its bright pink flowers lined with purple. A network of ridges and spines covers the unusual pods. The common name, borrowed from the French, simply means that this makes wholesome hay.

Status: probably introduced; mainly southern.

in spikes

large upper petal

striped

toothed

net-like pattern

fruits

paired leaflets

upright

SIMILAR SPECIES

Several plants with pink or purplish pea-flowers have longer pods lacking teeth.
1 Purple Milk-vetch *(Astragalus danicus)* has short stems and dense heads of purple flowers. **2 Crown Vetch** *(Coronilla varia)* has a ring of pink flowers and the long pods break into segments. **3 Goat's-rue** *(Galega officinalis)* is bushy, with lilac or white flowers.

purple

segmented   short

1

3

oblong   2   thin

SAINFOIN

Type	perennial
Height	30–60cm
Habitat	grassland; lime-rich soils
Flowering	June–August
STEMS AND LEAVES	
Stem	upright
Root	fibrous, with tiny nodules
Hairs	short, sparse
Stipules	oval, papery
Leaves	on alternate sides of stem, oblong or oval leaflets in 6–12 pairs, one at tip, each 10–30mm, not toothed
Leaf-stalk	short
FLOWERS	
Position	up to 50 in long-stalked, spike-like head from leaf-base
Bracts	minute
Type	⚥
Size	10–12mm
Colour	pink or red, purple veins
Stalk	much shorter than flower
Sepals	5, 5–8mm, bases joined into tube, teeth very narrow, longer than tube
Petals	5, 4–12mm, lower 2 joined, side 2 tiny, upper broad
Stamens	10, 9 joined at base
Stigma	1
Ovary	1, 1-celled
FRUIT	
Type	1, short pod, not opening, with network of ridges and bumps, 6–8 teeth on edge
Size	6–8mm
Seeds	1, not released

Wood-sorrel *Oxalis acetosella*

The delicate white flowers and clover-like leaves of Wood-sorrel carpet the floor of many deciduous woods in Spring. At night and in wet weather, the leaflets fold together. An elastic coat to the seeds enables them to be shot from the capsule. Most seeds develop from late, petal-less flowers.

Status: native; throughout area.

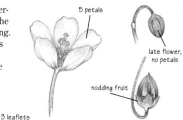

5 petals

late flower, no petals

nodding fruit

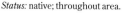

3 leaflets

white or lilac

from base

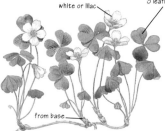

SIMILAR SPECIES

Several yellow-flowered species are naturalized. **1 Procumbent Yellow-sorrel** (*Oxalis corniculata*) has slender, trailing, rooting stems; **2 Bermuda-buttercup** (*Oxalis pes-caprae*), with large heads of flowers, occurs in the south-west. **3 Upright Yellow-sorrel** (*Oxalis europaea*) has thick, upright stems.

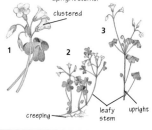

clustered

3

1

2

creeping

leafy stem

upright

WOOD-SORREL

Type	perennial
Height	5–15cm
Habitat	woods, hedgerows, among rocks; mostly acid soils
Flowering	April–May
STEMS AND LEAVES	
Stem	flowering stem upright
Root	fibrous from slender, scaly, underground stem
Hairs	sparse, pressed to surface
Stipules	absent
Leaves	at base of plant, with 3 leaflets, each 10–20mm, heart-shaped, yellowish green, notched, edge unbroken
Leaf-stalk	50–150mm
FLOWERS	
Position	single, at stem-tip
Bracts	2, small, at middle of stem
Type 1	☿, cup-shaped
Type 2	late, no petals, not opening
Size	15–30mm
Colour	white, rarely lilac or purple, lilac veins
Stalk	longer than flower
Sepals	5, 3–4mm, equal, oblong
Petals	5, 8–16mm, equal, notched
Stamens	10, 2 rings of 5
Stigmas	5
Ovary	1, 1-celled
FRUIT	
Type	1, capsule, 5-ridged
Size	4–7mm
Seeds	many, 2–2.5mm, egg-shaped, ridged, with fleshy coat

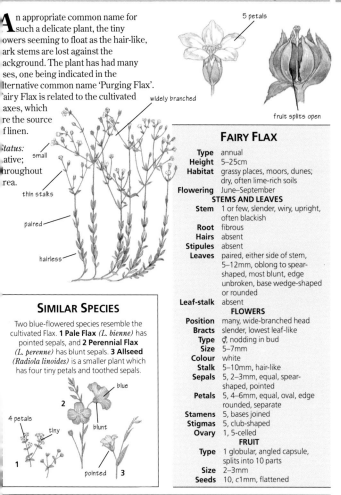

An appropriate common name for such a delicate plant, the tiny flowers seeming to float as the hair-like, dark stems are lost against the background. The plant has had many uses, one being indicated in the alternative common name 'Purging Flax'. Fairy Flax is related to the cultivated flaxes, which are the source of linen.

Status: native; throughout area.

5 petals

widely branched

fruit splits open

small

thin stalks

paired

hairless

SIMILAR SPECIES

Two blue-flowered species resemble the cultivated Flax. **1 Pale Flax** (*L. bienne*) has pointed sepals, and **2 Perennial Flax** (*L. perenne*) has blunt sepals. **3 Allseed** (*Radiola linoides*) is a smaller plant which has four tiny petals and toothed sepals.

4 petals
tiny
blue
2
blunt
1
pointed 3

FAIRY FLAX

Type	annual
Height	5–25cm
Habitat	grassy places, moors, dunes; dry, often lime-rich soils
Flowering	June–September
STEMS AND LEAVES	
Stem	1 or few, slender, wiry, upright, often blackish
Root	fibrous
Hairs	absent
Stipules	absent
Leaves	paired, either side of stem, 5–12mm, oblong to spear-shaped, most blunt, edge unbroken, base wedge-shaped or rounded
Leaf-stalk	absent
FLOWERS	
Position	many, wide-branched head
Bracts	slender, lowest leaf-like
Type	☿, nodding in bud
Size	5–7mm
Colour	white
Stalk	5–10mm, hair-like
Sepals	5, 2–3mm, equal, spear-shaped, pointed
Petals	5, 4–6mm, equal, oval, edge rounded, separate
Stamens	5, bases joined
Stigmas	5, club-shaped
Ovary	1, 5-celled
FRUIT	
Type	1 globular, angled capsule, splits into 10 parts
Size	2–3mm
Seeds	10, c1mm, flattened

89

Herb-Robert *Geranium robertianum*

Common in shady places, it attains its full glory on walls or rocks where the sun turns stems and leaves brilliant crimson. Native *Geranium* species are of a genus different from the Geraniums (*Pelargonium*) of gardens, but they are related and even smell similar.

Status: native or introduced; south-west of area, naturalized elsewhere.

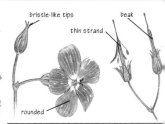

bristle-like tips · thin strand · beak · rounded · paired lobes · hairy · often turns reddish

SIMILAR SPECIES

Other species have leaves with shallower, radiating lobes. Two with notched petals are **1 Hedgerow Crane's-bill** (*G. pyrenaicum*), which has upright, perennial stems, and low-growing, annual **2 Dove's-foot Crane's-bill** (*G. molle*). **3 Shining Crane's-bill** (*G. lucidum*) is almost hairless, with glossy leaves and broad, angular sepals.

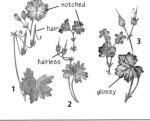

notched · hairy · hairless · 1 · glossy · 2 · 3

HERB-ROBERT

Type	annual or biennial
Height	10–50cm
Habitat	woods, hedges, rocks, walls
Flowering	May–September

STEMS AND LEAVES

Stem	angled upwards, branched from base, brittle
Root	slender tap-root
Hairs	dense below, sparse above
Stipules	small, oval
Leaves	basal or paired either side of stem, 15–65mm, deeply cut into 3–5 lobes, toothed, strong-smelling, often red-tinged
Leaf-stalk	lower long, upper short

FLOWERS

Position	1–2, from leaf-base
Bracts	scale-like
Type	♂
Size	16–20mm
Colour	purplish, pink, rarely white
Stalk	longer than flower
Sepals	5, 7–9mm, oval, bristle-like tip, upright
Petals	5, 9–13mm, equal, oval, rounded, base stalk-like
Stamens	10, orange or purple
Stigmas	5, slender
Ovary	1, 3–5-celled

FRUIT

Type	1, long-beaked capsule, strip from beak coils up with each segment
Size	12–20mm
Seeds	1 per segment, *c*2mm, oblong, smooth

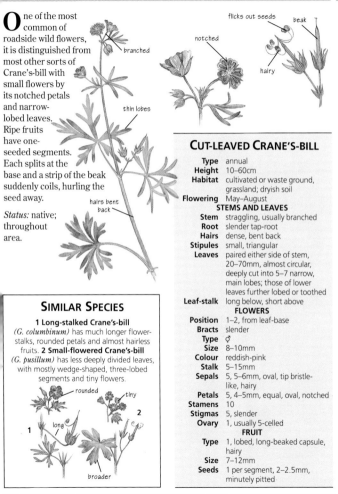

flicks out seeds

beak

notched

branched

hairy

thin lobes

hairs bent back

O ne of the most common of roadside wild flowers, it is distinguished from most other sorts of Crane's-bill with small flowers by its notched petals and narrow-lobed leaves. Ripe fruits have one-seeded segments. Each splits at the base and a strip of the beak suddenly coils, hurling the seed away.

Status: native; throughout area.

SIMILAR SPECIES

1 Long-stalked Crane's-bill
(*G. columbinum*) has much longer flower-stalks, rounded petals and almost hairless fruits. **2 Small-flowered Crane's-bill**
(*G. pusillum*) has less deeply divided leaves, with mostly wedge-shaped, three-lobed segments and tiny flowers.

rounded

tiny

1

long

2

broader

CUT-LEAVED CRANE'S-BILL

Type	annual
Height	10–60cm
Habitat	cultivated or waste ground, grassland; dryish soil
Flowering	May–August
STEMS AND LEAVES	
Stem	straggling, usually branched
Root	slender tap-root
Hairs	dense, bent back
Stipules	small, triangular
Leaves	paired either side of stem, 20–70mm, almost circular, deeply cut to 5–7 narrow, main lobes; those of lower leaves further lobed or toothed
Leaf-stalk	long below, short above
FLOWERS	
Position	1–2, from leaf-base
Bracts	slender
Type	♂
Size	8–10mm
Colour	reddish-pink
Stalk	5–15mm
Sepals	5, 5–6mm, oval, tip bristle-like, hairy
Petals	5, 4–5mm, equal, oval, notched
Stamens	10
Stigmas	5, slender
Ovary	1, usually 5-celled
FRUIT	
Type	1, lobed, long-beaked capsule, hairy
Size	7–12mm
Seeds	1 per segment, 2–2.5mm, minutely pitted

Meadow Crane's-bill *Geranium pratense*

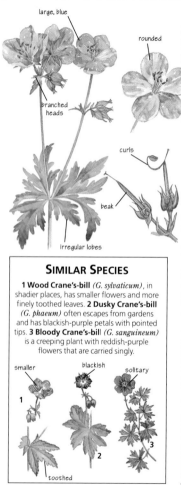

large, blue

rounded

branched heads

curls

beak

irregular lobes

A strikingly beautiful plant of summer meadows and grassy roadsides, it has bold, deeply lobed leaves and large, bluish-violet flowers. This is one of the few native plants that finds a permanent place in gardens, often as a double form.

Status: native, naturalized in parts of north; most of area.

MEADOW CRANE'S-BILL

Type	perennial
Height	30–80cm
Habitat	grassy, sunny places; mainly lime-rich soils
Flowering	June–September
STEMS AND LEAVES	
Stem	upright or angled upwards
Root	thick rhizome
Hairs	short, bent back below, long, dense above
Stipules	wide, papery, upper slender
Leaves	basal or on alternate sides of stem, 70–150mm, 3–7 deep, radiating lobes, each further toothed or lobed, tips pointed
Leaf-stalk	lower much longer than leaf, upper very short
FLOWERS	
Position	stalked pair from leaf-base
Bracts	narrowly triangular
Type	♂, cup-shaped
Size	30–40mm
Colour	bright bluish violet
Stalk	shorter than flower
Sepals	5, 11–15mm, oval, thin tip
Petals	5, 15–20mm, equal, broadly oval, tip rounded
Stamens	10
Stigmas	5, slender
Ovary	1, usually 5-celled
FRUIT	
Type	capsule, lobed, long-beaked, strip from beak coils up with each lobe
Size	25–30mm
Seeds	1 per segment, 3–4mm

SIMILAR SPECIES

1 Wood Crane's-bill *(G. sylvaticum)*, in shadier places, has smaller flowers and more finely toothed leaves. **2 Dusky Crane's-bill** *(G. phaeum)* often escapes from gardens and has blackish-purple petals with pointed tips. **3 Bloody Crane's-bill** *(G. sanguineum)* is a creeping plant with reddish-purple flowers that are carried singly.

smaller

blackish

solitary

1

2

3

toothed

sometimes spotted
many leaflets

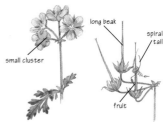

small cluster
long beak
spiral tail
fruit

A variable, mainly coastal species. Stickily hairy plants with slender stems and unspotted flowers are often regarded as a different subspecies, the typical version having stout stems and two dark-spotted petals. The beaked fruit of Stork's-bill splits from the top, each strip twisting spirally and parting with a one-seeded segment. This corkscrew-like structure twists and buries the seed.

Status: native, mostly near sea.

SIMILAR SPECIES

1 Musk Stork's-bill *(Erodium moschatum)* has blunt stipules, sticky leaves and larger flowers. **2 Sea Stork's-bill** *(Erodium maritimum)* has shallow-lobed leaves and tiny flowers.

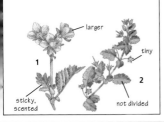

larger
tiny
1
2
sticky, scented
not divided

COMMON STORK'S-BILL

Type	annual
Height	to 60cm, rarely 100cm
Habitat	dunes, cultivated or waste ground; dry, sandy soil
Flowering	June–September
STEMS AND LEAVES	
Stem	variable, slender to stout
Root	slender to stout tap-root
Hairs	sparse to dense
Stipules	oval, papery, whitish
Leaves	most paired either side of stem, 20–200mm, paired leaflets are deeply lobed
Leaf-stalk	lower long, upper short
FLOWERS	
Position	1–9, in long-stalked head, from leaf-base
Bracts	oval, papery, brownish
Type	♂
Size	8–18mm
Colour	pinkish purple, often black spot at base of upper 2 petals
Stalk	longer than flower
Sepals	5, 3–7mm, oval, tip bristle-like
Petals	5, 4–11mm, often unequal
Stamens	5, orange
Stigmas	5, slender
Ovary	1, 5-celled
FRUIT	
Type	1, lobed, long-beaked capsule, beak splits, each strip twists spirally, parts with 1 segment
Size	15–40mm
Seeds	1 per segment, 3–4mm, elongated

Dog's Mercury *Mercurialis perennis*

A poisonous plant mainly of Oak, Ash or Beech woodland, where it carpets the floor with sombre green. Plants are either male or female, but because Dog's Mercury spreads more effectively by the creeping underground stems than by seed, large areas are of the same gender. The common name implies that this was a worthless version of the Annual Mercury, which was used medicinally.

Status: native or introduced in north and Ireland; most of area except extreme north.

labels: ♀; 2 stigmas; spikes of ♂ flowers; stalk; ♂; small teeth; many stamens; hairy; watery sap; paired; upright, unbranched

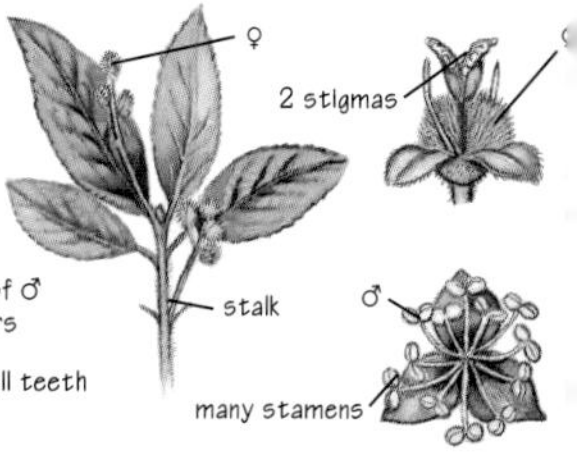

DOG'S MERCURY

Type	perennial
Height	15–40cm
Habitat	woods, hedges; fertile, often lime-rich soils
Flowering	February–April
STEMS AND LEAVES	
Stem	upright, unbranched, watery sap
Root	creeping underground stem
Hairs	throughout plant
Stipules	small
Leaves	paired either side of stem, 30–80mm, more or less elliptical, pointed, edge with rounded teeth
Leaf-stalk	3–10mm, shorter than blade
FLOWERS	
Position	♂ and ♀ flowers on different plants
Bracts	absent
Type 1	many ♂ flowers in stalked spike from leaf-base
Type 2	1–3 ♀ flowers on stalk from leaf-base
Size	4–5mm
Colour	green
Stalk	more or less absent
Perianth	3
Stamens	8–15
Stigmas	2
Ovary	1, hairy, 2-celled
FRUIT	
Type	capsule, broad, hairy, opening by 2 vertical splits
Size	6–8mm
Seeds	2, 3–3.5mm, globular, rough

SIMILAR SPECIES

Annual Mercury *(Mercurialis annua)* lacks underground stems and is more branched. Its leaves almost lack hairs and the female flowers their stalks.

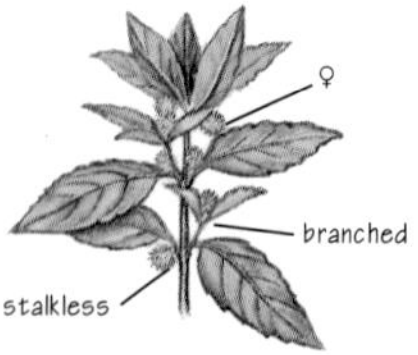

labels: ♀; branched; stalkless

A lthough the curious flowers lack sepals or petals, the bracts of Sun Spurge are yellowish and function like a large flower. This is the same structure as in the related, brightly coloured Poinsettia, most popular at Christmas. The milky sap is acrid and poisonous, and was formerly used to treat warts.

Status: native; throughout area.

yellowish bracts

cluster

toothed

scattered

milky sap

fruit opens

♂
♀

rounded glands

cup-like base

SIMILAR SPECIES

Three other spurges have horn-like ends to the glands of the flowers. **1 Petty Spurge** *(E. peplus)* has oval, green leaves, and **2 Dwarf Spurge** *(E. exigua)* narrow, bluish leaves. **3 Wood Spurge** *(E. amygdaloides)* is perennial, hairy, and has joined pairs of bracts below the flowers.

smaller

horned glands

3

joined

1

2

narrow

SUN SPURGE

Type	annual
Height	10–50cm
Habitat	cultivated and waste ground; fertile soil
Flowering	May–October
STEMS AND LEAVES	
Stem	single, upright, with 5 branches above, sap milky
Root	vertical main root
Hairs	more or less hairless
Stipules	absent
Leaves	spirally arranged around stem, 15–30mm, oval, broad above, blunt, minutely toothed, base wedge-shaped
Leaf-stalk	absent
FLOWERS	
Position	♂ and ♀ flowers on same plant, each ♀ with several ♂ flowers and cup-like base with 4–5 oval, green glands around lip
Bracts	leaf-like, yellowish green
Type 1	♂ a stamen on jointed stalk
Type 2	♀ a stalked ovary
Size	1–2mm
Colour	green
Stalk	elongating in fruit
Sepals	absent
Petals	absent
Stigmas	3, often forked
Ovary	1, 3-celled
FRUIT	
Type	1, broad, 3-angled, smooth capsule, opens by 3 splits
Size	3–5mm
Seeds	3, c2mm, brown, rough

Common Milkwort *Polygala vulgaris*

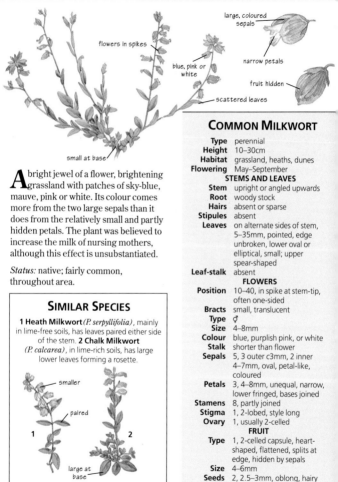

large, coloured sepals

flowers in spikes

narrow petals

blue, pink or white

fruit hidden

scattered leaves

small at base

A bright jewel of a flower, brightening grassland with patches of sky-blue, mauve, pink or white. Its colour comes more from the two large sepals than it does from the relatively small and partly hidden petals. The plant was believed to increase the milk of nursing mothers, although this effect is unsubstantiated.

Status: native; fairly common, throughout area.

SIMILAR SPECIES

1 Heath Milkwort *(P. serpyllifolia)*, mainly in lime-free soils, has leaves paired either side of the stem. **2 Chalk Milkwort** *(P. calcarea)*, in lime-rich soils, has large lower leaves forming a rosette.

smaller

paired

large at base

1   2

COMMON MILKWORT

Type	perennial
Height	10–30cm
Habitat	grassland, heaths, dunes
Flowering	May–September
STEMS AND LEAVES	
Stem	upright or angled upwards
Root	woody stock
Hairs	absent or sparse
Stipules	absent
Leaves	on alternate sides of stem, 5–35mm, pointed, edge unbroken, lower oval or elliptical, small; upper spear-shaped
Leaf-stalk	absent
FLOWERS	
Position	10–40, in spike at stem-tip, often one-sided
Bracts	small, translucent
Type	♂
Size	4–8mm
Colour	blue, purplish pink, or white
Stalk	shorter than flower
Sepals	5, 3 outer c3mm, 2 inner 4–7mm, oval, petal-like, coloured
Petals	3, 4–8mm, unequal, narrow, lower fringed, bases joined
Stamens	8, partly joined
Stigma	1, 2-lobed, style long
Ovary	1, usually 2-celled
FRUIT	
Type	1, 2-celled capsule, heart-shaped, flattened, splits at edge, hidden by sepals
Size	4–6mm
Seeds	2, 2.5–3mm, oblong, hairy

A spectacular plant that has hooded, pink flowers; stout, red-flushed stems; and purple, stalked glands at the leaf-bases. Walls of the ripe capsule are elastic and, at the slightest touch, rapidly roll back to fling out the seeds.

Status: introduced from the Himalaya; often common, most of area.

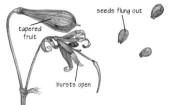

tapered fruit

seeds flung out

bursts open

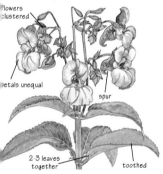

flowers clustered

petals unequal

spur

2-3 leaves together

toothed

SIMILAR SPECIES

The leaves of other Balsams are not paired.
1 Orange Balsam *(I. capensis)*, from North America, is fairly common in Britain and France. **2 Touch-me-not Balsam** *(I. noli-tangere)*, which has bright yellow flowers, is native. **3 Small Balsam** *(I. parviflora)* is Asiatic, and has much smaller, pale yellow flowers.

1 orange

3 small, pale

yellow 2

INDIAN BALSAM

Type	annual
Height	100–200cm
Habitat	river banks, lakesides, waste ground; damp soil
Flowering	July–October
STEMS AND LEAVES	
Stem	stout, fleshy, upright, often reddish
Root	thick, vertical main root
Hairs	more or less absent
Stipules	absent
Leaves	paired or in threes, 60–150mm, spear-shaped or elliptical, pointed, sharp-toothed
Leaf-stalk	shorter than blade, often with purple, stalked glands
FLOWERS	
Position	5–10, spike from leaf-base
Bracts	oval, pointed
Type	♂
Size	24–40mm
Colour	purplish pink, rarely white
Stalk	almost equalling flower
Sepals	3, 2 small, lower 12–27mm, hollow, tip spur-like
Petals	5, 2 joined each side, upper broad, 10–25mm
Stamens	5, mostly joined
Stigma	1, 5-toothed
Ovary	1, 5-celled
FRUIT	
Type	1, capsule, club-shaped, angled, walls elastic, sides coil back when ripe
Size	15–30mm
Seeds	few, 4–5mm, egg-shaped

Perforate St John's-wort *Hypericum perforatum*

A common plant of dry, grassy places, especially hedge-banks, its leaves are covered with translucent dots as if punctured, and are described in the common name. Stamens resembling a pin-cushion are gathered by their bases into three bundles. St John's-worts were long used to treat wounds and are still found in some medicines.

Status: native; throughout area.

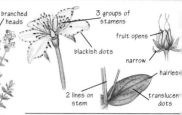

branched heads
3 groups of stamens
fruit opens
blackish dots
narrow
hairless
2 lines on stem
translucent dots
paired leaves

PERFORATE ST JOHN'S-WORT

Type	perennial
Height	30–90cm
Habitat	grassland, hedges, woods; mainly lime-rich soils
Flowering	June–September
STEMS AND LEAVES	
Stem	upright, woody at base, with 2 raised lines
Root	creeping underground stem
Hairs	absent
Stipules	absent
Leaves	paired either side of stem, 10–20mm, elliptical to narrowly oblong, blunt, edge unbroken, base narrowed, many translucent dots
Leaf-stalk	absent
FLOWERS	
Position	many in wide-branched head
Bracts	present, lower leaf-like
Type	♂
Size	17–25mm
Colour	yellow, petal-edge dotted with black
Stalk	shorter than flower
Sepals	5, 5–7mm, spear-shaped
Petals	5, 8–14mm, rather wedge-shaped with oblique end
Stamens	numerous
Stigmas	3, on long styles
Ovary	1, 3-celled
FRUIT	
Type	1, almost pear-shaped capsule, splits into 3
Size	c6mm
Seeds	many, c1mm, oblong, finely pitted

SIMILAR SPECIES

1 Slender St John's-wort (*H. pulchrum*) has blunt sepals and mostly heart-shaped leaf-bases. **2 Square-stalked St John's-wort** (*H. tetrapterum*) has four-angled stems and smaller flowers. **3 Marsh St John's-wort** (*H. elodes*), in wet ground, has softly hairy stems and sepals fringed with reddish glands.

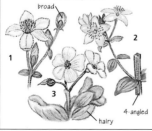

broad
2
1
3
4-angled
hairy

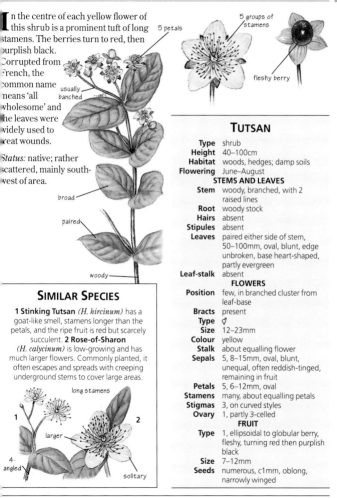

In the centre of each yellow flower of this shrub is a prominent tuft of long stamens. The berries turn to red, then purplish black. Corrupted from French, the common name means 'all wholesome' and the leaves were widely used to treat wounds.

Status: native; rather scattered, mainly south-west of area.

5 petals

5 groups of stamens

fleshy berry

usually banched

broad

paired

woody

TUTSAN

Type	shrub
Height	40–100cm
Habitat	woods, hedges; damp soils
Flowering	June–August
STEMS AND LEAVES	
Stem	woody, branched, with 2 raised lines
Root	woody stock
Hairs	absent
Stipules	absent
Leaves	paired either side of stem, 50–100mm, oval, blunt, edge unbroken, base heart-shaped, partly evergreen
Leaf-stalk	absent
FLOWERS	
Position	few, in branched cluster from leaf-base
Bracts	present
Type	♂
Size	12–23mm
Colour	yellow
Stalk	about equalling flower
Sepals	5, 8–15mm, oval, blunt, unequal, often reddish-tinged, remaining in fruit
Petals	5, 6–12mm, oval
Stamens	many, about equalling petals
Stigmas	3, on curved styles
Ovary	1, partly 3-celled
FRUIT	
Type	1, ellipsoidal to globular berry, fleshy, turning red then purplish black
Size	7–12mm
Seeds	numerous, c1mm, oblong, narrowly winged

SIMILAR SPECIES

1 Stinking Tutsan *(H. hircinum)* has a goat-like smell, stamens longer than the petals, and the ripe fruit is red but scarcely succulent. **2 Rose-of-Sharon** *(H. calycinum)* is low-growing and has much larger flowers. Commonly planted, it often escapes and spreads with creeping underground stems to cover large areas.

long stamens

1

larger

4-angled

2

solitary

Common Dog-violet *Viola riviniana*

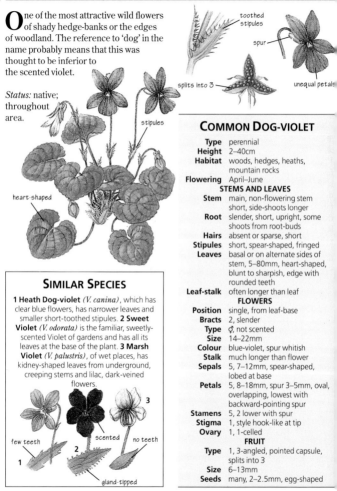

One of the most attractive wild flowers of shady hedge-banks or the edges of woodland. The reference to 'dog' in the name probably means that this was thought to be inferior to the scented violet.

Status: native; throughout area.

toothed stipules

spur

splits into 3

unequal petals

stipules

heart-shaped

SIMILAR SPECIES

1 Heath Dog-violet (*V. canina*), which has clear blue flowers, has narrower leaves and smaller short-toothed stipules. **2 Sweet Violet** (*V. odorata*) is the familiar, sweetly-scented Violet of gardens and has all its leaves at the base of the plant. **3 Marsh Violet** (*V. palustris*), of wet places, has kidney-shaped leaves from underground, creeping stems and lilac, dark-veined flowers.

few teeth

scented

no teeth

gland-tipped

COMMON DOG-VIOLET

Type	perennial
Height	2–40cm
Habitat	woods, hedges, heaths, mountain rocks
Flowering	April–June
STEMS AND LEAVES	
Stem	main, non-flowering stem short, side-shoots longer
Root	slender, short, upright, some shoots from root-buds
Hairs	absent or sparse, short
Stipules	short, spear-shaped, fringed
Leaves	basal or on alternate sides of stem, 5–80mm, heart-shaped, blunt to sharpish, edge with rounded teeth
Leaf-stalk	often longer than leaf
FLOWERS	
Position	single, from leaf-base
Bracts	2, slender
Type	☿, not scented
Size	14–22mm
Colour	blue-violet, spur whitish
Stalk	much longer than flower
Sepals	5, 7–12mm, spear-shaped, lobed at base
Petals	5, 8–18mm, spur 3–5mm, oval, overlapping, lowest with backward-pointing spur
Stamens	5, 2 lower with spur
Stigma	1, style hook-like at tip
Ovary	1, 1-celled
FRUIT	
Type	1, 3-angled, pointed capsule, splits into 3
Size	6–13mm
Seeds	many, 2–2.5mm, egg-shaped

often 3 coloured

splits into 3

short
spur

broad petals

lobed stipules

narrow leaves

Face-like markings on the flowers of Wild Pansy have long made it a favourite, the wild species of Pansy being developed as the familiar garden plants. Pansies differ from Violets mainly in the large, leaf-like stipules and flatter flowers with side petals angled upwards.

Status: native; throughout area.

SIMILAR SPECIES

1 Seaside Pansy *(V. tricolor subsp. curtisii)* is a low-growing perennial found by the coast. **2 Field Pansy** *(V. arvensis)*, usually a weed, has small petals about equalling the sepals. **3 Mountain Pansy** *(V. lutea)* is a perennial of hilly areas, spreading by underground stems to form large clumps on fairly lime-rich soils.

large

sepals

perennial

small flower

creeping stems

WILD PANSY

Type	usually annual
Height	15–30cm, rarely 45cm
Habitat	cultivated and waste ground, grassland; mainly lime-free soils
Flowering	April–September
STEMS AND LEAVES	
Stem	usually many-branched
Root	fibrous, rarely with short underground stems
Hairs	absent or very short
Stipules	large, with paired lobes
Leaves	on alternate sides of stem, 10–50mm, oval, spear-shaped or elliptical, blunt, with rounded teeth
Leaf-stalk	lower long, upper short
FLOWERS	
Position	solitary, from leaf-base
Bracts	2, tiny
Type	☿
Size	15–25mm, rarely 35mm
Colour	petals violet, yellow, pink or white with purplish marks
Stalk	long
Sepals	5, 5–14mm, spear-shaped
Petals	5, 7–17mm, unequal, oval, flattish, side petals turn upwards, lowest with spur
Stamens	5, 2 lower with spur
Stigma	1, club-shaped
Ovary	1, 1-celled
FRUIT	
Type	1, 3-angled capsule, splits into 3
Size	6–10mm
Seeds	many, 1.5–2mm, egg-shaped

Musk Mallow *Malva moschata*

These attractive, large, pink flowers resemble those of the related Hollyhock or Hibiscus, and have stamens joined into a club-shaped cluster. Mallows make copious mucilage, formerly used in cough-mixtures, poultices or to treat wasp-stings.

Status: native or naturalized in north; widespread except for much of north.

large, pink

stamens clustered

5 petals

hairy fruit

fruits in ring

deeply divided

mostly narrow lobes

MUSK MALLOW

Type	perennial
Height	30–80cm
Habitat	grassy places; mainly fertile soils
Flowering	July–August
STEMS AND LEAVES	
Stem	upright, rounded
Root	thick, branched stock
Hairs	sparse
Stipules	small, spear-shaped
Leaves	basal or on alternate sides of stem, variable, 50–80mm, 3–7 lobes, toothed, lower kidney-shaped, upper mostly cut into thin lobes
Leaf-stalk	lower long, upper short
FLOWERS	
Position	single from leaf-base or irregular head at stem-tip
Bracts	3 beneath base of sepals
Type	♂
Size	30–60mm
Colour	rose-pink, rarely white, veins crimson
Stalk	shorter than flower
Sepals	5, 6–12mm, oval, pointed
Petals	5, 14–25mm, twisted together in bud, equal, oval, squarish and notched
Stamens	many, in club-shaped head
Stigmas	numerous, slender
Ovary	1, usually many-celled
FRUIT	
Type	a ring of wedge-shaped, hairy, nut-like segments
Size	c2mm
Seeds	1 per segment, nearly circular, flattened

SIMILAR SPECIES

Other Mallows have leaves less divided. **1 Common Mallow** (*M. sylvestris*) has purplish, dark-striped flowers. **2 Dwarf Mallow** (*M. neglecta*) is a low-growing annual with small pale flowers. **3 Marsh-mallow** (*Althaea officinalis*), in marshy places near the sea, has soft, velvety leaves, pale pink flowers and more bracts beneath the sepals.

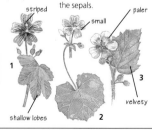

striped

paler

small

1

3

shallow lobes

2

velvety

Helianthemum nummularium **Common Rock-rose**

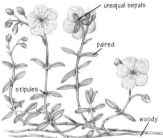

unequal sepals

paired

stipules

woody

5 petals

crumpled

fruit opens

A wiry-stemmed plant, its yellow petals crumpled like tissue-paper, opening in sunny weather and falling within a few hours. The flowers open with a tuft of stamens in the centre, so the first insect visitor is dusted with pollen. Once touched, the stamens move apart so that the flower can receive pollen from the next visitor.

Status: native; often common, absent from much of north, west and many islands.

SIMILAR SPECIES

1 White Rock-rose *(H. apenninum)* has narrow, greyish, woolly leaves and white flowers. **2 Spotted Rock-rose** *(Tuberaria guttata)* is an annual with a rosette of leaves at the base and smaller petals, often with a large red spot at the base.

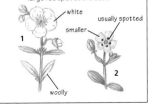

white

usually spotted

smaller

1

2

woolly

COMMON ROCK-ROSE

Type	perennial
Height	5–30cm
Habitat	grassland, scrub; lime-rich soils
Flowering	June–September
STEMS AND LEAVES	
Stem	many, woody below, low-growing or angled upwards
Root	thick, woody stock, vertical tap-root
Hairs	sparse or short; dense, whitish beneath leaves
Stipules	narrowly spear-shaped
Leaves	paired either side of stem, 5–20mm, oblong or oval, blunt, edge unbroken
Leaf-stalk	much shorter than blade
FLOWERS	
Position	1–12, in 1-sided, spike-like head from stem-tip
Bracts	narrowly spear-shaped
Type	♂
Size	14–25mm, rarely 30mm
Colour	usually bright yellow
Stalk	about equalling flower
Sepals	5, 2 slender, c2mm; 3 oval, c6mm
Petals	5, 6–12mm, equal, oval, crumpled, soon falling
Stamens	numerous, moving apart when touched
Stigma	1, 3-lobed on S-shaped style
Ovary	1, 1-celled
FRUIT	
Type	1, capsule, almost globular, splits into 3
Size	c6mm
Seeds	many, c2mm, egg-shaped

White Bryony *Bryonia cretica* subsp. *dioica*

Most noticeable in fruit, the stems bearing clusters of red berries hang like festoons in a leafless Autumn hedgerow. Although attractive, the berries are poisonous and can be fatal. White Bryony was cultivated for the massive rootstock; its uses included the treatment of rheumatic and arthritic pain.

Status: native or naturalized in north; sometimes common, rare in north.

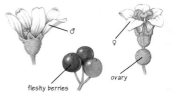

fleshy berries

ovary

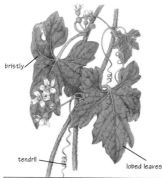

bristly

tendril

lobed leaves

SIMILAR SPECIES

Black Bryony *(Tamus communis)* is unrelated, although in fruit and with withered leaves the two look similar. This plant has twining stems, glossy, heart-shaped leaves, and six-petalled flowers, the males in long spikes.

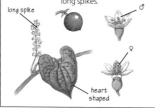

long spike

heart shaped

WHITE BRYONY

Type	perennial
Height	up to 400cm
Habitat	hedgerows, scrub, woods; mainly well-drained soils
Flowering	May–September
STEMS AND LEAVES	
Stem	long, angled, bristly; climbs with coiled tendrils at base of leaf-stalks
Root	large, swollen, stock
Hairs	stiff, swollen-based
Stipules	absent
Leaves	spirally placed around stem, 50–100mm, most with 5 radiating lobes, wavy-toothed
Leaf-stalk	shorter than blade
FLOWERS	
Position	♂ and ♀ flowers on different plants
Bracts	absent
Type 1	♂, 3–8 in long-stalked head
Type 2	♀, 2–5 in stalkless cluster from leaf-base, 10–12mm
Size	12–18mm
Colour	greenish white
Stalk	present
Sepals	5, triangular, bases joined
Petals	5, oblong, hairy, bases joined
Stamens	5, 4 joined in pairs
Stigmas	3, 2-lobed, on thick style
Ovary	1, globular, beneath petals, 3-celled
FRUIT	
Type	1, berry, globular, smooth, red when ripe
Size	5–8mm
Seeds	3–6, 4–5mm, flattened, black and yellow mottled

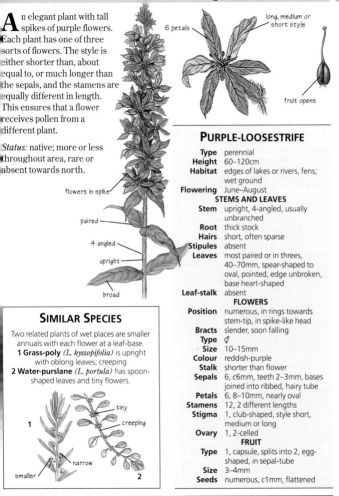

A n elegant plant with tall spikes of purple flowers. Each plant has one of three sorts of flowers. The style is either shorter than, about equal to, or much longer than the sepals, and the stamens are equally different in length. This ensures that a flower receives pollen from a different plant.

Status: native; more or less throughout area, rare or absent towards north.

long, medium or short style

6 petals

fruit opens

flowers in spike

paired

4-angled

upright

broad

SIMILAR SPECIES

Two related plants of wet places are smaller annuals with each flower at a leaf-base.
1 Grass-poly (*L. hyssopifolia*) is upright with oblong leaves; creeping
2 Water-purslane (*L. portula*) has spoon-shaped leaves and tiny flowers.

tiny

creeping

1

narrow

smaller

2

PURPLE-LOOSESTRIFE

Type	perennial
Height	60–120cm
Habitat	edges of lakes or rivers, fens; wet ground
Flowering	June–August
STEMS AND LEAVES	
Stem	upright, 4-angled, usually unbranched
Root	thick stock
Hairs	short, often sparse
Stipules	absent
Leaves	most paired or in threes, 40–70mm, spear-shaped to oval, pointed, edge unbroken, base heart-shaped
Leaf-stalk	absent
FLOWERS	
Position	numerous, in rings towards stem-tip, in spike-like head
Bracts	slender, soon falling
Type	♂
Size	10–15mm
Colour	reddish-purple
Stalk	shorter than flower
Sepals	6, c6mm, teeth 2–3mm, bases joined into ribbed, hairy tube
Petals	6, 8–10mm, nearly oval
Stamens	12, 2 different lengths
Stigma	1, club-shaped, style short, medium or long
Ovary	1, 2-celled
FRUIT	
Type	1, capsule, splits into 2, egg-shaped, in sepal-tube
Size	3–4mm
Seeds	numerous, c1mm, flattened

Large-flowered Evening-primrose
Oenothera erythrosepala

A tall, rather bushy plant, originally only a garden plant. At dusk the flowers open so rapidly that the petals move visibly. Within minutes, sepals split and petals unfurl. A delicate scent, like orange-blossom, and almost luminous, pale petals attract night-flying moths.

Status: introduced; often common, absent from north.

wavy-edged

large

bend back

fruit splits into 4

red-striped

red-based hairs

LARGE-FLOWERED EVENING-PRIMROSE

Type	biennial
Height	50–100cm
Habitat	waste ground, banks of roads and railways, dunes
Flowering	June–September

STEMS AND LEAVES

Stem	upright, stout, leafy
Root	thick, white tap-root
Hairs	mostly short, some long with swollen, red bases
Stipules	absent
Leaves	spirally arranged, 40–250mm, elliptical to spear-shaped, midrib white or pink, tip pointed, edge wavy, slightly toothed
Leaf-stalk	short or almost absent

FLOWERS

Position	in loose spike at stem-tip
Bracts	leaf-like below
Type	☿, scented
Size	80–100mm
Colour	pale yellow
Stalk	shorter than flower
Sepals	4, 35–50mm, bases joined, tubular, red-striped, bending back on opening
Petals	4, 40–50mm, twisted together in bud, broad, overlapping, notched
Stamens	8, bases curved
Stigma	1, 4-lobed, on long style
Ovary	1, below sepals, 4-celled

FRUIT

Type	1, capsule, splits into 4, oblong, tapered, hairy
Size	25–40mm
Seeds	numerous, 1–2mm, oblong

SIMILAR SPECIES

1 Common Evening-primrose *(O. biennis)* lacks red-based hairs and has smaller flowers with green sepals. **2 Fragrant Evening-primrose** *(O. stricta)* lacks red-based hairs and has more strongly scented flowers which turn red.

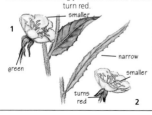

smaller

green

narrow

smaller

turns red

Circaea lutetiana **Enchanter's-nightshade**

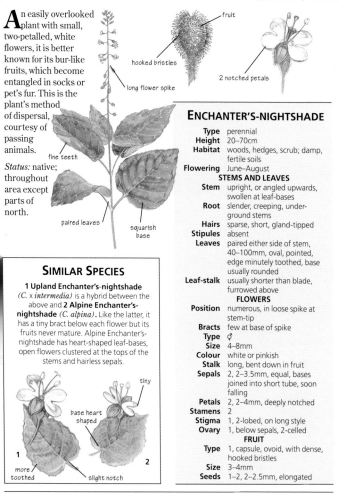

An easily overlooked plant with small, two-petalled, white flowers, it is better known for its bur-like fruits, which become entangled in socks or pet's fur. This is the plant's method of dispersal, courtesy of passing animals.

Status: native; throughout area except parts of north.

fruit

hooked bristles

long flower spike

2 notched petals

fine teeth

paired leaves

squarish base

ENCHANTER'S-NIGHTSHADE

Type	perennial
Height	20–70cm
Habitat	woods, hedges, scrub; damp, fertile soils
Flowering	June–August
STEMS AND LEAVES	
Stem	upright, or angled upwards, swollen at leaf-bases
Root	slender, creeping, underground stems
Hairs	sparse, short, gland-tipped
Stipules	absent
Leaves	paired either side of stem, 40–100mm, oval, pointed, edge usually toothed, base usually rounded
Leaf-stalk	usually shorter than blade, furrowed above
FLOWERS	
Position	numerous, in loose spike at stem-tip
Bracts	few at base of spike
Type	⚥
Size	4–8mm
Colour	white or pinkish
Stalk	long, bent down in fruit
Sepals	2, 2–3.5mm, equal, bases joined into short tube, soon falling
Petals	2, 2–4mm, deeply notched
Stamens	2
Stigma	1, 2-lobed, on long style
Ovary	1, below sepals, 2-celled
FRUIT	
Type	1, capsule, ovoid, with dense, hooked bristles
Size	3–4mm
Seeds	1–2, 2–2.5mm, elongated

SIMILAR SPECIES

1 Upland Enchanter's-nightshade (*C.* x *intermedia*) is a hybrid between the above and **2 Alpine Enchanter's-nightshade** (*C. alpina*). Like the latter, it has a tiny bract below each flower but its fruits never mature. Alpine Enchanter's-nightshade has heart-shaped leaf-bases, open flowers clustered at the tops of the stems and hairless sepals.

tiny

base heart shaped

1

more toothed

2

slight notch

Rosebay Willowherb *Chamerion angustifolium*

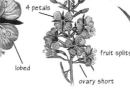

in spikes · 4 petals · long hairs · slightly unequal petals · lobed · fruit splits · ovary short · stalkless · spirally arranged

Spreading underground to form vast clumps, this plant bears slender spikes of rose-purple flowers. In Autumn it has fluffy masses of plumed seeds. Formerly rarer, the species has spread with the creation of railway embankments and demolition sites.

Status: native; throughout area, often common, rarer in Ireland and north.

ROSEBAY WILLOWHERB

Type	perennial
Height	30–120cm, rarely 250cm
Habitat	woodland clearings, scree, waste ground; mostly stony soils, often on burnt ground
Flowering	July–September
STEMS AND LEAVES	
Stem	upright, leafy
Root	woody, horizontal, creeping roots make new stems
Hairs	absent below, short above
Stipules	absent
Leaves	spirally arranged around stem, 50–150mm, narrowly spear-shaped or elliptical, pointed, edge unbroken or minutely toothed, wavy
Leaf-stalk	almost stalkless
FLOWERS	
Position	many, in spike at stem-tip
Bracts	leaf-like below
Type	♂
Size	20–30mm
Colour	deep pinkish purple
Stalk	10–15mm
Sepals	4, 8–12mm, slender, purple
Petals	4, 10–16mm, oval, notched, upper 2 broader than lower 2
Stamens	8
Stigma	1, 4-lobed, on long style
Ovary	1, below sepals, 4-celled
FRUIT	
Type	1, capsule, 4-angled, slender, splits into 4
Size	25–80mm
Seeds	many, 1–2mm, egg-shaped, with plume of long bristles

SIMILAR SPECIES

Other Willowherbs have mostly paired leaves and upright, equal-petalled flowers. **1 Great Willowherb** *(Epilobium hirsutum)* has hairy leaves which clasp the stem. Two species with smaller flowers are **2 Hoary Willowherb** *(E. parviflorum)*, which has hairy leaves, and **3 Broad-leaved Willowherb** *(E. montanum)* which has almost hairless leaves.

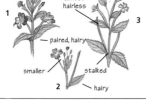

almost hairless · paired, hairy · smaller · stalked · hairy

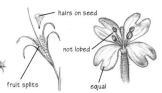

hairs on seed

not lobed

fruit splits

equal

O ne of the commonest Willowherbs but easily overlooked because it lacks showy flowers. In poorly-drained, cultivated ground it can be a troublesome weed as creeping stems root to make new plants. Willowherbs are larval food-plants for the Elephant Hawk-moth.

stalkless

Status: native; often common, most of area except parts of north and some islands.

longer than petals

lower paired

ovary

SHORT-FRUITED WILLOWHERB

Type	perennial
Height	30–60cm, rarely 80cm
Habitat	banks of streams, ditches, marshes; wet ground
Flowering	July–August

STEMS AND LEAVES

Stem	upright, 4 raised lines
Root	creeping, rooting stems at or below ground-level
Hairs	absent below, sparse above, pressed to surface
Stipules	absent
Leaves	lower paired, upper spirally arranged, 30–70mm, spear-shaped, edge with few, small teeth, base rounded, runs into lines on stem
Leaf-stalk	absent

FLOWERS

Position	many, in loose spike at stem-tip
Bracts	present, lowest leaf-like
Type	☿
Size	7–9mm
Colour	pinkish purple
Stalk	shorter than flower
Sepals	4, 3–4mm, spear-shaped, bases joined into tube
Petals	4, 5–6mm, deeply notched
Stamens	8
Stigma	1, on short style
Ovary	1, 4-celled

FRUIT

Type	slender, 4-angled capsule, downy, splits into 4
Size	40–60mm
Seeds	many, base c1mm, rough, with long plume of hairs

SIMILAR SPECIES

Two common species of similar wet places have rather smaller flowers.
1 Pale Willowherb (*E. roseum*) has stalked leaves and whitish, pink-streaked flowers.
2 Marsh Willowherb (*E. palustre*) has rounded stems without any raised lines. Its creeping stems end in bulb-like buds.

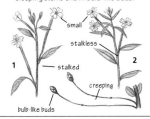

small

stalkless

1

2

stalked

creeping

bulb-like buds

Spiked Water-milfoil *Myriophyllum spicatum*

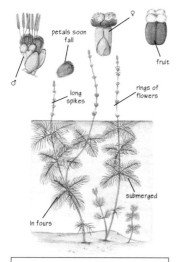

petals soon
fall

♂

♀

fruit

long
spikes

rings of
flowers

submerged

in fours

A submerged aquatic plant with feathery leaves mostly carried in fours. It is most noticeable in flower, when the slender, reddish flower-spikes appear above the water's surface.

Status: native; most of area, absent from some islands.

SPIKED WATER-MILFOIL

Type	perennial
Height	50–250cm
Habitat	lakes, ponds, ditches; still water, especially in lime-rich areas
Flowering	June–July
STEMS AND LEAVES	
Stem	slender, branched, leafless towards base
Root	creeping underground stems
Hairs	absent
Stipules	absent
Leaves	usually rings of 4 around stem, 15–30mm, deeply cut either side into 15–35 thin segments
Leaf-stalk	absent
FLOWERS	
Position	mostly rings of 4, in spike towards stem-tip
Bracts	nearly all not toothed, shorter than flowers
Type	lowest ♀, next ♂, upper ♂
Size	2–4mm
Colour	pinkish or dull red
Stalk	absent
Sepals	4, ♀ minute, ♂ c0.5mm
Petals	4, minute on ♀ flowers; ♂ c3mm, soon falling
Stamens	8
Stigmas	4, without a style
Ovary	1, below sepals, 4-celled
FRUIT	
Type	1, almost globular, splits into 4 nut-like parts
Size	2–3mm
Seeds	1 per segment, not released

SIMILAR SPECIES

1 Whorled Water-milfoil (*M. verticillatum*) has leaves in fives and toothed upper bracts. It overwinters in the form of club-shaped resting buds called 'turions'.
2 Alternate-flowered Water-milfoil (*M. alterniflorum*) has leaf-like lower bracts and the upper flowers are not in rings.
3 Rigid Hornwort (*Ceratophyllum demersum*) is unrelated and has rigid, repeatedly forked leaves. Each flower or spiny fruit is at the base of a leaf.

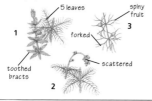

5 leaves

spiny
fruit

1

3

forked

toothed
bracts

scattered

2

berry-like fruits

lower leaves lobed

woody

upper not lobed

clinging roots

eads of flowers

5 petals

A woody climber with sombre, glossy leaves, Ivy is associated with death nd decay because it needs a support to climb up on and there is none better than an old, crumbling wall or a dying tree. Ivy as gained a reputation for killing trees – n unfounded slander, for it has little effect other than to increase the weight on the branches and trunk or to shade some leaves. The yellowish flowers are rather insignificant, but produce copious nectar at a time when little else is in flower and so are visited by large numbers of insects, particularly wasps and hornets. The berries are eaten by birds, such as thrushes and blackbirds, and the plant makes a favoured nesting-site. Ivy is a food-plant for caterpillars of both butterflies and moths, including the Holly Blue and the Swallow-tailed Moth. Many horticultural forms of Ivy are grown, differing greatly in habit and in form and colour of the leaves.

Status: native; common except in northernmost part of area.

Similar species: none.

IVY

Type	biennial
Height	up to 30cm
Habitat	woods, hedges, rocks, walls; most soils
Flowering	September–November

STEMS AND LEAVES

Stem	woody, up to 25cm across, climbs with clinging roots
Root	woody stock; stem roots
Hairs	mostly hairless; young shoots with branched hairs
Stipules	paired either side of stem
Leaves	spirally arranged, 40–100mm, most with 3–5 triangular, radiating lobes, glossy, evergreen, base heart-shaped; oval or diamond-shaped on flowering stems, not lobed, base rounded or wedge-shaped
Leaf-stalk	shorter than blade

FLOWERS

Position	many in compact, stalked heads towards stem-tip
Bracts	absent
Type	♂
Size	5–8mm
Colour	yellowish green
Stalk	about equalling flower
Sepals	5 minute, triangular teeth
Petals	5, 3–4mm, equal, oval
Stamens	5
Stigma	1, slender
Ovary	1, below sepals, 5-celled

FRUIT

Type	1, berry-like, leathery, almost globular, black
Size	6–8mm
Seeds	2–5, whitish, papery coat

Sea-holly *Eryngium maritimum*

A beautiful plant with a pale blue waxiness to both leaves and stems. Most unusually for a species of the Carrot family, the leaves have holly-like, spine-tipped teeth, and the flower-heads are compact and thistle-like. The thick, fleshy roots were peeled and boiled with sugar to make candied eryngoes.

Status: native; coasts except for extreme north.

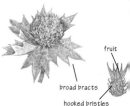

fruit

broad bracts

hooked bristles

spiny

head of florets

bluish

thick stem

SIMILAR SPECIES

1 Field Eryngo *(E.campestre)*, from southern parts, has more divided, greener leaves and narrow, often toothless bracts.
2 Astrantia *(Astrantia major)* is often naturalized and has flattened flower-heads encircled by greenish-white or pink, petal-like bracts.

narrow

petal-like

1

2

greener

not spiny

SEA-HOLLY

Type	perennial
Height	15–60cm
Habitat	sand-dunes, shingle banks
Flowering	July–August
STEMS AND LEAVES	
Stem	more or less upright, thick, branched, hollow
Root	long, thick, fleshy
Hairs	absent
Stipules	absent
Leaves	basal or on alternate sides of stem, 40–120mm, with radiating lobes and spine-tipped teeth, pale bluish-green or purple-tinged, base heart-shaped, upper leaves clasp stem
Leaf-stalk	present or upper absent
FLOWERS	
Position	many in almost globular, stalked head, 15–30mm long
Bracts	leaf-like, spiny below head; 3-toothed below flowers
Type	♂
Size	6–8mm
Colour	whitish or pale blue
Stalk	absent
Sepals	5, 4–5mm, thin, spine-tipped
Petals	5, 3–4mm, narrow, notched
Stamens	5, curved inwards
Stigmas	2, slender
Ovary	1, below sepals, 2-celled
FRUIT	
Type	1, dry, egg-shaped, corky-walled, covered with hooked spines, splits into 2
Size	5–6mm
Seeds	1 per half, not released

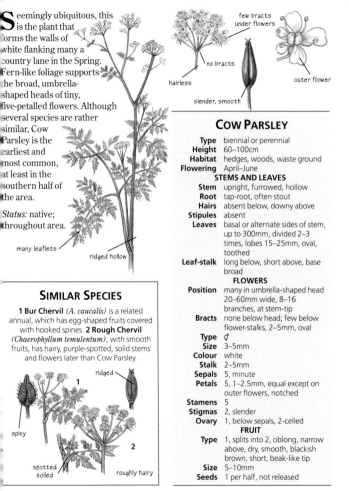

S eemingly ubiquitous, this is the plant that forms the walls of white flanking many a country lane in the Spring. Fern-like foliage supports the broad, umbrella-shaped heads of tiny, five-petalled flowers. Although several species are rather similar, Cow Parsley is the earliest and most common, at least in the southern half of the area.

Status: native; throughout area.

many leaflets

ridged hollow

few bracts under flowers

no bracts

hairless

slender, smooth

outer flower

COW PARSLEY

Type	biennial or perennial
Height	60–100cm
Habitat	hedges, woods, waste ground
Flowering	April–June

STEMS AND LEAVES

Stem	upright, furrowed, hollow
Root	tap-root, often stout
Hairs	absent below, downy above
Stipules	absent
Leaves	basal or alternate sides of stem, up to 300mm, divided 2–3 times, lobes 15–25mm, oval, toothed
Leaf-stalk	long below, short above, base broad

FLOWERS

Position	many in umbrella-shaped head 20–60mm wide, 8–16 branches, at stem-tip
Bracts	none below head; few below flower-stalks, 2–5mm, oval
Type	♂
Size	3–5mm
Colour	white
Stalk	2–5mm
Sepals	5, minute
Petals	5, 1–2.5mm, equal except on outer flowers, notched
Stamens	5
Stigmas	2, slender
Ovary	1, below sepals, 2-celled

FRUIT

Type	1, splits into 2, oblong, narrow above, dry, smooth, blackish brown, short, beak-like tip
Size	5–10mm
Seeds	1 per half, not released

SIMILAR SPECIES

1 Bur Chervil (*A. caucalis*) is a related annual, which has egg-shaped fruits covered with hooked spines. **2 Rough Chervil** (*Chaerophyllum temulentum*), with smooth fruits, has hairy, purple-spotted, solid stems and flowers later than Cow Parsley.

ridged

spiny

spotted solled

roughly hairy

Alexanders *Smyrnium olusatrum*

lower leaves large

blackish

greenish-yellow

smooth ridges

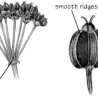

few bracts

leaflets in threes

broad

grooved

A robust plant of coastal districts, with glossy, dark green foliage, umbrella-shaped, greenish-yellow flower-heads and almost globular, blackish fruits. Probably brought by the Romans as a pot-herb, it was long used for the celery-like leaf-bases.

Status: introduced, or native in extreme south; mostly near southern coasts.

SIMILAR SPECIES

1 Scots Lovage (*Ligusticum scoticum*) is native on northern coasts. A smaller plant, with fewer leaflets, whitish flowers and flattened fruits, it is also edible.

2 Lovage (*Levisticum officinale*), a garden herb that often escapes, has leaves with fewer, coarser teeth and smaller fruits.

white

few leaflets

small

1

2

flattened

few teeth

ALEXANDERS

Type	biennial
Height	50–150cm
Habitat	grassy banks, hedges, cliffs
Flowering	April–June

STEMS AND LEAVES

Stem	upright, stout, solid or oldest hollow, furrowed
Root	tap-root
Hairs	absent
Stipules	absent
Leaves	basal, scattered or upper paired, up to 300mm, divided 1–3 times, leaflets in 3s, oval, glossy dark green, toothed or lobed
Leaf-stalk	broad base sheaths stem, long or upper short

FLOWERS

Position	many in umbrella-shaped head, 7–20 branches, at stem-tip
Bracts	few or absent
Type	♂
Size	1.5–3.5mm
Colour	greenish yellow
Stalk	about equalling flower
Sepals	absent
Petals	5, 0.7–1.5mm, spear-shaped, tip curved in
Stamens	5
Stigmas	2, slender
Ovary	1, below petals, 2-celled

FRUIT

Type	1, splits into 2, nearly globular, dry, smooth or 3-ridged, almost black
Size	7–8mm
Seeds	1 per half, not released

Crithmum maritimum **Rock Samphire**

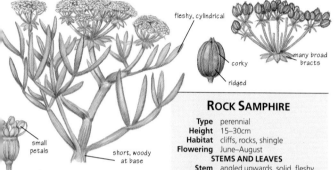

fleshy, cylindrical

corky

ridged

many broad bracts

small petals

short, woody at base

A curious member of the Carrot family, with the normal umbrella-shaped heads of flowers but swollen, succulent, aromatic leaves. These leaves can be made into a pickle or sauce, uses that were formerly commonplace but are now rarely tried. Rock Samphire commonly inhabits inaccessible ledges of sea-cliffs and its collection was an exceedingly hazardous and often lethal trade. Eating the plant was believed to aid digestion and have beneficial effects on the kidneys and bladder. Rock Samphire was sometimes grown as a vegetable on well-drained soils, especially in England and France. The succulent leaves, with a thick, translucent coat, are an adaptation to drought, for even though the plant may be drenched by spray from a rough sea, the salt in the water tends to dry out an unprotected leaf and makes it difficult for roots to take up usable water.

Status: native; coastal, from Scotland southwards.

Similar species: none.

ROCK SAMPHIRE

Type	perennial
Height	15–30cm
Habitat	cliffs, rocks, shingle
Flowering	June–August
STEMS AND LEAVES	
Stem	angled upwards, solid, fleshy, woody at base
Root	woody stock
Hairs	absent
Stipules	absent
Leaves	on alternate sides of stem, divided 1–2 times into slender, smoothly rounded, fleshy, pointed segments, each 10–40mm, edge unbroken
Leaf-stalk	short with broad base sheathing stem
FLOWERS	
Position	many, in umbrella-shaped head 30–60mm across, 8–20 branches, at stem-tip
Bracts	many, spear-shaped, below head and flower-stalks
Type	♂
Size	1.5–2.5mm
Colour	yellowish green
Stalk	about equalling flower
Sepals	5, minute
Petals	5, 0.6–1mm, heart-shaped
Stamens	5
Stigmas	2, slender
Ovary	1, below petals, 2-celled
FRUIT	
Type	1, splits into 2, corky, egg-shaped, angled, sometimes purplish
Size	5–6mm
Seeds	1 per half, not released

Burnet-saxifrage *Pimpinella saxifraga*

no bracts

ridged, smooth

Like a curious mixture of other plants, this has umbrella-shaped flower-heads like Wild Carrot but lower leaves like Salad Burnet. Like true Saxifrages, it was used to treat kidney stones. The root has a goat-like smell.

upper narrow

Status: native; most of area except extreme north and many islands.

broad lower leaves

BURNET-SAXIFRAGE

Type	perennial
Height	30–100cm
Habitat	grassy places; mostly dry, lime-rich soils
Flowering	July–August
STEMS AND LEAVES	
Stem	upright, mostly solid, slightly ridged
Root	slender stock, fibres from old leaves, strong-smelling
Hairs	short, often sparse
Stipules	absent
Leaves	basal with 6–14 leaflets, mostly paired, each 10–25mm, oval, toothed; stem-leaves scattered, cut 1–2 times into thin leaflets
Leaf-stalk	lower long, upper with base sheathing stem
FLOWERS	
Position	many, in umbrella-shaped heads 20–50mm wide, 10–20 branches, at stem-tip
Bracts	absent
Type	mostly ♂
Size	2–3mm
Colour	white
Stalk	longer than flower
Sepals	5, minute
Petals	5, 0.8–1.5mm, tip curved in
Stamens	5
Stigmas	2, slender, short styles
Ovary	1, below sepals, 2-celled
FRUIT	
Type	1, splits into 2, dry, nearly globular, ridged
Size	2–3mm
Seeds	1 per half, not released

SIMILAR SPECIES

1 Greater Burnet-saxifrage (*P. major*) is larger, and has ridged, hollow stems, longer, pointed lower leaflets, and grows in shadier places. Two grassland species have lumpy edible tubers. **2 Pignut** (*Conopodium majus*) has hollow stems, long styles and narrow-beaked fruits. **3 Great Pignut** (*Bunium bulbocastanum*) has solid stems, short styles and fruits with a short, bent beak.

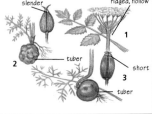

slender

ridged, hollow

1

tuber

short

3

2

tuber

tuber

116

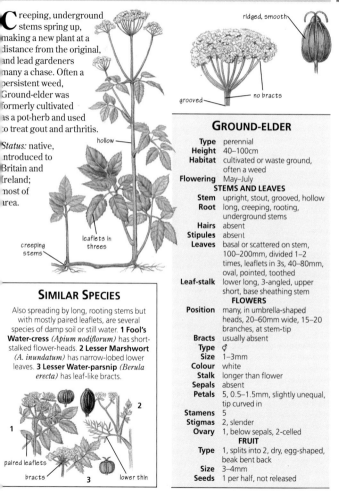

Creeping, underground stems spring up, making a new plant at a distance from the original, and lead gardeners many a chase. Often a persistent weed, Ground-elder was formerly cultivated as a pot-herb and used to treat gout and arthritis.

Status: native, introduced to Britain and Ireland; most of area.

ridged, smooth

grooved

no bracts

hollow

leaflets in threes

creeping stems

SIMILAR SPECIES

Also spreading by long, rooting stems but with mostly paired leaflets, are several species of damp soil or still water. **1 Fool's Water-cress** *(Apium nodiflorum)* has short-stalked flower-heads. **2 Lesser Marshwort** *(A. inundatum)* has narrow-lobed lower leaves. **3 Lesser Water-parsnip** *(Berula erecta)* has leaf-like bracts.

paired leaflets

bracts

lower thin

1

2

3

GROUND-ELDER

Type	perennial
Height	40–100cm
Habitat	cultivated or waste ground, often a weed
Flowering	May–July
STEMS AND LEAVES	
Stem	upright, stout, grooved, hollow
Root	long, creeping, rooting, underground stems
Hairs	absent
Stipules	absent
Leaves	basal or scattered on stem, 100–200mm, divided 1–2 times, leaflets in 3s, 40–80mm, oval, pointed, toothed
Leaf-stalk	lower long, 3-angled, upper short, base sheathing stem
FLOWERS	
Position	many, in umbrella-shaped heads, 20–60mm wide, 15–20 branches, at stem-tip
Bracts	usually absent
Type	♂
Size	1–3mm
Colour	white
Stalk	longer than flower
Sepals	absent
Petals	5, 0.5–1.5mm, slightly unequal, tip curved in
Stamens	5
Stigmas	2, slender
Ovary	1, below sepals, 2-celled
FRUIT	
Type	1, splits into 2, dry, egg-shaped, beak bent back
Size	3–4mm
Seeds	1 per half, not released

Hemlock Water-dropwort *Oenanthe crocata*

A robust plant of wet places, with large, much-divided lower leaves and umbrella-shaped flower-heads, it is extremely poisonous and often kills livestock. The tubers are attached to the base of the plant by thread-like roots, and this is the origin of the name 'dropwort'.

Status: native; fairly common, south-west of region.

bracts

grooved, hollow

many leaflets

narrow, ridged

HEMLOCK WATER-DROPWORT

Type	perennial
Height	50–150cm
Habitat	wet ditches, edge of water
Flowering	June–July
STEMS AND LEAVES	
Stem	upright, stout, grooved, hollow
Root	elongated tubers
Hairs	absent
Stipules	absent
Leaves	basal or scattered on stem, up to 400mm, divided 2–4 times; leaflets many, oval to narrowly spear-shaped, toothed or lobed
Leaf-stalk	base sheathing stem, lower long, upper short
FLOWERS	
Position	many, in umbrella-shaped heads 50–100mm wide, 12–40 branches, at stem-tip
Bracts	many, slender, below head and flower-stalks
Type	♂ and ♀ in same head
Size	2–4mm
Colour	white
Stalk	longer than flower
Sepals	5, small, pointed
Petals	5, 1–2mm, notched, unequal on outer flowers
Stamens	5, anthers crimson
Stigmas	2, slender
Ovary	1, below sepals, 2-celled
FRUIT	
Type	1, splits into 2, dry, nearly cylindrical, ridged
Size	4–6mm
Seeds	1 per half, not released

SIMILAR SPECIES

1 Fine-leaved Water-dropwort (*O. aquatica*) has tiny leaflets and no bracts.
2 Parsley Water-dropwort (*O. lachenalii*) has bracts but few, slender leaflets.
3 Tubular Water-dropwort (*O. fistulosa*) has curious, swollen stem-segments and flower-heads with few branches and no bracts.

few branches

no bracts

swollen

thin

1

2

3

Conium maculatum **Hemlock**

rough ridges

A tall, rather elegant plant with fern-like foliage, purple-spotted stems and white, lacy flower-heads. Marring this image is a strong smell which hints at the extremely poisonous nature of the plant. Its powerful alkaloids can paralyse the respiratory system of animals or humans. In ancient times, preparations were made as a method of execution and, apparently, used by the Greeks to kill Socrates. Children should be warned of this plant: hollow stems cut for use as pea-shooters have proved fatal, although the toxicity of the plant varies greatly between different areas. Hemlock has been used as a drastic antidote to strychnine. In times long past it was used as an external treatment for herpes and breast tumours, and in controlled doses, equally misguidedly, to treat epilepsy and certain nervous afflictions; this practice has ceased because such usage can lead to paralysis or death. There are no plants quite like Hemlock, although several others, such as Rough Chervil, have purple-spotted stems.

Status: native; throughout area, rarer in north.

Similar species: none.

purple-spotted, hollow

small bracts

many leaflets

fall

HEMLOCK

Type	perennial
Height	50–250cm
Habitat	woodland edges, waste ground; mostly damp soils
Flowering	June–July

STEMS AND LEAVES

Stem	upright, grooved, smooth, purple-spotted, hollow
Root	stout tap-root
Hairs	absent
Stipules	absent
Leaves	basal or scattered on stem, up to 300mm, divided 2–3 times; leaflets 10–20mm, spear-shaped to triangular, coarsely toothed
Leaf-stalk	lower long, upper very short, base broad

FLOWERS

Position	many in umbrella-shaped heads 20–50mm wide, 10–20 branches
Bracts	few, bent back, below head and flower-stalks
Type	♀in head at stem-tip, ♂ in head from leaf-base
Size	2–3mm
Colour	white
Stalk	longer than flower
Sepals	absent
Petals	5, 1–1.5mm, oval, notched
Stamens	5
Stigmas	2, on slender styles
Ovary	1, below petals, 2-celled

FRUIT

Type	1, splits into 2, nearly globular
Size	3–4mm
Seeds	1 per half, not released

119

Wild Parsnip *Pastinaca sativa*

Yellow, umbrella-shaped flower-heads and coarse, hairy foliage of Wild Parsnip are common by many roadsides in high Summer. The whole plant has a strong smell of Parsnips, for this is the same species as the cultivated plant. Wild roots are slender and often woody.

Status: native, escaped from cultivation in north; often common, most of area.

yellow

flattened fruits

no bracts

upright

hairy

5 petals

divided

all ♂

SIMILAR SPECIES

Two yellow-flowered species have finely divided, hairless leaves and oblong, wingless fruits. **1 Fennel** *(Foeniculum vulgare)* is more robust, the aniseed-scented foliage having almost hair-like segments. **2 Pepper-saxifrage** *(Silaum silaus)* has spear-shaped segments and fruits with the beak curved back.

1

very thin

ridged

2

ridged

narrow

WILD PARSNIP

Type	biennial
Height	30–150cm
Habitat	grassy and waste ground; mainly lime-rich soil
Flowering	July–August
STEMS AND LEAVES	
Stem	upright, ridged, hollow
Root	tap-root, strong-smelling
Hairs	straight, throughout plant
Stipules	absent
Leaves	basal or scattered on stem, up to 300mm, divided 1–2 times; leaflets oval, lobed, toothed
Leaf-stalk	mostly short, base sheathing stem
FLOWERS	
Position	many in umbrella-shaped heads 30–100mm wide, 5–15 unequal branches, at stem-tip
Bracts	absent or few, soon falling
Type	♂
Size	1.5–2.5mm
Colour	yellow
Stalk	little longer than flower
Sepals	absent
Petals	5, oval, curved inwards
Stamens	5
Stigmas	2, styles short
Ovary	1, below petals, 2-celled
FRUIT	
Type	1, splits into 2, broad, flattened with encircling wing, ridged, dark-lined
Size	5–8mm
Seeds	1 per half, not released

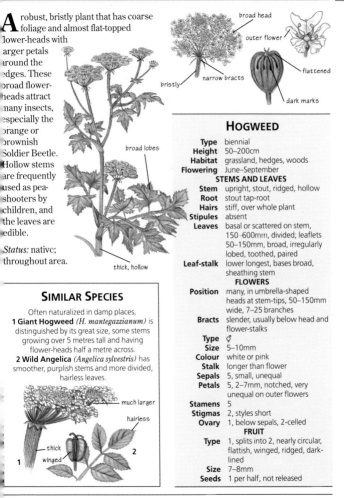

A robust, bristly plant that has coarse foliage and almost flat-topped flower-heads with larger petals around the edges. These broad flower-heads attract many insects, especially the orange or brownish Soldier Beetle. Hollow stems are frequently used as pea-shooters by children, and the leaves are edible.

Status: native; throughout area.

broad head
outer flower
bristly
narrow bracts
flattened
dark marks

broad lobes

thick, hollow

SIMILAR SPECIES

Often naturalized in damp places,
1 Giant Hogweed *(H. mantegazzianum)* is distinguished by its great size, some stems growing over 5 metres tall and having flower-heads half a metre across.
2 Wild Angelica *(Angelica sylvestris)* has smoother, purplish stems and more divided, hairless leaves.

much larger
hairless
thick
winged
1
2

HOGWEED

Type	biennial
Height	50–200cm
Habitat	grassland, hedges, woods
Flowering	June–September
STEMS AND LEAVES	
Stem	upright, stout, ridged, hollow
Root	stout tap-root
Hairs	stiff, over whole plant
Stipules	absent
Leaves	basal or scattered on stem, 150–600mm, divided; leaflets 50–150mm, broad, irregularly lobed, toothed, paired
Leaf-stalk	lower longest, bases broad, sheathing stem
FLOWERS	
Position	many, in umbrella-shaped heads at stem-tips, 50–150mm wide, 7–25 branches
Bracts	slender, usually below head and flower-stalks
Type	⚥
Size	5–10mm
Colour	white or pink
Stalk	longer than flower
Sepals	5, small, unequal
Petals	5, 2–7mm, notched, very unequal on outer flowers
Stamens	5
Stigmas	2, styles short
Ovary	1, below sepals, 2-celled
FRUIT	
Type	1, splits into 2, nearly circular, flattish, winged, ridged, dark-lined
Size	7–8mm
Seeds	1 per half, not released

121

Upright Hedge-parsley *Torilis japonica*

One of the later-flowering hedgerow species of the Carrot family, with lacy umbrella-shaped heads of pinkish flowers. Spiny fruits and many slender bracts distinguish it from most other native species of the family.

Status: native; often very common, most of area except extreme north.

slender

spiny

umbrella-shaped heads

many bracts

solid, smooth

SIMILAR SPECIES

1 Knotted Hedge-parsley *(T. nodosa)* has almost stalkless flower-heads with few branches. **2 Spreading Hedge-parsley** *(T. arvensis)* has heads with fewer branches and usually one bract.
3 Fool's Parsley *(Aethusa cynapium)* has long, downward-pointing bracts below the flower-stalks, and smoothly ridged fruits.

few branches

stemless head

half spiny

smooth, ridged

long

1

2

3

UPRIGHT HEDGE-PARSLEY

Type	annual
Height	5–125cm
Habitat	hedges, grassy places
Flowering	July–August
STEMS AND LEAVES	
Stem	more or less upright, solid
Root	slender tap-root
Hairs	short, pressed to surface
Stipules	absent
Leaves	on alternate sides of stem, divided 1–3 times; leaflets 10–20mm, oval to spear-shaped, lobed or toothed
Leaf-stalk	lower longest
FLOWERS	
Position	many, in umbrella-shaped heads 15–40mm wide, 5–12 branches, most at stem-tip
Bracts	many, unequal, thin, below head and flower-stalks
Type	♂
Size	2–3mm
Colour	white tinged pink or purple
Stalk	longer than flower
Sepals	5, small, triangular
Petals	5, 1–1.5mm, unequal, notched, tip curved in
Stamens	5
Stigmas	2, styles short
Ovary	1, below sepals, 2-celled
FRUIT	
Type	1, splits into 2, egg-shaped, ridged, covered with spines, beak-like tips curved back
Size	3–4mm
Seeds	1 per half, not released

Daucus carota subsp. *carota* **Wild Carrot**

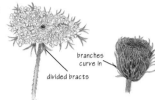

dark middle

branches curve in

divided bracts

Distinct among the many species of the family because of the conspicuous, divided bracts beneath the flower-heads. In the middle of the white flower-head there is usually a single purple flower. The fruiting head curls up like a ball and bristles with spiny fruits. Cultivated Carrot belongs to a different subspecies.

Status: native or introduced in extreme north; throughout area.

spiny

WILD CARROT

Type	biennial
Height	30–100cm, rarely 150cm
Habitat	grassland, often lime-rich soils
Flowering	June–August
STEMS AND LEAVES	
Stem	upright, ridged, solid
Root	usually thin tap-root
Hairs	stems stiffly hairy
Stipules	absent
Leaves	on alternate sides of stem, divided 2–3 times; leaflets 4–7mm, slender, lobed
Leaf-stalk	lower longest, base sheathing stem
FLOWERS	
Position	many, in umbrella-shaped heads at stem-tips 30–70mm wide, many branches
Bracts	7–13 below head, deeply cut into thin lobes, undivided below flowers, edges papery
Type	♂
Size	2–4mm
Colour	white, middle flower usually purple or red
Stalk	about equalling flower
Sepals	5, small
Petals	5, 1–2mm, notched, unequal on outer flowers
Stamens	5
Stigmas	2, styles short
Ovary	1, below sepals, 2-celled
FRUIT	
Type	1, splits into 2, nearly oblong, ridged, spiny
Size	2.5–4mm
Seeds	1 per half, not released

SIMILAR SPECIES

Sea Carrot *(D. carota* subsp. *gummifer)*, from the Atlantic coasts of Britain and France, is often short-stemmed, with more triangular leaves having broader, fleshier segments, and the fruiting heads are flat or slightly domed.

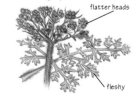

flatter heads

fleshy

Thorow-wax *Bupleurum rotundifolium*

A most peculiar member of the Carrot family, its stems appear to pass straight through the bluish, undivided leaves, as referred to in the common name. Broad bracts and dull yellow flowers look rather like some sort of Spurge. Once a common cornfield weed, it became extinct in many areas with seed-cleaning and selective herbicides.

Status: native or introduced; uncommon, south of area.

fruit

smooth ridges

small flowers

few branches

leaf surrounds stem

broad bracts

SIMILAR SPECIES

Warty fruits are found on **1 False Thorow-wax** (*B. subovatum*), with narrower leaves, and **2 Slender Hare's-ear** (*B. tenuissimum*), with grass-like leaves. **3 Sickle-leaved Hare's-ear** (*B. falcatum*) is perennial, and has smooth fruits and narrow, often curved leaves.

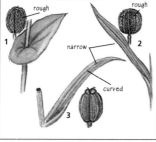

rough

rough

narrow

curved

THOROW-WAX

Type	annual
Height	15–30cm
Habitat	cornfields, waste ground; mostly dry soils
Flowering	June–July
STEMS AND LEAVES	
Stem	upright, smooth, hollow
Root	fibrous
Hairs	absent
Stipules	absent
Leaves	scattered around stem, 20–50mm, elliptical to almost circular, bluish green, edge unbroken, upper with stem passing through blade
Leaf-stalk	absent or short on lower
FLOWERS	
Position	few, umbrella-shaped heads 10–30mm wide, 3–8 branches, at stem-tip or leaf-base
Bracts	none below head, large below flower-stalks, oval, yellowish
Type	♂
Size	1.5–2mm
Colour	yellow
Stalk	about equalling flower
Sepals	absent
Petals	5, 0.5–0.8mm, equal, oval
Stamens	5
Stigmas	2, styles slender
Ovary	1, below petals, 2-celled
FRUIT	
Type	1, splits into 2, egg-shaped, ridged, blackish
Size	2–3mm
Seeds	1 per half, not released

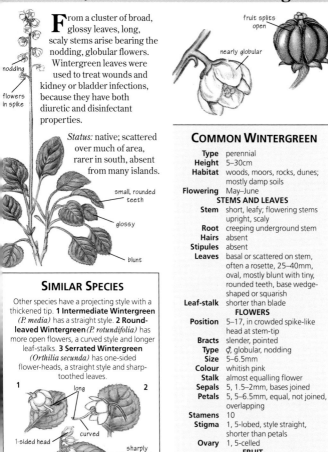

From a cluster of broad, glossy leaves, long, scaly stems arise bearing the nodding, globular flowers. Wintergreen leaves were used to treat wounds and kidney or bladder infections, because they have both diuretic and disinfectant properties.

Status: native; scattered over much of area, rarer in south, absent from many islands.

fruit splits open

nearly globular

nodding

flowers in spike

small, rounded teeth

glossy

blunt

SIMILAR SPECIES

Other species have a projecting style with a thickened tip. **1 Intermediate Wintergreen** *(P. media)* has a straight style. **2 Round-leaved Wintergreen** *(P. rotundifolia)* has more open flowers, a curved style and longer leaf-stalks. **3 Serrated Wintergreen** *(Orthilia secunda)* has one-sided flower-heads, a straight style and sharp-toothed leaves.

long

1-sided head

curved

sharply toothed

1

2

3

COMMON WINTERGREEN

Type	perennial
Height	5–30cm
Habitat	woods, moors, rocks, dunes; mostly damp soils
Flowering	May–June
STEMS AND LEAVES	
Stem	short, leafy; flowering stems upright, scaly
Root	creeping underground stem
Hairs	absent
Stipules	absent
Leaves	basal or scattered on stem, often a rosette, 25–40mm, oval, mostly blunt with tiny, rounded teeth, base wedge-shaped or squarish
Leaf-stalk	shorter than blade
FLOWERS	
Position	5–17, in crowded spike-like head at stem-tip
Bracts	slender, pointed
Type	☿, globular, nodding
Size	5–6.5mm
Colour	whitish pink
Stalk	almost equalling flower
Sepals	5, 1.5–2mm, bases joined
Petals	5, 5–6.5mm, equal, not joined, overlapping
Stamens	10
Stigma	1, 5-lobed, style straight, shorter than petals
Ovary	1, 5-celled
FRUIT	
Type	1, capsule, globular, splits into 5
Size	4–5mm
Seeds	numerous, minute

Bell Heather *Erica cinerea*

A wiry, evergreen, dwarf shrub with needle-like leaves and nodding, bell-shaped flowers. Garden forms have varying flowering times and colours. Species of Heathers can be so prolific that they change the colour of vast tracts of land as flowering commences.

bell-like

nodding

narrow mouth

Status: native; most of area, commoner in west.

fruit opens

hairless

needle-like

woody

SIMILAR SPECIES

1 Cross-leaved Heath *(E. tetralix)* has leaves in fours, edged with long, gland-tipped hairs. **2 Cornish Heath** *(E. vagans)* is larger with long flower-stalks and projecting stamens. **3 Heather** *(Calluna vulgaris)*, or Ling, has small, closely-packed leaves and the large, purple sepals are longer than the petals.

stamens

fours

hairy

long stalk

tiny

BELL HEATHER

Type	dwarf, evergreen shrub
Height	15–75cm
Habitat	heaths, moors, woodland edges; dryish, acid soils
Flowering	July–September
STEMS AND LEAVES	
Stem	many, branched, woody, rooting, almost upright
Root	woody stock
Hairs	only on young shoots
Stipules	absent
Leaves	rings of 3, 5–7mm, slender, straight-sided, pointed, edges curved under
Leaf-stalk	very short
FLOWERS	
Position	many in head, 10–70mm, at stem-tip
Bracts	3 tiny bracts below sepals
Type	☿, nodding
Size	4–7mm
Colour	reddish purple
Stalk	shorter than flower
Sepals	4, 2–3mm, pointed, bases joined
Petals	4, 4–7mm, joined except at tips, bell-shaped with narrow mouth
Stamens	8, not projecting
Stigma	1, club-shaped, on long style, projecting
Ovary	1, 4-celled
FRUIT	
Type	1, capsule, splits open, enclosed by dry petals
Size	1.5–2mm
Seeds	numerous, minute

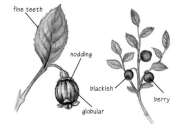

fine teeth

nodding

blackish

globular

berry

A small deciduous shrub of moors and heaths, with globular pink flowers followed by globular black fruits. The berries have a bluish 'bloom', as on black grapes. Although small and rather watery, they are edible and often eaten in pies, tarts or with cream.

Status: native; most of area, on mountains in south.

woody

BILBERRY

Type	deciduous shrub
Height	15–60cm
Habitat	moors, heaths, woods; acid soils
Flowering	July–September

STEMS AND LEAVES

Stem	upright, many, young shoots 3-angled
Root	creeping underground stem
Hairs	absent
Stipules	absent
Leaves	on alternate sides of stem, 10–30mm, oval, pointed, finely toothed
Leaf-stalk	shorter than blade

FLOWERS

Position	mostly single, at leaf-base
Bracts	2, scale-like
Type	⚥, nodding
Size	4–6mm
Colour	pink, sometimes greenish
Stalk	about equalling flower
Sepals	4–5, joined, forming scarcely lobed ring
Petals	4–5, 4–6mm, joined, globular, tips bent back
Stamens	8–10
Stigma	1, club-shaped, long style
Ovary	1, below sepals, 4–5-celled

FRUIT

Type	1, berry, globular, black with bluish, waxy bloom, edible
Size	6–10mm
Seeds	many, small

SIMILAR SPECIES

1 Cowberry *(V. vitis-idaea)* is evergreen with glossy leaves, bell-shaped flowers and red fruits. **2 Cranberry** *(V. oxycoccos)* has long-stalked, red fruits, and petals bent sharply back revealing purple stamens. Although with blue-black fruits, **3 Crowberry** *(Empetrum nigrum)* is unrelated, having heather-like leaves and six-petalled flowers.

glossy

red

long

long

narrow

Primrose *Primula vulgaris*

Few sights are more welcome after a bleak Winter, than a bank covered with the soft yellow flowers of Primroses. Two forms of flower differ by the look of the tube-mouth. One has five stamens ('thrum-eyed'), the other a stigma ('pin-eyed'), an arrangement enhancing the chances of cross-pollination.

Status: native; most parts except extreme north.

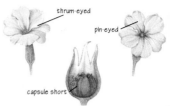

thrum-eyed

pin-eyed

capsule short

sepals joined

flowers from base

SIMILAR SPECIES

Other species have stalked flower-clusters.
1 Cowslip (*P. veris*) has small, often darker petals; **2 Oxlip** (*P. elatior*) has large, whitish-yellow petals and a long capsule.
3 Bird's-eye Primrose (*P. farinosa*) has floury-looking leaves and lilac flowers.

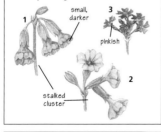

small, darker

3

pinkish

1

2

stalked cluster

PRIMROSE

Type	perennial
Height	10–20cm
Habitat	woods, hedgerows, grassy banks; damp soils
Flowering	December–May

STEMS AND LEAVES

Stem	very short
Root	short underground stem; thick, white roots
Hairs	few below leaves, none above; long on flower-stalks and sepals
Stipules	absent
Leaves	rosette at base, 80–200mm, oval to spoon-shaped, widest above middle, blunt, irregularly toothed
Leaf-stalk	short or absent

FLOWERS

Position	in cluster at base or on very short stem
Bracts	present
Type	⚥, facing upwards
Size	width 20–40mm
Colour	pale yellow, deeper marks around throat, rarely pink
Stalk	50–200mm, with long hairs
Sepals	5, joined into tube, 15–17mm, teeth 4–6mm
Petals	5, 20–40mm, base forms tube
Stamens	5, at tube-mouth or middle
Stigma	1, club-shaped, style long, at mouth of tube or middle
Ovary	1, 1-celled

FRUIT

Type	1, capsule, nearly globular
Size	5–7mm
Seeds	numerous, c1mm, angular

bent back

fruit opens

nodding

stem coils

small lobes

swollen stem

long stalk

some angled

A delightful little plant, the upswept petals of its nodding, pink flowers spotted purple at the base. Leaves arise singly from the underground stem and only as the flowers fade, and are often marked with silver above and tinged purple below. The young capsule's stalk spirals from the tip until it lies on the ground, looking like a coil-spring. Cyclamen multiplies readily by seed and becomes naturalized.

Status: introduced from southern Europe; scattered, mainly southern.

SIMILAR SPECIES

One species *C. purpurascens* is native in the south-eastern part of the area. It has scented flowers, rounded leaves, and purplish petals lacking basal lobes.

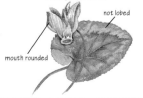

not lobed

mouth rounded

CYCLAMEN

Type	perennial
Height	10–30cm
Habitat	woods, hedges, near gardens
Flowering	August–September
STEMS AND LEAVES	
Stem	very short
Root	underground, swollen stem to 100mm wide, globular or hollow upper face
Hairs	more or less absent
Leaves	at base, 30–140mm, oval to kidney-shaped, 5–9-angled, often pale marks above and purple below, blunt, finely toothed, appearing after flowers
Leaf-stalk	often longer than blade
FLOWERS	
Position	single, from base
Bracts	absent
Type	♂, nodding
Size	15–25mm
Colour	pink with purple blotches at base, rarely white
Stalk	10–30mm, nearly upright
Sepals	5, 4–8mm, oval, bases joined
Petals	5, 15–25mm, equal, elliptical, bases joined into 5-angled tube, each petal bent back, 2 small lobes at base
Stamens	5, forming short cone
Stigma	1, scarcely projecting
Ovary	1, 1-celled
FRUIT	
Type	1, capsule, globular, splits from middle, purple-flecked, centre sticky; stalk coiled
Size	10–18mm
Seeds	many, 2–4mm, angular

Yellow Pimpernel *Lysimachia nemorum*

Rather a delicate, trailing plant with starry, yellow flowers dotted over a shady woodland floor. Paired oval leaves and long-stalked flowers look rather like those of the Scarlet Pimpernel.

Status: native; most of area except extreme north.

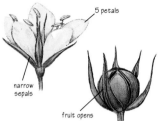

5 petals

narrow sepals

fruit opens

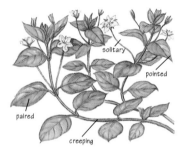

solitary

pointed

paired

creeping

SIMILAR SPECIES

Often escaping from cultivation, **1 Creeping-Jenny** (*L. nummularia*) has rounded leaves and larger flowers with much broader sepals. Two related species with upright stems are **2 Yellow Loosestrife** (*L. vulgaris*), with clusters of flowers towards the stem-tips, and **3 Tufted Loosestrife** (*L. thyrsiflora*) with spikes of narrow-petalled flowers from the upper leaf-bases.

rounded

broader

clustered

thin petals

1

2

3

upright

YELLOW PIMPERNEL

Type	perennial
Height	10–45cm
Habitat	woods, hedges; mostly damp soils
Flowering	May–September
STEMS AND LEAVES	
Stem	slender, low-growing
Root	fibrous
Hairs	absent
Stipules	absent
Leaves	paired either side of stem, 20–40mm, oval, evergreen, pointed, edge unbroken, base rounded
Leaf-stalk	shorter than blade
FLOWERS	
Position	solitary, at leaf-base
Bracts	absent
Type	♂
Size	6–8.5mm
Colour	yellow
Stalk	much longer than flower, hair-like
Sepals	5, 3.5–6mm, very slender, pointed
Petals	5, 6–8.5mm, equal, bases joined, wide-spreading
Stamens	5
Stigma	1, slender, style long
Ovary	1, 1-celled
FRUIT	
Type	1, capsule, globular, splits in 5
Size	3–4mm
Seeds	many, 1.5–2mm, circular, flattened

Anagallis arvensis **Scarlet Pimpernel**

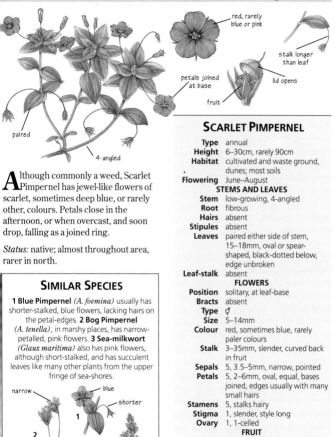

red, rarely
blue or pink

stalk longer
than leaf

lid opens

petals joined
at base

fruit

paired

4-angled

Although commonly a weed, Scarlet Pimpernel has jewel-like flowers of scarlet, sometimes deep blue, or rarely other, colours. Petals close in the afternoon, or when overcast, and soon drop, falling as a joined ring.

Status: native; almost throughout area, rarer in north.

SIMILAR SPECIES

1 Blue Pimpernel (*A. foemina*) usually has shorter-stalked, blue flowers, lacking hairs on the petal-edges. **2 Bog Pimpernel** (*A. tenella*), in marshy places, has narrow-petalled, pink flowers. **3 Sea-milkwort** (*Glaux maritima*) also has pink flowers, although short-stalked, and has succulent leaves like many other plants from the upper fringe of sea-shores.

narrow

blue
shorter

1

long

2

small

3

fleshy

SCARLET PIMPERNEL

Type	annual
Height	6–30cm, rarely 90cm
Habitat	cultivated and waste ground, dunes; most soils
Flowering	June–August

STEMS AND LEAVES

Stem	low-growing, 4-angled
Root	fibrous
Hairs	absent
Stipules	absent
Leaves	paired either side of stem, 15–18mm, oval or spear-shaped, black-dotted below, edge unbroken
Leaf-stalk	absent

FLOWERS

Position	solitary, at leaf-base
Bracts	absent
Type	♂
Size	5–14mm
Colour	red, sometimes blue, rarely paler colours
Stalk	3–35mm, slender, curved back in fruit
Sepals	5, 3.5–5mm, narrow, pointed
Petals	5, 2–6mm, oval, equal, bases joined, edges usually with many small hairs
Stamens	5, stalks hairy
Stigma	1, slender, style long
Ovary	1, 1-celled

FRUIT

Type	1, capsule, globular, top splits off
Size	2.5–4mm
Seeds	12–45, 1–1.5mm, nearly circular, slightly flattened

131

Water Violet *Hottonia palustris*

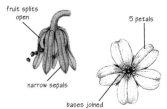

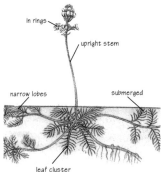

A most attractive plant that has rings of lilac, yellow-eyed flowers quite like those of some garden Primulas, but with very different foliage. This water-plant has feathery leaves on submerged stems which turn up at the tip and emerge from the water before flowering.

Status: native, introduced to Ireland and elsewhere; scattered through much of area except parts of north.

SIMILAR SPECIES

No species is quite like Water Violet but **Bogbean** *(Menyanthes trifoliata)* is also aquatic and has stalked spikes of pale flowers, although pink, with fringed petals. The leaves have three broad leaflets and are carried above the water.

WATER VIOLET

Type	perennial
Height	30–90cm
Habitat	ponds, ditches; shallow, still, fresh water
Flowering	May–June
STEMS AND LEAVES	
Stem	submerged or floating, turns upright to flower above water
Root	fibrous; stems root
Hairs	absent except for flowers
Stipules	absent
Leaves	in rings or scattered around stem, 20–130mm, cut 1–2 times into very slender lobes, some float
Leaf-stalk	shorter than blade
FLOWERS	
Position	3–8 in a ring, 3–9 rings around stem
Bracts	5–10mm, thin, pointed
Type	♂
Size	20–25mm
Colour	lilac with yellow centre
Stalk	about equalling flower
Sepals	5, 5–10mm, narrowly oblong
Petals	5, 12–17mm, bases joined into slender tube
Stamens	5, attached to petals
Stigma	1, club-shaped, style short or long
Ovary	1, 1-celled
FRUIT	
Type	1, capsule, globular, splits into 5 except at tip
Size	3–6mm
Seeds	numerous, c1mm, angular

Trientalis europaea **Chickweed Wintergreen**

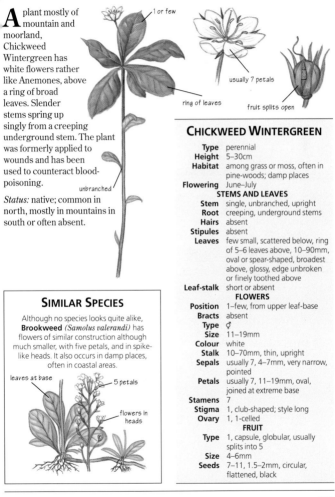

A plant mostly of mountain and moorland, Chickweed Wintergreen has white flowers rather like Anemones, above a ring of broad leaves. Slender stems spring up singly from a creeping underground stem. The plant was formerly applied to wounds and has been used to counteract blood-poisoning.

Status: native; common in north, mostly in mountains in south or often absent.

1 or few

usually 7 petals

ring of leaves

fruit splits open

unbranched

SIMILAR SPECIES

Although no species looks quite alike, **Brookweed** *(Samolus valerandi)* has flowers of similar construction although much smaller, with five petals, and in spike-like heads. It also occurs in damp places, often in coastal areas.

leaves at base

5 petals

flowers in heads

CHICKWEED WINTERGREEN

Type	perennial
Height	5–30cm
Habitat	among grass or moss, often in pine-woods; damp places
Flowering	June–July
STEMS AND LEAVES	
Stem	single, unbranched, upright
Root	creeping, underground stems
Hairs	absent
Stipules	absent
Leaves	few small, scattered below, ring of 5–6 leaves above, 10–90mm, oval or spear-shaped, broadest above, glossy, edge unbroken or finely toothed above
Leaf-stalk	short or absent
FLOWERS	
Position	1–few, from upper leaf-base
Bracts	absent
Type	♂
Size	11–19mm
Colour	white
Stalk	10–70mm, thin, upright
Sepals	usually 7, 4–7mm, very narrow, pointed
Petals	usually 7, 11–19mm, oval, joined at extreme base
Stamens	7
Stigma	1, club-shaped; style long
Ovary	1, 1-celled
FRUIT	
Type	1, capsule, globular, usually splits into 5
Size	4–6mm
Seeds	7–11, 1.5–2mm, circular, flattened, black

Thrift *Armeria maritima*

A distinctive plant of coastal areas. On exposed cliff-tops, the leaves disappear among grassy tufts so that the pink heads, held aloft above the short turf, provide the first indication of the plant's presence. The only common *Armeria* in the area.

Status: native; common in coastal areas, sometimes on inland mountains.

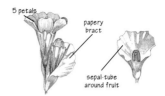

5 petals
papery bract
sepal-tube around fruit

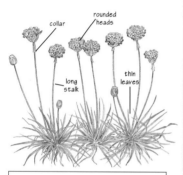

collar
rounded heads
long stalk
thin leaves

SIMILAR SPECIES

Although at first sight rather different, Sea-lavenders grow in similar places, have much the same growth-habit and similar flowers. **Common Sea-lavender** (*Limonium vulgare*) prefers muddy salt-marshes and has bluish-purple flowers in widely-branched heads.

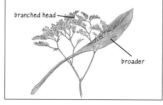

branched head
broader

THRIFT

Type	perennial
Height	5–30cm
Habitat	coastal cliffs, rocks, salt-marshes
Flowering	April–October
STEMS AND LEAVES	
Stem	leafy part very short; stalk of flower-head upright, unbranched
Root	woody, branched stock
Hairs	short or absent
Stipules	absent
Leaves	basal, forming rosette, 20–150mm, grass-like, rather thick, edge unbroken
Leaf-stalk	absent
FLOWERS	
Position	small clusters grouped into rounded head at stalk-tip
Bracts	lowest form tubular sheath up to 20mm long, around stalk-tip; innermost papery
Type	☿, slightly scented
Size	7–10mm; heads 15–25mm
Colour	pink, rarely red or white
Stalk	shorter than flower
Sepals	5, 5–10mm, joined, papery, funnel-shaped, 5 hairy ribs
Petals	5, equal, oval, bases joined
Stamens	5
Stigmas	5, slender; long styles
Ovary	1, 1-celled
FRUIT	
Type	1, oblong capsule, opening irregularly, surrounded by sepals and withered petals
Size	2.5–3mm
Seeds	1, 2–2.5mm, egg-shaped

A delicate plant with slender stems, glossy leaves and pink petals. It is very variable in height, branching, and the size and number of the flowers. Common Centaury is a bitter-tasting herb, formerly taken to stimulate appetite and to treat digestive disorders. It was also used to combat fevers and treat anaemia.

Status: native; absent from much of north.

branched heads

5 petals

bases joined

narrow fruit

narrow

upright

paired

hairless

COMMON CENTAURY

Type	annual or biennial
Height	2–50cm
Habitat	mostly grassy places or dunes; dry soils
Flowering	June–October
STEMS AND LEAVES	
Stem	1–few, upright, often branched
Root	small tap-root
Hairs	absent
Stipules	absent
Leaves	basal forming rosette or paired either side of stem, 10–50mm, oval or elliptical 3–7 main veins, blunt or sharpish, edge unbroken; upper smaller
Leaf-stalk	absent
FLOWERS	
Position	many in branched, crowded, flattish-topped heads
Bracts	present
Type	⚥, facing upwards
Size	10–14mm
Colour	pink, rarely white
Stalk	short or absent
Sepals	5, 5–8mm, narrow, pointed, bases joined
Petals	5, lobes 5–6mm, equal, bases joined into tube
Stamens	5, at top of petal-tube
Stigmas	2; style forked
Ovary	1, 1-celled
FRUIT	
Type	1, slender capsule, pointed
Size	8–12mm
Seeds	many, 0.8–1mm, rounded

SIMILAR SPECIES

1 Lesser Centaury *(C. pulchellum)* has distinctly stalked flowers in less crowded heads; **2 Seaside Centaury** *(C. littorale)* has narrower, oblong leaves. **3 Yellow-wort** *(Blackstonia perfoliata)* is more distantly related, has the upper leaves joined, and flowers with six to eight yellow petals.

less crowded

yellow

narrower

joined

1

2

3

135

Field Gentian *Gentianella campestris*

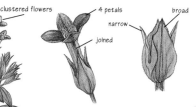

clustered flowers

4 petals

narrow

joined

broad

A small-flowered relative of the garden Gentians, with clusters of purplish, tubular flowers. Field Gentian is bitter-tasting and one of several plants used to flavour ales before the introduction of Hops. Native species were sometimes made into a tonic used medicinally and to stimulate appetite.

Status: native; common, especially in north.

paired

SIMILAR SPECIES

1 Autumn Gentian (*G. amarella*) has narrower, equal, non-overlapping sepals. True Gentians have non-fringed petal-lobes separated by small lobes. Of these, **2 Marsh Gentian** (*Gentiana pneumonanthe*) has a broad, green-striped petal-tube, and **3 Spring Gentian** (*G. verna*) has a slender, deep-blue petal-tube.

all narrow

blue

narrow tube

broad tube

1

2

3

FIELD GENTIAN

Type	annual or biennial
Height	10–30cm
Habitat	grassy places, dunes; mostly lime-free soils
Flowering	July–October
STEMS AND LEAVES	
Stem	upright, branched above
Root	fibrous
Hairs	absent
Stipules	absent
Leaves	basal or paired either side of stem, 10–30mm, oval to oblong, blunt or pointed, edge unbroken
Leaf-stalk	absent
FLOWERS	
Position	many, in branched heads
Bracts	present
Type	♂
Size	15–30mm
Colour	bluish lilac, rarely white
Stalk	shorter than flower
Sepals	4, 10–18mm, very unequal, bases joined, 2 outer oval, widest below middle, pointed, 2 inner narrow
Petals	4, 15–30mm, equal, joined into long tube, the oblong lobes fringed at base
Stamens	4
Stigmas	2, somewhat flattened
Ovary	1, 1-celled
FRUIT	
Type	1, elongated capsule, splits lengthwise
Size	20–25mm
Seeds	many, 0.8–1mm, globular

petals joined at base

fruit splits

An evergreen, carpeting shady bank-
sides with glossy leaves and a
sprinkling of bluish-purple, white-eyed
blooms. Cultivated for many centuries, it
has often escaped. Species of Periwinkle
have had many medicinal uses, including
staunching bleeding and
reducing blood-
pressure; other
members of
the family
provide anti-
cancer drugs.

Status: native,
introduced in
north-west;
scattered
through area
except extreme
north.

paired leaflets

upright

rooting

LESSER PERIWINKLE

Type	evergreen perennial
Height	300–600cm
Habitat	woods, hedges; often dry, lime-rich soils
Flowering	March–May

STEMS AND LEAVES

Stem	trailing with short, upright flowering stems
Root	woody stock; stems root
Hairs	absent
Stipules	absent
Leaves	paired either side of stem, 25–40mm, oval to elliptical, pointed or blunt, edge unbroken
Leaf-stalk	shorter than blade

FLOWERS

Position	1, rarely 2, at leaf-base
Bracts	absent
Type	♂
Size	25–32mm
Colour	bluish purple, rarely white or pink
Stalk	about equalling flower
Sepals	5, 4–5mm, spear-shaped
Petals	5, 12–16mm, equal, bases joined into tube, lobes broad, twisted together in bud, spreading widely, tip asymmetrical
Stamens	5, joined to petal-tube
Stigmas	forming broad head; styles joined
Ovaries	2, 1-celled

FRUIT

Type	2, dry, pointed, spreading apart, splitting lengthwise
Size	20–25mm
Seeds	1–4, 5–6mm, oblong, grooved

SIMILAR SPECIES

Greater Periwinkle *(V. major)* is more
robust, with larger leaves and flowers. The
stems arch over and root at the tips,
springing up again as a new plant.

larger flowers

arching stems

Cleavers *Galium aparine*

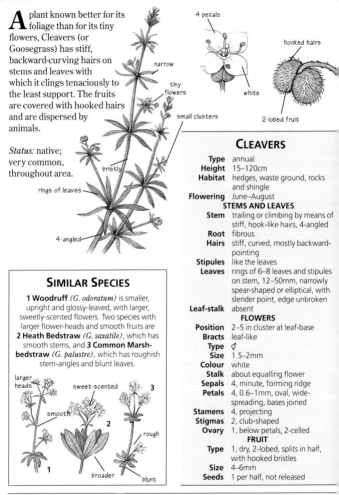

A plant known better for its foliage than for its tiny flowers, Cleavers (or Goosegrass) has stiff, backward-curving hairs on stems and leaves with which it clings tenaciously to the least support. The fruits are covered with hooked hairs and are dispersed by animals.

Status: native; very common, throughout area.

4 petals

white

hooked hairs

2-lobed fruit

narrow

tiny flowers

small clusters

bristly

rings of leaves

4-angled

SIMILAR SPECIES

1 Woodruff *(G. odoratum)* is smaller, upright and glossy-leaved, with larger, sweetly-scented flowers. Two species with larger flower-heads and smooth fruits are **2 Heath Bedstraw** *(G. saxatile)*, which has smooth stems, and **3 Common Marsh-bedstraw** *(G. palustre)*, which has roughish stem-angles and blunt leaves.

larger heads

sweet-scented

smooth

rough

broader

blunt

CLEAVERS

Type	annual
Height	15–120cm
Habitat	hedges, waste ground, rocks and shingle
Flowering	June–August
STEMS AND LEAVES	
Stem	trailing or climbing by means of stiff, hook-like hairs, 4-angled
Root	fibrous
Hairs	stiff, curved, mostly backward-pointing
Stipules	like the leaves
Leaves	rings of 6–8 leaves and stipules on stem, 12–50mm, narrowly spear-shaped or elliptical, with slender point, edge unbroken
Leaf-stalk	absent
FLOWERS	
Position	2–5 in cluster at leaf-base
Bracts	leaf-like
Type	♂
Size	1.5–2mm
Colour	white
Stalk	about equalling flower
Sepals	4, minute, forming ridge
Petals	4, 0.6–1mm, oval, wide-spreading, bases joined
Stamens	4, projecting
Stigmas	2, club-shaped
Ovary	1, below petals, 2-celled
FRUIT	
Type	1, dry, 2-lobed, splits in half, with hooked bristles
Size	4–6mm
Seeds	1 per half, not released

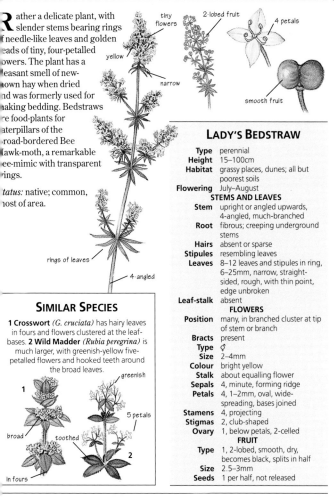

Rather a delicate plant, with slender stems bearing rings of needle-like leaves and golden heads of tiny, four-petalled flowers. The plant has a pleasant smell of new-mown hay when dried and was formerly used for making bedding. Bedstraws are food-plants for caterpillars of the Broad-bordered Bee Hawk-moth, a remarkable bee-mimic with transparent wings.

Status: native; common, most of area.

labels on illustration: tiny flowers; 2-lobed fruit; 4 petals; yellow; narrow; smooth fruit; rings of leaves; 4-angled

SIMILAR SPECIES

1 Crosswort *(G. cruciata)* has hairy leaves in fours and flowers clustered at the leaf-bases. **2 Wild Madder** *(Rubia peregrina)* is much larger, with greenish-yellow five-petalled flowers and hooked teeth around the broad leaves.

labels: greenish; 5 petals; broad; toothed; in fours

LADY'S BEDSTRAW

Type	perennial
Height	15–100cm
Habitat	grassy places, dunes; all but poorest soils
Flowering	July–August

STEMS AND LEAVES

Stem	upright or angled upwards, 4-angled, much-branched
Root	fibrous; creeping underground stems
Hairs	absent or sparse
Stipules	resembling leaves
Leaves	8–12 leaves and stipules in ring, 6–25mm, narrow, straight-sided, rough, with thin point, edge unbroken
Leaf-stalk	absent

FLOWERS

Position	many, in branched cluster at tip of stem or branch
Bracts	present
Type	♂
Size	2–4mm
Colour	bright yellow
Stalk	about equalling flower
Sepals	4, minute, forming ridge
Petals	4, 1–2mm, oval, wide-spreading, bases joined
Stamens	4, projecting
Stigmas	2, club-shaped
Ovary	1, below petals, 2-celled

FRUIT

Type	1, 2-lobed, smooth, dry, becomes black, splits in half
Size	2.5–3mm
Seeds	1 per half, not released

Hedge Bindweed *Calystegia sepium*

A spectacular climber with funnel-shaped flowers of pure white, just as large as those of many treasured garden plants. Gardeners shun Hedge Bindweed because it has long, creeping underground stems which sprout up all around, and its vigorous growth swamps all but the most robust plants. This rampant vine is beneficial in that it covers abandoned ruins, refuse tips, even a scrapped car or telegraph pole.

Status: native; throughout area except for extreme north.

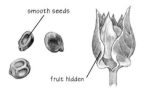

smooth seeds

funnel-shaped

petals joined

fruit hidden

stems twine

SIMILAR SPECIES

1 Large Bindweed (*C. silvatica*) has larger flowers and larger, balloon-like bracts. **2 Hairy Bindweed** (*C. pulchra*) has pink flowers and short hairs on young stems, stalks and bracts.

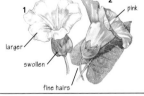

larger

1

2

pink

swollen

fine hairs

HEDGE BINDWEED

Type	perennial
Height	100–300cm
Habitat	hedges, woods, waste and cultivated ground
Flowering	April–July
STEMS AND LEAVES	
Stem	climbs by twining anticlockwise, some creeping
Root	long, white, rooting, underground stems
Hairs	absent
Stipules	absent
Leaves	spirally placed on stem, to 150mm, heart- or arrow-shaped, blunt or with small point, edge unbroken
Leaf-stalk	mostly shorter than blade
FLOWERS	
Position	solitary, at leaf-base
Bracts	2 below sepals, 10–30mm, broad, nearly flat
Type	☿
Size	30–55mm
Colour	white
Stalk	shorter than flower
Sepals	5, 9–12mm, oval, bases joined, enclosed by bracts
Petals	5, 30–50mm, equal, almost completely joined into tube
Stamens	5, at base of petal-tube
Stigmas	2, broad; style forked
Ovary	1, 1-celled
FRUIT	
Type	1, capsule, globular, hidden by sepals
Size	7–12mm
Seeds	4, 4–7mm, angular brown

Convolvulus arvensis **Field Bindweed**

A climber with delightful pink and white, candy-striped flowers; its funnel-shaped petal-tube is pleated and opens fan-like by day, attracting many sorts of insect. On bare ground, such as railway ballast, long, radiating stems of Field Bindweed spread in a circle and sometimes twist together, using each other for support. This species is unwelcome in gardens because it has extremely invasive underground stems.

Status: native; throughout area, rarer in north.

rough seeds

pink and white

fruit exposed

lobed base

petals joined

twining

SIMILAR SPECIES

Sea Bindweed *(Calystegia soldanella)* is a trailing plant from sand-dunes and shingle, with kidney-shaped leaves and larger flowers.

larger

kidney-shaped

trailing

FIELD BINDWEED

Type	perennial
Height	20–100cm, rarely to 200cm
Habitat	cultivated and waste ground, often near sea
Flowering	June–September
STEMS AND LEAVES	
Stem	trailing or climbing by twisting anticlockwise
Root	long, creeping, underground stems
Hairs	absent or on young shoots
Stipules	absent
Leaves	on alternate sides of stem, 20–50mm, oblong, oval or arrow-shaped, blunt, edge more or less unbroken
Leaf-stalk	shorter than blade
FLOWERS	
Position	1–3, in stalked cluster at leaf-base
Bracts	2, small, below flower-stalks
Type	☿, scented
Size	10–30mm
Colour	pink and white
Stalk	shorter than flower
Sepals	5, 4–6mm, bases joined
Petals	5, 9–25mm, almost completely joined, funnel-shaped
Stamens	5, at base of petal-tube
Stigmas	2, slender; style forked
Ovary	1, 2-celled
FRUIT	
Type	1, capsule, almost globular
Size	3–5mm
Seeds	2–4, 2.5–4mm, angular, rough

141

Dodder *Cuscuta epithymum*

A most curious plant, with leafless, tendril-like stems. Individually scarcely noticeable, these stems can swamp a clump of Heather or Dwarf Gorse with a tangled mass of lurid pink and yellow threads. Dodder lacks green pigment because it is a parasite, drawing nourishment through sucker-like, modified roots which are firmly attached to the stem of another plant. It is rooted in the ground only as a seedling.

Status: native; common in many localities, scattered through area except extreme north.

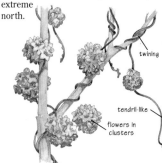

petals joined — long styles

fruit opens

twining

tendril-like

flowers in clusters

SIMILAR SPECIES

Greater Dodder *(C. europaea)* usually attacks nettles or hops and has larger petals.

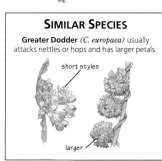

short styles

larger

DODDER

Type	annual, parasite
Height	15–120cm
Habitat	mainly on species of Heather, Gorse and Clover
Flowering	July–September

STEMS AND LEAVES

Stem	thread-like, white or yellow tinged with red or purple, twining, branched
Root	sucker-like, on stem, attached to other plants
Hairs	absent
Stipules	absent
Leaves	on alternate sides of stem, 0.5–2mm, scale-like, pointed, edge unbroken
Leaf-stalk	absent

FLOWERS

Position	8–17, crowded in rounded heads 5–10mm wide
Bracts	minute, below each flower
Type	♂
Size	2.5–5mm
Colour	white tinged pink or red
Stalk	absent
Sepals	5, 1–2mm, joined below
Petals	5, 2.5–4mm, joined, lobes pointed, spreading, with scales at base closing mouth of tube
Stamens	5, between petal-lobes
Stigmas	2, slender
Ovary	1, 2-celled

FRUIT

Type	1, capsule, globular, splits near base, hidden by withered petals
Size	1.5–2mm
Seeds	2–4, 1–1.5mm, angled

Callitriche stagnalis **Common Water-starwort**

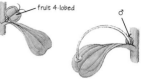
floating rosette — broad — fruit 4-lobed

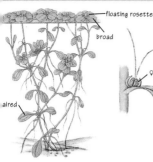
aired

A plant usually noticed as fresh green rosettes of small leaves, floating on the surface of a pond or stream. It is very variable, the shape of the leaves changing with the depth and speed of the water and the flowering or fruiting state. Plants growing on mud look very different. Closely related species are identified only with difficulty, and if ripe fruit is present.

Status: native; common, most of area.

SIMILAR SPECIES

Other aquatic plants include **1 Canadian Waterweed** (*Elodea canadensis*), with leaves in threes and long-stalked flowers, and **2 Nuttall's Waterweed** (*E. nuttallii*) with narrower, pointed leaves. **3 Mare's-tail** (*Hippuris vulgaris*) has leaves in rings of six to twelve.

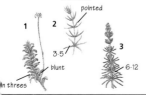
1   2   pointed   3
3-5   blunt   6-12
In threes

COMMON WATER-STARWORT

Type	annual or perennial
Height	10–60cm
Habitat	ponds, streams; shallow fresh water or wet mud
Flowering	May–September
STEMS AND LEAVES	
Stem	submerged or low-growing
Root	fibrous; stems root
Hairs	absent
Stipules	absent
Leaves	paired or in rosette at stem-tip, 10–20mm, rounded or notched, edge unbroken; lower usually submerged, elliptical or spoon-shaped; upper usually floating, broader, forming rosette
Leaf-stalk	shorter than blade
FLOWERS	
Position	solitary, at base of upper leaf, separate ♂ and ♀
Bracts	2, curved
Type 1	♂, with stamen
Type 2	♀, with ovary
Size	1.5–2mm
Colour	white or green
Stalk	shorter than flower
Sepals	absent
Petals	absent
Stamen	1, c2mm
Stigmas	2; styles curved, 2–3mm
Ovary	1, 4-celled
FRUIT	
Type	1, splits into 4, nearly circular, 4-ridged
Size	1.6–2mm
Seeds	4, 1.4–1.8mm, winged

143

Field Gromwell *Lithospermum arvense*

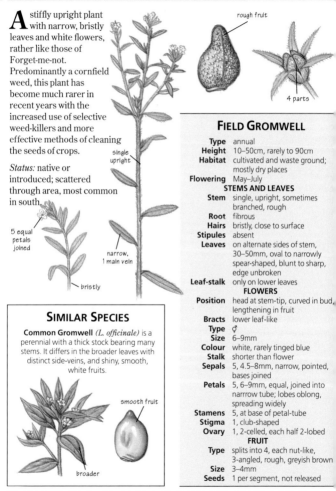

A stiffly upright plant with narrow, bristly leaves and white flowers, rather like those of Forget-me-not. Predominantly a cornfield weed, this plant has become much rarer in recent years with the increased use of selective weed-killers and more effective methods of cleaning the seeds of crops.

Status: native or introduced; scattered through area, most common in south.

rough fruit

4 parts

single upright

5 equal petals joined

narrow, 1 main vein

bristly

SIMILAR SPECIES

Common Gromwell (*L. officinale*) is a perennial with a thick stock bearing many stems. It differs in the broader leaves with distinct side-veins, and shiny, smooth, white fruits.

smooth fruit

broader

FIELD GROMWELL

Type	annual
Height	10–50cm, rarely to 90cm
Habitat	cultivated and waste ground; mostly dry places
Flowering	May–July
STEMS AND LEAVES	
Stem	single, upright, sometimes branched, rough
Root	fibrous
Hairs	bristly, close to surface
Stipules	absent
Leaves	on alternate sides of stem, 30–50mm, oval to narrowly spear-shaped, blunt to sharp, edge unbroken
Leaf-stalk	only on lower leaves
FLOWERS	
Position	head at stem-tip, curved in bud, lengthening in fruit
Bracts	lower leaf-like
Type	♂
Size	6–9mm
Colour	white, rarely tinged blue
Stalk	shorter than flower
Sepals	5, 4.5–8mm, narrow, pointed, bases joined
Petals	5, 6–9mm, equal, joined into narrow tube; lobes oblong, spreading widely
Stamens	5, at base of petal-tube
Stigma	1, club-shaped
Ovary	1, 2-celled, each half 2-lobed
FRUIT	
Type	splits into 4, each nut-like, 3-angled, rough, greyish brown
Size	3–4mm
Seeds	1 per segment, not released

Symphytum officinale **Common Comfrey**

This bristly plant has blades of the upper leaves running down the stem as wings. Curved heads of tubular, nodding flowers are variously cream, pink, red or purple. Leaves were once used to dress cuts or bruises and roots made into cough-medicine.

Status: native, or naturalized in north; throughout region.

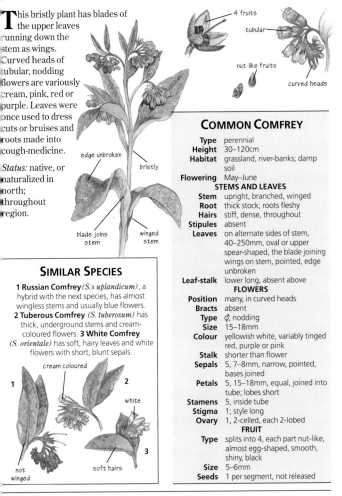

4 fruits

tubular

nut-like fruits

curved heads

edge unbroken

bristly

blade joins stem

winged stem

COMMON COMFREY

Type	perennial
Height	30–120cm
Habitat	grassland, river-banks; damp soil
Flowering	May–June
STEMS AND LEAVES	
Stem	upright, branched, winged
Root	thick stock; roots fleshy
Hairs	stiff, dense, throughout
Stipules	absent
Leaves	on alternate sides of stem, 40–250mm, oval or upper spear-shaped, the blade joining wings on stem, pointed, edge unbroken
Leaf-stalk	lower long, absent above
FLOWERS	
Position	many, in curved heads
Bracts	absent
Type	⚥, nodding
Size	15–18mm
Colour	yellowish white, variably tinged red, purple or pink
Stalk	shorter than flower
Sepals	5, 7–8mm, narrow, pointed, bases joined
Petals	5, 15–18mm, equal, joined into tube; lobes short
Stamens	5, inside tube
Stigma	1; style long
Ovary	1, 2-celled, each 2-lobed
FRUIT	
Type	splits into 4, each part nut-like, almost egg-shaped, smooth, shiny, black
Size	5–6mm
Seeds	1 per segment, not released

SIMILAR SPECIES

1 Russian Comfrey *(S. x uplandicum)*, a hybrid with the next species, has almost wingless stems and usually blue flowers.
2 Tuberous Comfrey *(S. tuberosum)* has thick, underground stems and cream-coloured flowers. **3 White Comfrey** *(S. orientale)* has soft, hairy leaves and white flowers with short, blunt sepals.

cream coloured

white

not winged

soft hairs

Field Forget-me-not *Myosotis arvensis*

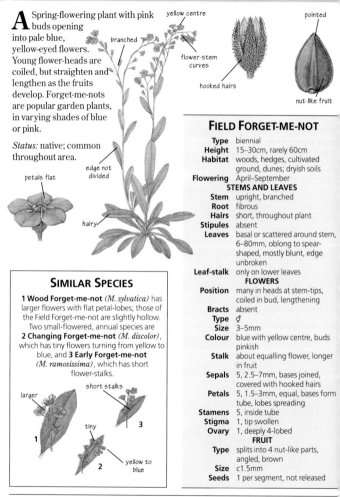

A Spring-flowering plant with pink buds opening into pale blue, yellow-eyed flowers. Young flower-heads are coiled, but straighten and lengthen as the fruits develop. Forget-me-nots are popular garden plants, in varying shades of blue or pink.

Status: native; common throughout area.

yellow centre

branched

flower-stem curves

hooked hairs

pointed

nut-like fruit

edge not divided

petals flat

hairy

SIMILAR SPECIES

1 Wood Forget-me-not *(M. sylvatica)* has larger flowers with flat petal-lobes; those of the Field Forget-me-not are slightly hollow. Two small-flowered, annual species are **2 Changing Forget-me-not** *(M. discolor)*, which has tiny flowers turning from yellow to blue, and **3 Early Forget-me-not** *(M. ramosissima)*, which has short flower-stalks.

larger

short stalks

tiny

1

3

2

yellow to blue

FIELD FORGET-ME-NOT

Type	biennial
Height	15–30cm, rarely 60cm
Habitat	woods, hedges, cultivated ground, dunes; dryish soils
Flowering	April–September
STEMS AND LEAVES	
Stem	upright, branched
Root	fibrous
Hairs	short, throughout plant
Stipules	absent
Leaves	basal or scattered around stem, 6–80mm, oblong to spear-shaped, mostly blunt, edge unbroken
Leaf-stalk	only on lower leaves
FLOWERS	
Position	many in heads at stem-tips, coiled in bud, lengthening
Bracts	absent
Type	♂
Size	3–5mm
Colour	blue with yellow centre, buds pinkish
Stalk	about equalling flower, longer in fruit
Sepals	5, 2.5–7mm, bases joined, covered with hooked hairs
Petals	5, 1.5–3mm, equal, bases form tube, lobes spreading
Stamens	5, inside tube
Stigma	1, tip swollen
Ovary	1, deeply 4-lobed
FRUIT	
Type	splits into 4 nut-like parts, angled, brown
Size	c1.5mm
Seeds	1 per segment, not released

Tufted Forget-me-not
Myosotis laxa subsp. *caespitosa*

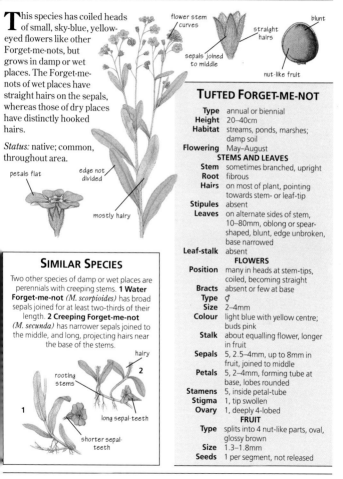

This species has coiled heads of small, sky-blue, yellow-eyed flowers like other Forget-me-nots, but grows in damp or wet places. The Forget-me-nots of wet places have straight hairs on the sepals, whereas those of dry places have distinctly hooked hairs.

Status: native; common, throughout area.

flower stem curves

straight hairs

blunt

sepals joined to middle

nut-like fruit

petals flat

edge not divided

mostly hairy

SIMILAR SPECIES

Two other species of damp or wet places are perennials with creeping stems. **1 Water Forget-me-not** *(M. scorpioides)* has broad sepals joined for at least two-thirds of their length. **2 Creeping Forget-me-not** *(M. secunda)* has narrower sepals joined to the middle, and long, projecting hairs near the base of the stems.

hairy

rooting stems

long sepal-teeth

shorter sepal-teeth

TUFTED FORGET-ME-NOT

Type	annual or biennial
Height	20–40cm
Habitat	streams, ponds, marshes; damp soil
Flowering	May–August
STEMS AND LEAVES	
Stem	sometimes branched, upright
Root	fibrous
Hairs	on most of plant, pointing towards stem- or leaf-tip
Stipules	absent
Leaves	on alternate sides of stem, 10–80mm, oblong or spear-shaped, blunt, edge unbroken, base narrowed
Leaf-stalk	absent
FLOWERS	
Position	many in heads at stem-tips, coiled, becoming straight
Bracts	absent or few at base
Type	♀
Size	2–4mm
Colour	light blue with yellow centre; buds pink
Stalk	about equalling flower, longer in fruit
Sepals	5, 2.5–4mm, up to 8mm in fruit, joined to middle
Petals	5, 2–4mm, forming tube at base, lobes rounded
Stamens	5, inside petal-tube
Stigma	1, tip swollen
Ovary	1, deeply 4-lobed
FRUIT	
Type	splits into 4 nut-like parts, oval, glossy brown
Size	1.3–1.8mm
Seeds	1 per segment, not released

Vervain *Verbena officinalis*

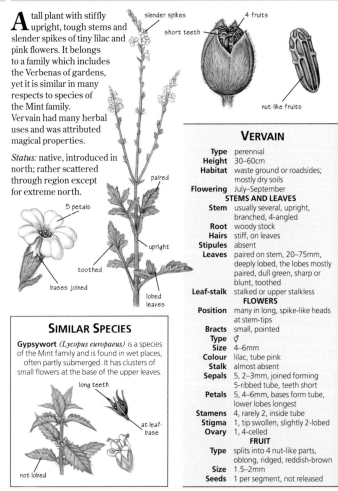

A tall plant with stiffly upright, tough stems and slender spikes of tiny lilac and pink flowers. It belongs to a family which includes the Verbenas of gardens, yet it is similar in many respects to species of the Mint family. Vervain had many herbal uses and was attributed magical properties.

Status: native, introduced in north; rather scattered through region except for extreme north.

slender spikes

short teeth

4 fruits

nut-like fruits

5 petals

paired

upright

toothed

bases joined

lobed leaves

SIMILAR SPECIES

Gypsywort (*Lycopus europaeus*) is a species of the Mint family and is found in wet places, often partly submerged. It has clusters of small flowers at the base of the upper leaves.

long teeth

at leaf-base

not lobed

VERVAIN

Type	perennial
Height	30–60cm
Habitat	waste ground or roadsides; mostly dry soils
Flowering	July–September
STEMS AND LEAVES	
Stem	usually several, upright, branched, 4-angled
Root	woody stock
Hairs	stiff, on leaves
Stipules	absent
Leaves	paired on stem, 20–75mm, deeply lobed, the lobes mostly paired, dull green, sharp or blunt, toothed
Leaf-stalk	stalked or upper stalkless
FLOWERS	
Position	many in long, spike-like heads at stem-tips
Bracts	small, pointed
Type	♂
Size	4–6mm
Colour	lilac, tube pink
Stalk	almost absent
Sepals	5, 2–3mm, joined forming 5-ribbed tube, teeth short
Petals	5, 4–6mm, bases form tube, lower lobes longest
Stamens	4, rarely 2, inside tube
Stigma	1, tip swollen, slightly 2-lobed
Ovary	1, 4-celled
FRUIT	
Type	splits into 4 nut-like parts, oblong, ridged, reddish-brown
Size	1.5–2mm
Seeds	1 per segment, not released

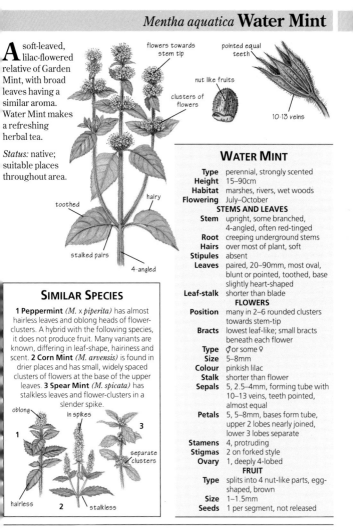

A soft-leaved, lilac-flowered relative of Garden Mint, with broad leaves having a similar aroma. Water Mint makes a refreshing herbal tea.

Status: native; suitable places throughout area.

flowers towards stem tip

clusters of flowers

nut like fruits

pointed equal teeth

10-13 veins

toothed

hairy

stalked pairs

4-angled

SIMILAR SPECIES

1 Peppermint *(M.* x *piperita)* has almost hairless leaves and oblong heads of flower-clusters. A hybrid with the following species, it does not produce fruit. Many variants are known, differing in leaf-shape, hairiness and scent. **2 Corn Mint** *(M. arvensis)* is found in drier places and has small, widely spaced clusters of flowers at the base of the upper leaves. **3 Spear Mint** *(M. spicata)* has stalkless leaves and flower-clusters in a slender spike.

oblong

in spikes

3

separate clusters

hairless

1

2

stalkless

WATER MINT

Type	perennial, strongly scented
Height	15–90cm
Habitat	marshes, rivers, wet woods
Flowering	July–October

STEMS AND LEAVES

Stem	upright, some branched, 4-angled, often red-tinged
Root	creeping underground stems
Hairs	over most of plant, soft
Stipules	absent
Leaves	paired, 20–90mm, most oval, blunt or pointed, toothed, base slightly heart-shaped
Leaf-stalk	shorter than blade

FLOWERS

Position	many in 2–6 rounded clusters towards stem-tip
Bracts	lowest leaf-like; small bracts beneath each flower
Type	♂ or some ♀
Size	5–8mm
Colour	pinkish lilac
Stalk	shorter than flower
Sepals	5, 2.5–4mm, forming tube with 10–13 veins, teeth pointed, almost equal
Petals	5, 5–8mm, bases form tube, upper 2 lobes nearly joined, lower 3 lobes separate
Stamens	4, protruding
Stigmas	2 on forked style
Ovary	1, deeply 4-lobed

FRUIT

Type	splits into 4 nut-like parts, egg-shaped, brown
Size	1–1.5mm
Seeds	1 per segment, not released

Wood Sage *Teucrium scorodonia*

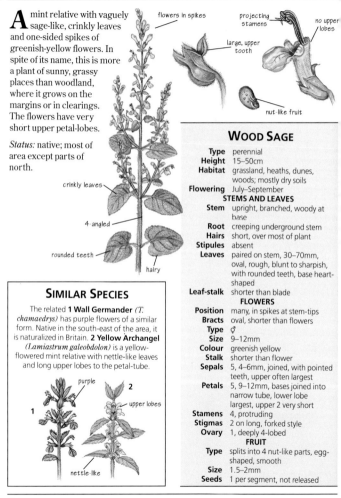

A mint relative with vaguely sage-like, crinkly leaves and one-sided spikes of greenish-yellow flowers. In spite of its name, this is more a plant of sunny, grassy places than woodland, where it grows on the margins or in clearings. The flowers have very short upper petal-lobes.

Status: native; most of area except parts of north.

flowers in spikes

crinkly leaves

4-angled

rounded teeth

hairy

projecting stamens

no upper lobes

large, upper tooth

nut-like fruit

SIMILAR SPECIES

The related **1 Wall Germander** (*T. chamaedrys*) has purple flowers of a similar form. Native in the south-east of the area, it is naturalized in Britain. **2 Yellow Archangel** (*Lamiastrum galeobdolon*) is a yellow-flowered mint relative with nettle-like leaves and long upper lobes to the petal-tube.

purple

1

2

upper lobes

nettle-like

WOOD SAGE

Type	perennial
Height	15–50cm
Habitat	grassland, heaths, dunes, woods; mostly dry soils
Flowering	July–September
STEMS AND LEAVES	
Stem	upright, branched, woody at base
Root	creeping underground stem
Hairs	short, over most of plant
Stipules	absent
Leaves	paired on stem, 30–70mm, oval, rough, blunt to sharpish, with rounded teeth, base heart-shaped
Leaf-stalk	shorter than blade
FLOWERS	
Position	many, in spikes at stem-tips
Bracts	oval, shorter than flowers
Type	♂
Size	9–12mm
Colour	greenish yellow
Stalk	shorter than flower
Sepals	5, 4–6mm, joined, with pointed teeth, upper often largest
Petals	5, 9–12mm, bases joined into narrow tube, lower lobe largest, upper 2 very short
Stamens	4, protruding
Stigmas	2 on long, forked style
Ovary	1, deeply 4-lobed
FRUIT	
Type	splits into 4 nut-like parts, egg-shaped, smooth
Size	1.5–2mm
Seeds	1 per segment, not released

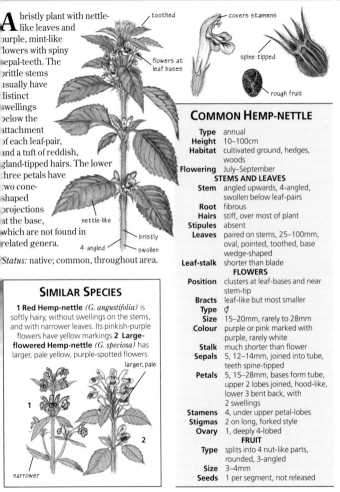

A bristly plant with nettle-like leaves and purple, mint-like flowers with spiny sepal-teeth. The brittle stems usually have distinct swellings below the attachment of each leaf-pair, and a tuft of reddish, gland-tipped hairs. The lower three petals have two cone-shaped projections at the base, which are not found in related genera.

toothed

covers stamens

flowers at leaf bases

spine-tipped

nettle-like

bristly

4-angled

swollen

rough fruit

Status: native; common, throughout area.

COMMON HEMP-NETTLE

Type	annual
Height	10–100cm
Habitat	cultivated ground, hedges, woods
Flowering	July–September

STEMS AND LEAVES

Stem	angled upwards, 4-angled, swollen below leaf-pairs
Root	fibrous
Hairs	stiff, over most of plant
Stipules	absent
Leaves	paired on stems, 25–100mm, oval, pointed, toothed, base wedge-shaped
Leaf-stalk	shorter than blade

FLOWERS

Position	clusters at leaf-bases and near stem-tip
Bracts	leaf-like but most smaller
Type	♂
Size	15–20mm, rarely to 28mm
Colour	purple or pink marked with purple, rarely white
Stalk	much shorter than flower
Sepals	5, 12–14mm, joined into tube, teeth spine-tipped
Petals	5, 15–28mm, bases form tube, upper 2 lobes joined, hood-like, lower 3 bent back, with 2 swellings
Stamens	4, under upper petal-lobes
Stigmas	2 on long, forked style
Ovary	1, deeply 4-lobed

FRUIT

Type	splits into 4 nut-like parts, rounded, 3-angled
Size	3–4mm
Seeds	1 per segment, not released

SIMILAR SPECIES

1 Red Hemp-nettle *(G. angustifolia)* is softly hairy, without swellings on the stems, and with narrower leaves. Its pinkish-purple flowers have yellow markings. **2 Large-flowered Hemp-nettle** *(G. speciosa)* has larger, pale yellow, purple-spotted flowers.

larger, pale

1

2

narrower

White Dead-nettle *Lamium album*

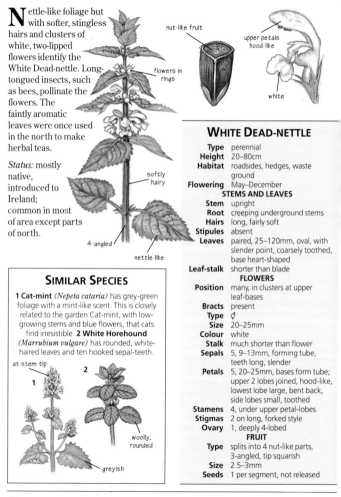

Nettle-like foliage but with softer, stingless hairs and clusters of white, two-lipped flowers identify the White Dead-nettle. Long-tongued insects, such as bees, pollinate the flowers. The faintly aromatic leaves were once used in the north to make herbal teas.

Status: mostly native, introduced to Ireland; common in most of area except parts of north.

nut-like fruit

upper petals hood-like

flowers in rings

white

softly hairy

4-angled

nettle-like

SIMILAR SPECIES

1 Cat-mint *(Nepeta cataria)* has grey-green foliage with a mint-like scent. This is closely related to the garden Cat-mint, with low-growing stems and blue flowers, that cats find irresistible. **2 White Horehound** *(Marrubium vulgare)* has rounded, white-haired leaves and ten hooked sepal-teeth.

at stem-tip

1

2

woolly, rounded

greyish

WHITE DEAD-NETTLE

Type	perennial
Height	20–80cm
Habitat	roadsides, hedges, waste ground
Flowering	May–December
STEMS AND LEAVES	
Stem	upright
Root	creeping underground stems
Hairs	long, fairly soft
Stipules	absent
Leaves	paired, 25–120mm, oval, with slender point, coarsely toothed, base heart-shaped
Leaf-stalk	shorter than blade
FLOWERS	
Position	many, in clusters at upper leaf-bases
Bracts	present
Type	♂
Size	20–25mm
Colour	white
Stalk	much shorter than flower
Sepals	5, 9–13mm, forming tube, teeth long, slender
Petals	5, 20–25mm, bases form tube; upper 2 lobes joined, hood-like, lowest lobe large, bent back, side lobes small, toothed
Stamens	4, under upper petal-lobes
Stigmas	2 on long, forked style
Ovary	1, deeply 4-lobed
FRUIT	
Type	splits into 4 nut-like parts, 3-angled, tip squarish
Size	2.5–3mm
Seeds	1 per segment, not released

Lamium purpureum **Red Dead-nettle**

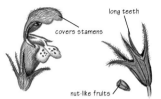

long teeth

covers stamens

nut-like fruits

A vaguely nettle-like plant but with stingless hairs on the leaves and four-angled stems, with flowers and clusters of four nut-like fruits typical of the Mint family. The creeping, rooting, basal parts of the plant were formerly used as pig-feed. In complete contrast, the flowers were crystallized in sugar and eaten as sweets.

Status: native; very common, throughout area.

in clusters

paired

stalk

4-angled

rounded teeth

rooting

SIMILAR SPECIES

1 Henbit Dead-nettle (*L. amplexicaule*) has stalkless upper leaves. **2 Cut-leaved Dead-nettle** (*L. hybridum*) has deeply lobed leaves with few teeth. **3 Black Horehound** (*Ballota nigra*) is a more robust perennial, with short, broad sepal-teeth.

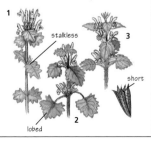

stalkless

short

lobed

1

2

3

RED DEAD-NETTLE

Type	annual
Height	10–45cm
Habitat	cultivated and waste ground
Flowering	March–October

STEMS AND LEAVES

Stem	base branched, often rooting, upper parts upright, 4-angled, purplish
Root	fibrous
Hairs	short, over most of plant
Stipules	absent
Leaves	paired on stem, 10–50mm, oval, blunt, with rounded teeth, base heart-shaped
Leaf-stalk	lowest long, upper short

FLOWERS

Position	few, in clusters towards stem-tip
Bracts	similar to leaves
Type	♂
Size	10–18mm
Colour	pinkish purple
Stalk	very short
Sepals	5, 5–7mm, bases joined, teeth long, pointed
Petals	5, 10–18mm, bases form tube, upper 2 lobes joined, hood-like, lowest large, 2-lobed, side 2 short, toothed
Stamens	4, under upper petal-lobes
Stigmas	2 on long, forked style
Ovary	1, deeply 4-lobed

FRUIT

Type	splits into 4 nut-like parts, 3-angled, tip square
Size	2–2.5mm
Seeds	1 per segment, not released

Betony *Stachys officinalis*

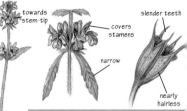

towards stem-tip

covers stamens

narrow

slender teeth

nearly hairless

Almost leafless stems of Betony arise from a basal tuft of long-stalked leaves, and each bears a fairly compact, cylindrical head of reddish-purple flowers at the tip. To Betony was attributed many properties, both medicinal and magical, and it was used in herbal tea and herbal tobacco.

Status: native; common in south, absent from parts of north.

sparse hairs

paired

nut-like fruits

long stalk

rounded teeth

SIMILAR SPECIES

Related species lack leaves at the base but have many on the stems. Stem-leaves of **1 Hedge Woundwort** (*S. sylvatica*) are long-stalked, whereas those of **2 Marsh Woundwort** (*S. palustris*) are stalkless. **3 Field Woundwort** (*S. arvensis*) is a small-flowered annual with broad stem-leaves.

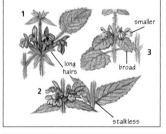

long hairs

smaller

broad

3

stalkless

1

2

BETONY

Type	perennial
Height	15–60cm
Habitat	woods, hedges, grassy places; light soils
Flowering	June–September
STEMS AND LEAVES	
Stem	upright, mostly unbranched
Root	woody underground stem
Hairs	sparse
Stipules	absent
Leaves	most basal, 2–4 pairs on stem, 30–70mm, oval to oblong, blunt, with rounded teeth, base heart-shaped
Leaf-stalk	lowest twice as long as blade, uppermost stalkless
FLOWERS	
Position	many, in clusters around stem, towards stem-tip
Bracts	lowest leaf-like
Type	⚥
Size	12–18mm
Colour	bright reddish purple
Stalk	much shorter than flower
Sepals	5, 5–9mm, bases form tube, teeth sharply pointed
Petals	5, 12–18mm, bases form tube, upper 2 lobes joined, hood-like, other lobes bent back
Stamens	4, under upper lobes
Stigmas	2 on long, forked style
Ovary	1, deeply 4-lobed
FRUIT	
Type	splits into 4 nut-like parts, 3-angled, tip rounded
Size	2.5–3mm
Seeds	1 per segment, not released

A very variable plant, usually with spikes of violet, 2-lipped flowers and pairs of rough, lobed leaves. Some specimens produce flowers which never open fully, being pollinated in bud and setting a full crop of nut-like fruits. Height, lobing of the leaves and size of the flowers vary considerably. The fruits swell and become sticky when wet.

Status: native; scattered localities, mainly in south-west of area, north to Scotland.

towards stem-tip

upper stalkless

stamens project

hairy

3 short teeth

2 long teeth

nut-like fruits

paired

lower often lobed

4-angled

WILD CLARY

Type	perennial
Height	30–80cm
Habitat	grassy places; dry soils
Flowering	May–August
STEMS AND LEAVES	
Stem	upright, hardly branched, 4-angled
Root	tough stock
Hairs	short, gland-tipped above
Stipules	absent
Leaves	basal or 2–3 pairs on stem, 40–120mm, oblong or oval, rough, blunt, toothed, lowest often deeply lobed
Leaf-stalk	lowest long, upper absent
FLOWERS	
Position	6–10, in rings, clustered in spikes at stem-tips
Bracts	oval, shorter than sepals
Type	♂ or ♀, some not opening
Size	6–15mm
Colour	bluish violet
Stalk	much shorter than flower
Sepals	5, 6–8mm, with long, white hairs, bases form tube; 3 upper lobes nearly joined, lower 2 longer than tube
Petals	5, 6–15mm, bases form tube, upper 2 lobes joined, hood-like, lower lobes bent back
Stamens	2, under upper petal-lobes
Stigmas	2 on long, forked style
Ovary	1, deeply 4-lobed
FRUIT	
Type	splits into 4 nut-like parts, egg-shaped
Size	1.5–2mm
Seeds	1 per segment, not released

SIMILAR SPECIES

Meadow Clary *(S. pratensis)* has larger flowers with long, curved, hood-like upper petal-lobes, and lacks white hairs on the sepal-tube.

larger, sticky

not lobed

155

Ground-ivy *Glechoma hederacea*

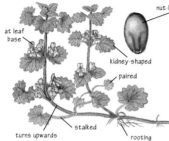

at leaf base

nut-like fruits

kidney-shaped

paired

stalked

turns upwards

rooting

♂

♀

5 equal teeth

A charming plant with violet-coloured, two-lipped flowers, creeping beneath hedgerows and over woodland floors. It is sometimes grown in gardens, often as a variegated form used to trail over hanging baskets. Ground-ivy was formerly known best as a bitter herb used for flavouring ale, although it also had medicinal uses.

Status: native; common, most of area.

SIMILAR SPECIES

1 Skullcap *(Scutellaria galericulata)* also has violet, two-lipped flowers. It has elongated leaves, a swelling on the upper side of the sepal-tube, and grows in wet, sunny places. **2 Lesser Skullcap** *(S. minor)* has smaller, pinkish flowers and sparsely toothed leaves.

elongated

2

1

hardly toothed

lobe on sepals

GROUND-IVY

Type	perennial
Height	10–50cm
Habitat	hedges, woods, grassy places; usually damp soil
Flowering	March–May
STEMS AND LEAVES	
Stem	creeping, rooting, angled upwards to flower
Root	fibrous, stems root
Hairs	soft, fairly long
Stipules	absent
Leaves	paired on stem, 5–35mm, kidney-shaped to nearly oval, blunt, coarsely-toothed, base heart-shaped
Leaf-stalk	most longer than blade
FLOWERS	
Position	clusters of 2–4 towards stem-tips
Bracts	resembling leaves
Type	♂ or sometimes ♀
Size	15–22mm
Colour	bluish violet, spotted reddish purple
Stalk	much shorter than flower
Sepals	5, 5–6.5mm, bases joined, teeth nearly equal, pointed
Petals	5, 15–22mm, bases joined; upper 2 lobes nearly joined, hood-like, lower 3 larger
Stamens	4, under upper petal-lobes
Stigmas	2 on long, forked style
Ovary	1, deeply 4-lobed
FRUIT	
Type	splits into 4 nut-like parts, egg-shaped, smooth
Size	2–3mm
Seeds	1 per segment, not released

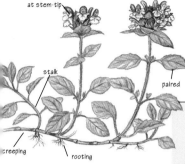

at stem-tip

stalk

paired

creeping

rooting

broad upper lip

nut-like fruit

A grassland plant, often thriving in close-grazed or mown turf, from which it raises its compact, cylindrical heads of deep violet-coloured flowers. It was much prized as a herb for treating wounds and also taken for sore throats.

Status: native; very common, throughout area.

SIMILAR SPECIES

1 Cut-leaved Selfheal (*P. laciniata*) has divided upper leaves and cream-coloured flowers. It is native only in the south of the area but is naturalized in Britain. **2 Bugle** (*Ajuga reptans*) has more widely spaced clusters of flowers with larger bracts, often tinged with blackish violet and contrasting vividly with the bluish flowers.

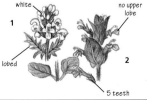

white

no upper lobe

1

lobed

2

5 teeth

SELFHEAL

Type	perennial
Height	5–50cm
Habitat	grassland, woodland clearings; most soils
Flowering	June–September
STEMS AND LEAVES	
Stem	angled upwards or upright
Root	short underground stem
Hairs	sparse, short
Stipules	absent
Leaves	paired on stem, 20–50mm, oval or diamond-shaped, edge toothed or unbroken
Leaf-stalk	shorter than blade
FLOWERS	
Position	rings of 6, in compact, oblong head at stem-tip
Bracts	circular, stalkless, often purple-tinged
Type	♂
Size	10–15mm
Colour	violet, rarely pink or white
Stalk	much shorter than flower
Sepals	5, 8–9mm, bases joined, upper 3 teeth almost joined, lower 2 longer
Petals	5, 10–15mm, bases form tube, upper 2 lobes joined, hood-like, lower 3 bent back
Stamens	4, under upper petal-lobes
Stigmas	2 on long, forked style
Ovary	1, deeply 4-lobed
FRUIT	
Type	splits into 4 nut-like parts, oblong, smooth
Size	2–2.5mm
Seeds	1 per segment, not released

Marjoram *Origanum vulgare*

Usually found among tall grasses, this rather bushy plant has branched heads of pink flowers and contrasting purple bracts. It is sometimes used as a pot-herb and is related to Oregano, which derives from Mediterranean plants. Native plants were widely used to treat coughs and headaches.

Status: native; most of area, most common in south.

widely branched clusters

at stem-tip

nut-like fruits

5 teeth equal

nearly hairless

most not toothed

paired

MARJORAM

Type	perennial
Height	30–90cm
Habitat	grassy places, scrub; dry, often lime-rich soils
Flowering	July–September
STEMS AND LEAVES	
Stem	upright, usually branched
Root	woody, creeping underground stem
Hairs	usually scattered
Stipules	absent
Leaves	paired on stem, 10–45mm, oval, strongly scented, blunt or sharp, edge unbroken or hardly toothed
Leaf-stalk	shorter than blade
FLOWERS	
Position	many, in widely branched clusters of short spikes
Bracts	oval, smaller than leaves, usually purple
Type	⚥ or sometimes ♀
Size	4–8mm
Colour	pinkish purple or white
Stalk	much shorter than flower
Sepals	5, 2–4mm, bases joined, teeth nearly equal
Petals	5, 4–8mm, bases joined, lower 3 lobes longer than upper 2
Stamens	4, usually protruding
Stigmas	2 on long, forked style
Ovary	1, deeply 4-lobed
FRUIT	
Type	splits into 4 nut-like parts
Size	1.5–2mm
Seeds	1 per segment, not released

SIMILAR SPECIES

Two other species have longer, less crowded heads of larger flowers and unequal, hairier sepal-teeth. **1 Wild Basil** *(Clinopodium vulgare)* has almost stalkless flower-clusters and a curved sepal-tube, whereas **2 Common Calamint** *(Calamintha sylvatica subsp. ascendens)* has stalked clusters of flowers.

hairy

thinner

stalked

Thymus praecox subsp. *arcticus* **Wild Thyme**

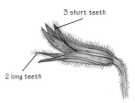

short cluster

nut-like fruits

3 short teeth

not toothed

paired

2 long teeth

creeping   rooting

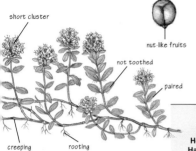

A mat-forming plant of dry places, that has short flowering stems bearing compact heads of purple flowers. The leaves have a faint but distinctive aroma of Thyme as used in the kitchen. Species of Thyme formerly had medicinal as well as culinary uses.

Status: native; common in south, absent from much of north.

SIMILAR SPECIES

1 Large Thyme (*T. pulegioides*) usually has much taller stems, with cylindrical heads of larger flowers. The stems are more upright, sharply four-angled, and the whole plant is more strongly scented. **2 Basil Thyme** (*Acinos arvensis*) is a much hairier plant, with toothed leaves and larger flowers.

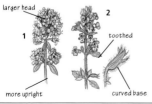

larger head

2

1

toothed

more upright

curved base

WILD THYME

Type	perennial, aromatic
Height	1–8cm
Habitat	grasslands, heaths, dunes, rocks; dry soils
Flowering	May–August

STEMS AND LEAVES

Stem	long, creeping, forming mats, branches angled upwards to flower
Root	woody stock; stems root
Hairs	on 2 sides of stem, long on leaf-edges
Stipules	absent
Leaves	paired on stem, 4–8mm, elliptical or oval, blunt, edge unbroken
Leaf-stalk	very short

FLOWERS

Position	short heads at stem-tips
Bracts	lowest leaf-like
Type	♂ or ♀
Size	4–7mm
Colour	pinkish purple
Stalk	much shorter than flower
Sepals	5, 3–4mm, bases form tube, upper 3 teeth short, lower 2 long
Petals	5, 4–7mm, bases joined, upper 2 lobes nearly joined
Stamens	4, protruding on ♂ flowers
Stigmas	2 on long, forked style
Ovary	1, deeply 4-lobed

FRUIT

Type	splits into 4 nut-like parts, egg-shaped, smooth
Size	0.7–1mm
Seeds	1 per segment, not released

159

Deadly Nightshade *Atropa belladonna*

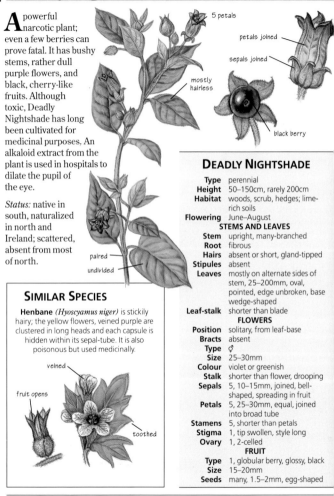

A powerful narcotic plant; even a few berries can prove fatal. It has bushy stems, rather dull purple flowers, and black, cherry-like fruits. Although toxic, Deadly Nightshade has long been cultivated for medicinal purposes. An alkaloid extract from the plant is used in hospitals to dilate the pupil of the eye.

Status: native in south, naturalized in north and Ireland; scattered, absent from most of north.

5 petals

petals joined

sepals joined

mostly hairless

black berry

paired

undivided

SIMILAR SPECIES

Henbane *(Hyoscyamus niger)* is stickily hairy; the yellow flowers, veined purple are clustered in long heads and each capsule is hidden within its sepal-tube. It is also poisonous but used medicinally.

veined

fruit opens

toothed

DEADLY NIGHTSHADE

Type	perennial
Height	50–150cm, rarely 200cm
Habitat	woods, scrub, hedges; lime-rich soils
Flowering	June–August
STEMS AND LEAVES	
Stem	upright, many-branched
Root	fibrous
Hairs	absent or short, gland-tipped
Stipules	absent
Leaves	mostly on alternate sides of stem, 25–200mm, oval, pointed, edge unbroken, base wedge-shaped
Leaf-stalk	shorter than blade
FLOWERS	
Position	solitary, from leaf-base
Bracts	absent
Type	♂
Size	25–30mm
Colour	violet or greenish
Stalk	shorter than flower, drooping
Sepals	5, 10–15mm, joined, bell-shaped, spreading in fruit
Petals	5, 25–30mm, equal, joined into broad tube
Stamens	5, shorter than petals
Stigma	1, tip swollen, style long
Ovary	1, 2-celled
FRUIT	
Type	1, globular berry, glossy, black
Size	15–20mm
Seeds	many, 1.5–2mm, egg-shaped

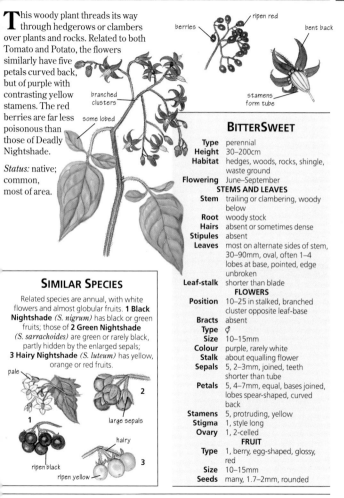

This woody plant threads its way through hedgerows or clambers over plants and rocks. Related to both Tomato and Potato, the flowers similarly have five petals curved back, but purple with contrasting yellow stamens. The red berries are far less poisonous than those of Deadly Nightshade.

Status: native; common, most of area.

berries

ripen red

bent back

branched clusters

some lobed

stamens form tube

BitterSweet

Type	perennial
Height	30–200cm
Habitat	hedges, woods, rocks, shingle, waste ground
Flowering	June–September

STEMS AND LEAVES

Stem	trailing or clambering, woody below
Root	woody stock
Hairs	absent or sometimes dense
Stipules	absent
Leaves	most on alternate sides of stem, 30–90mm, oval, often 1–4 lobes at base, pointed, edge unbroken
Leaf-stalk	shorter than blade

FLOWERS

Position	10–25 in stalked, branched cluster opposite leaf-base
Bracts	absent
Type	♀
Size	10–15mm
Colour	purple, rarely white
Stalk	about equalling flower
Sepals	5, 2–3mm, joined, teeth shorter than tube
Petals	5, 4–7mm, equal, bases joined, lobes spear-shaped, curved back
Stamens	5, protruding, yellow
Stigma	1, style long
Ovary	1, 2-celled

FRUIT

Type	1, berry, egg-shaped, glossy, red
Size	10–15mm
Seeds	many, 1.7–2mm, rounded

SIMILAR SPECIES

Related species are annual, with white flowers and almost globular fruits. **1 Black Nightshade** (*S. nigrum*) has black or green fruits; those of **2 Green Nightshade** (*S. sarrachoides*) are green or rarely black, partly hidden by the enlarged sepals; **3 Hairy Nightshade** (*S. luteum*) has yellow, orange or red fruits.

pale

large sepals

2

1

hairy

ripen black

ripen yellow

3

161

Great Mullein *Verbascum thapsus*

A stiffly upright plant that has slender, crowded spikes of yellow flowers and is clothed with whitish wool. Innumerable branched hairs give the leaves a softness and warmth. Dried tops of plants were used to make tapers for burning; leaves provided shoe-liners; and flowers a cough medicine.

Status: native; most of area except north.

flowers in spike
short-stalked
crowded
5 petals
blade joins stem
whitish hairs on stamens

fruit splits open
thick hairs
lower large

GREAT MULLEIN

Type	biennial
Height	30–200cm
Habitat	grassy banks, waste ground; dry, often sandy soil
Flowering	June–August

STEMS AND LEAVES

Stem	upright, usually unbranched
Root	tap-root
Hairs	dense, woolly, whitish
Stipules	absent
Leaves	basal rosette or spirally placed on stem, 40–500mm, oval to oblong, most pointed, edge unbroken or fine-toothed, upper blades run down stem as wings
Leaf-stalk	lowest short, upper absent

FLOWERS

Position	in dense spike at stem-tip
Bracts	narrowly triangular, pointed
Type	♂
Size	12–30mm
Colour	yellow
Stalk	much shorter than flowers
Sepals	5, 8–12mm, bases joined, lobes equal, oval, pointed
Petals	5, 6–14mm, almost equal, bases joined, lobes rounded, spreading widely
Stamens	5, upper 3 with long, white hairs, lower 2 hairless
Stigma	1, tip swollen
Ovary	1, 2-celled

FRUIT

Type	1, egg-shaped capsule, splits lengthwise
Size	7–10mm
Seeds	many, 0.8–1mm, oblong, pitted

SIMILAR SPECIES

1 White Mullein *(V. lychnitis)* has wide-spaced, whitish, smaller flowers, and all stamens are hairy. Two species have stamens with purple hairs: **2 Dark Mullein** *(V. nigrum)* has dark green, rather hairy leaves; **3 Moth Mullein** *(V. blattaria)* has almost hairless leaves and long-stalked, widely-spaced flowers.

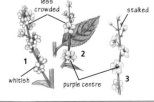

less crowded
stalked
whitish
purple centre

A tall, perhaps sombre plant, with broad, dark leaves and dull, brownish-purple flowers. Small flowers, rather unpleasantly scented, are pollinated mainly by wasps. Leaves of Figwort were used as poultices for skin complaints.

Status: native; common; almost throughout area.

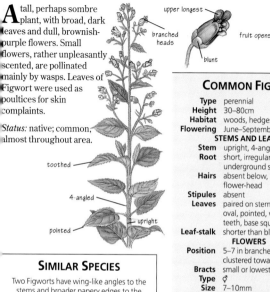

COMMON FIGWORT

Type	perennial
Height	30–80cm
Habitat	woods, hedges; damp soils
Flowering	June–September
STEMS AND LEAVES	
Stem	upright, 4-angled
Root	short, irregularly swollen, underground stem
Hairs	absent below, gland-tipped in flower-head
Stipules	absent
Leaves	paired on stem, 60–130mm, oval, pointed, with uneven teeth, base squarish
Leaf-stalk	shorter than blade
FLOWERS	
Position	5–7 in branched heads, clustered towards stem-tip
Bracts	small or lowest leaf-like
Type	♂
Size	7–10mm
Colour	green below, reddish brown on upper petal-lobes
Stalk	2–3 times length of flower
Sepals	5, 2–3.5mm, joined, lobes oval, blunt, edge papery
Petals	5, 7–10mm, bases joined, nearly globular, upper 2 lobes rounded, lower shorter
Stamens	4 normal, 1 broad, sterile
Stigma	1, tip swollen, style short
Ovary	1, 2-celled
FRUIT	
Type	1, capsule, egg-shaped, pointed, splits lengthwise
Size	5–10mm
Seeds	many, c1mm, oblong, pitted

SIMILAR SPECIES

Two Figworts have wing-like angles to the stems and broader papery edges to the sepals. **1 Water Figwort** *(S. auriculata)* has blunt leaves with rounded teeth and often two lobes at the base. **2 Green Figwort** *(S. umbrosa)* has more pointed leaves with pointed teeth and lacks lobes. **3 Yellow Figwort** *(S. vernalis)* is softly hairy, and has pointed sepals and yellow flowers.

Ivy-leaved Toadflax *Cymbalaria muralis*

Labels on illustrations: trailing, fold, rough seed, fruit opens, lobed, short spur, flower-stalk, stalked

Lilac, Snapdragon-like flowers, backed by broad, lobed, glossy leaves make this a charming plant. In full sun, stems, stalks and the base of the flowers have a purple tinge which is lacking in shady places. Long stalks hold flowers clear of the foliage but, in fruit, curve round to bury the seeds in crevices.

Status: introduced, from southern Europe; most common in south.

IVY-LEAVED TOADFLAX

Type	perennial
Height	5–15cm
Habitat	walls, rocks, shingle, railway ballast; dry places
Flowering	May–September
STEMS AND LEAVES	
Stem	trailing, hanging, to 80cm long, often tinged purple
Root	fibrous, stems root
Hairs	absent
Stipules	absent
Leaves	most on alternate sides of stem, lowest paired, 7–25mm, kidney-shaped, 5–9 rounded or triangular lobes
Leaf-stalk	longer than blade
FLOWERS	
Position	single from base of leaf
Bracts	absent
Type	♂
Size	9–15mm
Colour	lilac, yellow on fold of lower petals, violet veins
Stalk	much longer than flower, bends down in fruit
Sepals	5, 2–2.5mm, spear-shaped, pointed, bases joined
Petals	5, 9–15mm, bases form tube, spur at base, lower 3 lobes with fold closing tube
Stamens	4, inside petal-tube
Stigma	1, tip swollen
Ovary	1, 2-celled
FRUIT	
Type	capsule, sides split open
Size	2.5–4mm
Seeds	many, 0.8–1mm, globular, irregularly ridged, black

SIMILAR SPECIES

Fluellens, of cornfields or waste ground, have capsules with circular lids and pitted seeds. **1 Sharp-leaved Fluellen** *(Kickxia elatine)* has arrow-shaped leaves, with backward-pointing lobes; **2 Round-leaved Fluellen** *(K. spuria)* lacks the lobes and has sepals that enlarge in fruit.

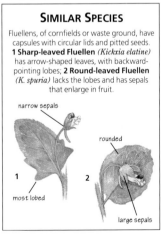

Labels: narrow sepals, rounded, 1, most lobed, 2, large sepals

rounded sepals

fruit has 3 openings

broad tube

A popular garden plant that has often escaped, known to generations of children for the mouth-like flower which snaps open when the sides are pressed. Snapdragon originated in the western Mediterranean region, but the exact location has been obscured by many centuries of cultivation outside its original range.

flowers in spike

Status: introduced; mainly south of area, often near coasts.

edge unbroken

scattered leaves

fold

upright

SNAPDRAGON

Type	perennial
Height	30–80cm
Habitat	walls, cliffs; dry soils
Flowering	July–September
STEMS AND LEAVES	
Stem	upright, base woody
Root	fibrous
Hairs	absent below, sticky, gland-tipped in flower-head
Stipules	absent
Leaves	spirally placed on stem or lowest paired, 30–50mm, spear-shaped or oblong, edge unbroken, base tapered
Leaf-stalk	absent
FLOWERS	
Position	many, in spike at stem-tip
Bracts	oval, smaller than leaves
Type	♂
Size	30–40mm
Colour	reddish purple with yellow mark, some pink or white
Stalk	much shorter than flower
Sepals	5, 6–8mm, slightly unequal, bases joined, lobed oval
Petals	5, bases form broad tube, lower 3 lips with fold closing mouth of tube
Stamens	4, inside petal-tube
Stigma	1, tip swollen
Ovary	1, 2-celled
FRUIT	
Type	1, egg-shaped capsule, sides unequal, 3 pores at tip
Size	10–14mm
Seeds	many, 1–1.2mm, egg-shaped, with net-like ridges

SIMILAR SPECIES

1 Lesser Snapdragon (*Misopates orontium*) is a native annual that has small flowers, long sepals and seeds with one face smooth, the other encircled by a ridge. **2 Asarina** (*Asarina procumbens*) is sometimes naturalized and has large, yellow flowers, trailing stems and kidney-shaped, lobed leaves.

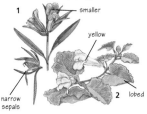

smaller

yellow

narrow sepals

1

2 lobed

Small Toadflax *Chaenorhinum minus*

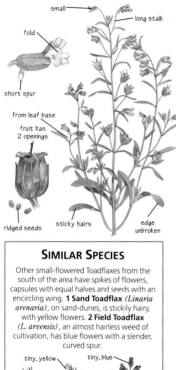

small — long stalk
fold
short spur
from leaf-base
fruit has 2 openings
ridged seeds — sticky hairs — edge unbroken

A delicate annual, Small Toadflax has tiny flowers like those of Snapdragon but with a small spur at the base. Mainly a weed of arable fields, it thrives on railway ballast although recent use of weedkillers has led to a decline.

Status: native or introduced; mainly south of region.

SMALL TOADFLAX

Type	annual
Height	8–25cm
Habitat	cultivated and waste ground, railway ballast
Flowering	May–October
STEMS AND LEAVES	
Stem	upright, branched
Root	fibrous
Hairs	short, gland-tipped
Stipules	absent
Leaves	lower paired, upper on alternate sides of stem, 5–25mm, narrow, spear-shaped to oblong, blunt, edge unbroken, tapered
Leaf-stalk	short
FLOWERS	
Position	each at base of upper leaf
Bracts	absent
Type	♂
Size	6–9mm
Colour	whitish, lobes and veins purple
Stalk	mostly longer than flower
Sepals	5, 2–5mm, unequal, narrow, blunt, bases joined
Petals	5, 6–9mm, bases form tube, with spur, fold of lower 3 lobes closes tube-mouth
Stamens	4, inside petal-tube
Stigma	1, tip swollen
Ovary	1, 2-celled
FRUIT	
Type	1, egg-shaped capsule, sides unequal, 2 pores at tip
Size	3–6mm
Seeds	many, 0.5–0.8mm, egg-shaped, ridged lengthwise

SIMILAR SPECIES

Other small-flowered Toadflaxes from the south of the area have spikes of flowers, capsules with equal halves and seeds with an encircling wing. **1 Sand Toadflax** *(Linaria arenaria)*, on sand-dunes, is stickily hairy, with yellow flowers. **2 Field Toadflax** *(L. arvensis)*, an almost hairless weed of cultivation, has blue flowers with a slender, curved spur.

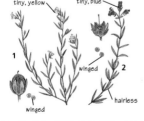

tiny, yellow — tiny, blue
1
winged — 2
winged — hairless

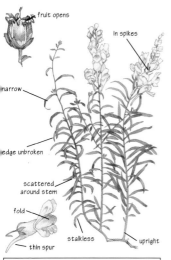

fruit opens

in spikes

narrow

edge unbroken

scattered around stem

fold

stalkless

upright

thin spur

F lowering in late Summer, commonly on grassy banks, many stems arise from creeping roots. Pollination is almost solely by bees, which have enough weight and strength to open the flower, and a long tongue to reach the nectar at the base.

Status: native; common, most of area.

COMMON TOADFLAX

Type	perennial
Height	30–80cm
Habitat	grassy and waste places, railway embankments
Flowering	July–October
STEMS AND LEAVES	
Stem	many, upright, branched
Root	fibrous, long, creeping roots produce new stems
Hairs	absent or sticky hairs above
Stipules	absent
Leaves	spirally around stem, lowest in ring or paired, 20–60mm, narrow, straight-sided or spear-shaped, pointed, edge unbroken
Leaf-stalk	absent
FLOWERS	
Position	5–30, in crowded spike
Bracts	small, oval, pointed
Type	♂
Size	20–33mm
Colour	yellow, darker fold at base of lower petal-lobes
Stalk	shorter than flower
Sepals	5, 3–6mm, oval, pointed
Petals	5, 20–33mm, forming tube, spur at base, fold of lower 3 lobes closes tube-mouth
Stamens	4, paired
Stigma	1, style slender
Ovary	1, 2-celled
FRUIT	
Type	1, oblong capsule, 2 pores at tip
Size	5–11mm
Seeds	many, 2–3mm, flattened, encircling wing, black

SIMILAR SPECIES

Two species have purplish flowers and wingless seeds. **1 Purple Toadflax** *(L. purpurea)* has long spikes of flowers each with a slender, curved spur. **2 Pale Toadflax** *(L. repens)* has fewer flowers with a short, straight spur; it sometimes forms hybrids with Common Toadflax. **3 Prostrate Toadflax** *(L. supina)* is low-growing, its pale yellow flowers with longer petal-lobes than those of Common Toadflax.

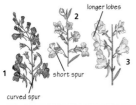

longer lobes

2

1

short spur

3

curved spur

Monkeyflower *Mimulus guttatus*

L arge, bright yellow flowers of Monkeyflower brighten many a stream and look so well established that they appear native. But this is an introduced plant that has often escaped from cultivation and spread widely along water-courses. Other species and hybrids are often cultivated in gardens.

Status: introduced from North America; common, much of area.

stickily hairy

toothed

long lower lobes

small red spots

unequal teeth

turns upwards

hairless below

paired leaves

MONKEYFLOWER

Type	perennial
Height	5–50cm
Habitat	streams, slow rivers; wet ground or shallow water
Flowering	July–September
STEMS AND LEAVES	
Stem	low-growing, angled upwards, hollow
Root	fibrous; stems root
Hairs	absent below, stickily hairy in flower-head
Stipules	absent
Leaves	paired on stem, 10–70mm, oval to circular, blunt to pointed, irregularly toothed
Leaf-stalk	lower short, upper absent
FLOWERS	
Position	few to many, in heads towards stem-tips
Bracts	leaf-like or upper smaller
Type	♂
Size	25–45mm
Colour	yellow, red-spotted in tube
Stalk	nearly equalling flower
Sepals	5, 15–20mm, bases form 5-angled tube, inflated in fruit, teeth unequal
Petals	5, 25–45mm, bases form tube, lower 3 lobes longer, folds nearly close tube-mouth
Stamens	4, paired, inside tube
Stigma	1, 2 flat lobes; style long
Ovary	1, 2-celled
FRUIT	
Type	1, oblong capsule, splits lengthwise
Size	8–12mm
Seeds	many, 0.7–0.9mm, oblong

SIMILAR SPECIES

1 Blood-drop-emlets *(M. luteus)* has large, red blotches on the flowers and is almost hairless. The hybrid with Monkeyflower is often more common than either species. **2 Musk** *(M. moschatus)* has smaller, unspotted flowers and stickily hairy foliage.

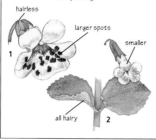

hairless

larger spots

smaller

all hairy

1

2

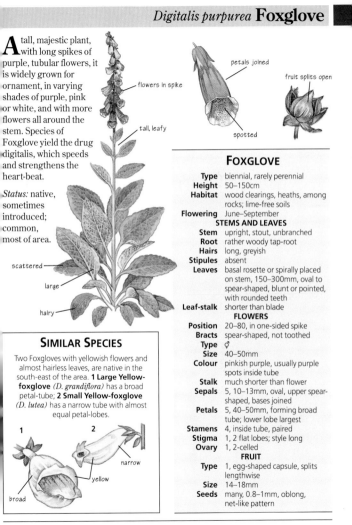

A tall, majestic plant, with long spikes of purple, tubular flowers, it is widely grown for ornament, in varying shades of purple, pink or white, and with more flowers all around the stem. Species of Foxglove yield the drug digitalis, which speeds and strengthens the heart-beat.

Status: native, sometimes introduced; common, most of area.

petals joined

fruit splits open

flowers in spike

tall, leafy

spotted

scattered

large

hairy

SIMILAR SPECIES

Two Foxgloves with yellowish flowers and almost hairless leaves, are native in the south-east of the area. **1 Large Yellow-foxglove** *(D. grandiflora)* has a broad petal-tube; **2 Small Yellow-foxglove** *(D. lutea)* has a narrow tube with almost equal petal-lobes.

1

2

narrow

yellow

broad

FOXGLOVE

Type	biennial, rarely perennial
Height	50–150cm
Habitat	wood clearings, heaths, among rocks; lime-free soils
Flowering	June–September
STEMS AND LEAVES	
Stem	upright, stout, unbranched
Root	rather woody tap-root
Hairs	long, greyish
Stipules	absent
Leaves	basal rosette or spirally placed on stem, 150–300mm, oval to spear-shaped, blunt or pointed, with rounded teeth
Leaf-stalk	shorter than blade
FLOWERS	
Position	20–80, in one-sided spike
Bracts	spear-shaped, not toothed
Type	♂
Size	40–50mm
Colour	pinkish purple, usually purple spots inside tube
Stalk	much shorter than flower
Sepals	5, 10–13mm, oval, upper spear-shaped, bases joined
Petals	5, 40–50mm, forming broad tube; lower lobe largest
Stamens	4, inside tube, paired
Stigma	1, 2 flat lobes; style long
Ovary	1, 2-celled
FRUIT	
Type	1, egg-shaped capsule, splits lengthwise
Size	14–18mm
Seeds	many, 0.8–1mm, oblong, net-like pattern

169

Germander Speedwell *Veronica chamaedrys*

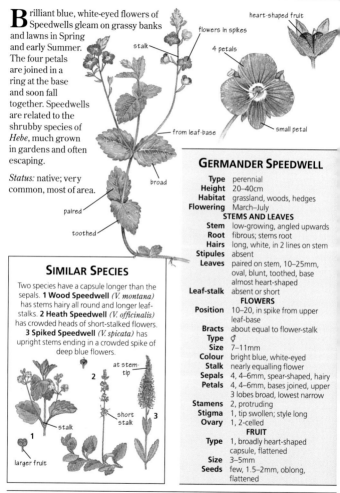

Brilliant blue, white-eyed flowers of Speedwells gleam on grassy banks and lawns in Spring and early Summer. The four petals are joined in a ring at the base and soon fall together. Speedwells are related to the shrubby species of *Hebe*, much grown in gardens and often escaping.

Status: native; very common, most of area.

heart-shaped fruit

flowers in spikes

stalk

4 petals

from leaf-base

small petal

broad

paired

toothed

SIMILAR SPECIES

Two species have a capsule longer than the sepals. **1 Wood Speedwell** *(V. montana)* has stems hairy all round and longer leaf-stalks. **2 Heath Speedwell** *(V. officinalis)* has crowded heads of short-stalked flowers. **3 Spiked Speedwell** *(V. spicata)* has upright stems ending in a crowded spike of deep blue flowers.

at stem-tip

2

short stalk

3

stalk

1

larger fruit

GERMANDER SPEEDWELL

Type	perennial
Height	20–40cm
Habitat	grassland, woods, hedges
Flowering	March–July
STEMS AND LEAVES	
Stem	low-growing, angled upwards
Root	fibrous; stems root
Hairs	long, white, in 2 lines on stem
Stipules	absent
Leaves	paired on stem, 10–25mm, oval, blunt, toothed, base almost heart-shaped
Leaf-stalk	absent or short
FLOWERS	
Position	10–20, in spike from upper leaf-base
Bracts	about equal to flower-stalk
Type	♂
Size	7–11mm
Colour	bright blue, white-eyed
Stalk	nearly equalling flower
Sepals	4, 4–6mm, spear-shaped, hairy
Petals	4, 4–6mm, bases joined, upper 3 lobes broad, lowest narrow
Stamens	2, protruding
Stigma	1, tip swollen; style long
Ovary	1, 2-celled
FRUIT	
Type	1, broadly heart-shaped capsule, flattened
Size	3–5mm
Seeds	few, 1.5–2mm, oblong, flattened

Veronica beccabunga **Brooklime**

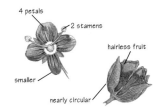

4 petals
2 stamens
hairless fruit
smaller
nearly circular

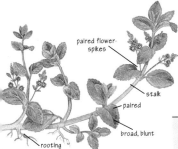

paired flower-spikes
stalk
paired
broad, blunt
rooting

Spikes of deep blue flowers, set against glossy dark foliage, make this an attractive plant often cultivated in ornamental ponds. It is one of the Speedwells, of which species in wet places are more robust than their counterparts of dry grassland, and are mostly hairless.

Status: native; common, throughout area.

SIMILAR SPECIES

Three species have elongated, stalkless leaves. **1 Blue Water-speedwell** (*V. anagallis-aquatica*) has long heads of flowers from both leaves of a pair. **2 Pink Water-speedwell** (*V. catenata*) is similar but with smaller, pink flowers on widely spreading stalks. **3 Marsh Speedwell** (*V. scutellata*) has sparsely-flowered heads from only one leaf of a pair.

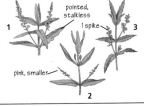

pointed, stalkless
1 spike
1
3
pink, smaller
2

BROOKLIME

Type	perennial
Height	20–60cm
Habitat	streams, ponds, wet meadows; wet places
Flowering	May–September
STEMS AND LEAVES	
Stem	creeping, angled upwards, fleshy
Root	fibrous; stems root
Hairs	absent
Stipules	absent
Leaves	paired on stem, 30–60mm, oval or oblong, thick, tip blunt, edge shallow-toothed, base rounded
Leaf-stalk	shorter than blade
FLOWERS	
Position	10–30, in spike at base of both leaves of pair
Bracts	small, narrow, pointed
Type	♂
Size	5–8mm
Colour	usually deep blue
Stalk	nearly equal to flower
Sepals	4, 2–4mm, unequal, oval, pointed
Petals	4, 2.5–4mm, bases joined, lobes flat, upper largest
Stamens	2, protruding
Stigma	1, tip swollen; style long
Ovary	1, 2-celled
FRUIT	
Type	1, nearly circular capsule, flattened, notched
Size	2–4mm
Seeds	few, 0.8–1mm, oblong, flattened

Common Field-speedwell *Veronica persica*

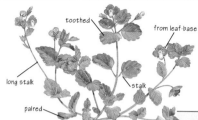

toothed · from leaf-base · heart-shaped · long stalk · stalk · paired · pale · 4 petals

Sky-blue flowers with the lowest petal white make this an attractive weed for the short time that the flowers endure. Seeds germinate and flowers open in almost any month of the year. Introduced from Asia nearly two centuries ago, in many parts of Europe this is now the most common of all Speedwells.

Status: introduced; common weed, throughout area.

SIMILAR SPECIES

1 Wall Speedwell (*V. arvensis*) has short-stalked flowers clustered in a rather lax spike at the stem-tip. **2 Green Field-speedwell** (*V. agrestis*) has small, pale flowers with shorter stalks. **3 Ivy-leaved Speedwell** (*V. hederifolia*) has leaves with few, large lobes and broad-based sepals.

short stalk · smaller · 1 · 2 · lobed · 3

COMMON FIELD-SPEEDWELL

Type	annual
Height	10–40cm
Habitat	arable fields, gardens
Flowering	January–December
STEMS AND LEAVES	
Stem	low-growing, branches angled upwards
Root	fibrous
Hairs	almost throughout plant
Stipules	absent
Leaves	on alternate sides of stem or lower paired, 10–30mm, oval, blunt, coarsely toothed, base squarish
Leaf-stalk	shorter than blade
FLOWERS	
Position	solitary, from leaf-base
Bracts	absent
Type	♂
Size	8–12mm
Colour	bright blue, lower petal paler or white
Stalk	longer than leaf at base, bent down in fruit
Sepals	4, 5–7mm, unequal, oval, enlarging in fruit
Petals	4, 4–6mm, bases joined, upper broadest
Stamens	2, protruding
Stigma	1, tip swollen; style long
Ovary	1, 2-celled
FRUIT	
Type	2-lobed, flattened capsule, lobes spread apart
Size	5–10mm
Seeds	few, 1.5–1.8mm, oblong, one face hollow

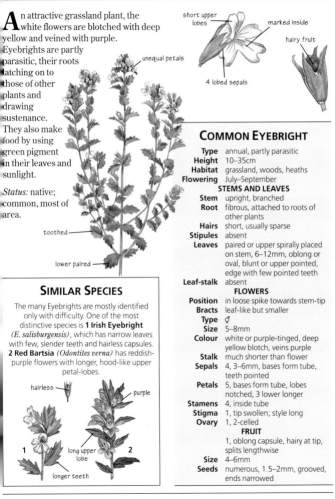

An attractive grassland plant, the white flowers are blotched with deep yellow and veined with purple. Eyebrights are partly parasitic, their roots latching on to those of other plants and drawing sustenance. They also make food by using green pigment in their leaves and sunlight.

Status: native; common, most of area.

short upper lobes

marked inside

hairy fruit

unequal petals

4 lobed sepals

toothed

lower paired

COMMON EYEBRIGHT

Type	annual, partly parasitic
Height	10–35cm
Habitat	grassland, woods, heaths
Flowering	July–September

STEMS AND LEAVES

Stem	upright, branched
Root	fibrous, attached to roots of other plants
Hairs	short, usually sparse
Stipules	absent
Leaves	paired or upper spirally placed on stem, 6–12mm, oblong or oval, blunt or upper pointed, edge with few pointed teeth
Leaf-stalk	absent

FLOWERS

Position	in loose spike towards stem-tip
Bracts	leaf-like but smaller
Type	♂
Size	5–8mm
Colour	white or purple-tinged, deep yellow blotch, veins purple
Stalk	much shorter than flower
Sepals	4, 3–6mm, bases form tube, teeth pointed
Petals	5, bases form tube, lobes notched, 3 lower longer
Stamens	4, inside tube
Stigma	1, tip swollen; style long
Ovary	1, 2-celled

FRUIT

	1, oblong capsule, hairy at tip, splits lengthwise
Size	4–6mm
Seeds	numerous, 1.5–2mm, grooved, ends narrowed

SIMILAR SPECIES

The many Eyebrights are mostly identified only with difficulty. One of the most distinctive species is **1 Irish Eyebright** (*E. salisburgensis*), which has narrow leaves with few, slender teeth and hairless capsules. **2 Red Bartsia** (*Odontites verna*) has reddish-purple flowers with longer, hood-like upper petal-lobes.

hairless

purple

long upper lobe

1

2

longer teeth

Marsh Lousewort *Pedicularis palustris*

A striking plant, especially in water-meadows, where its purplish, finely-divided foliage and pink flowers stand out. The species is partly parasitic, attaching itself to roots of grasses and deriving nourishment from them. Grazing animals were thought to catch liver-fluke from Louseworts but it is now known that both fluke and plant just flourish in the same places.

Status: native; fairly common, most of area.

fruit splits open

lobed sepals

hood-like

flowers towards stem-tip

4 teeth

hairy sepals

broad lower petals

hairless

deeply lobed

MARSH LOUSEWORT

Type	biennial or annual, partly parasitic
Height	8–60cm
Habitat	meadows, heaths; wet places
Flowering	May–September
STEMS AND LEAVES	
Stem	single, branched below
Root	fibrous, attached to roots of other plants
Hairs	almost absent
Stipules	absent
Leaves	on alternate sides of stem, 20–40mm, deeply divided into paired, toothed lobes, often tinged purple
Leaf-stalk	shorter than blade
FLOWERS	
Position	many in spike at stem-tip
Bracts	leaf-like but smaller
Type	♂
Size	20–25mm
Colour	purplish pink
Stalk	much shorter than flower
Sepals	5, joined, hairy, lobes unequal, toothed, tube swollen in fruit
Petals	5, 18–25mm, upper 2 lobes joined, hood-like, 2 teeth each side
Stamens	4, under upper petal-lobes
Stigma	1, tip swollen; style long
Ovary	1, 2-celled
FRUIT	
Type	1, capsule, curved, flattened, pointed
Size	10–12mm
Seeds	few, 2–3mm, oblong, with net-like pattern

SIMILAR SPECIES

The perennial **1 Lousewort** (*P. sylvatica*), of moors and heaths, is generally smaller with hairless sepals. **2 Leafy Lousewort** (*P. foliosa*), from mountains in the south-east of the area, has leafy spikes of pale yellow flowers.

hairless sepals

smaller

pale

1

larger

2

A plant of sunny, grassy places, with yellow, hooded flowers, but best known in fruit when the seeds rattle inside the capsule and papery sepal-tube. This is another partial parasite, some of its nourishment coming from grasses and other herbs through joined roots.

Status: native; common, most of area.

flowers towards stem-tip

hood-like

hides fruit

swollen, papery

broad sepal tube

paired

toothed

upright

YELLOW-RATTLE

Type	annual, partly parasitic
Height	12–50cm
Habitat	grassland, marshes, mountains
Flowering	May–August
STEMS AND LEAVES	
Stem	upright, usually black-spotted, sometimes branched
Root	fibrous, attached to those of other plants
Hairs	short, rough
Stipules	absent
Leaves	paired on stem, 10–50mm, oblong, toothed
Leaf-stalk	absent
FLOWERS	
Position	in spike at stem-tip
Bracts	triangular, leaf-like
Type	♂
Size	12–15mm
Colour	yellow or purple-tinged
Stalk	much shorter than flower
Sepals	4, 12–18mm, bases joined, flattened, enlarged in fruit, almost hairless
Petals	5, 12–15mm, bases form tube, upper 2 lobes joined, hood-like
Stamens	4, under upper petal-lobes
Stigma	1, tip swollen; style long
Ovary	1, 2-celled
FRUIT	
Type	1, rounded, flattened capsule, splits lengthwise
Size	10–12mm
Seeds	few, 4–5mm, flattened, with encircling wing

SIMILAR SPECIES

1 Greater Yellow-rattle (*R. angustifolius*) is a larger plant of arable fields, and has yellowish, long-toothed bracts and a curved petal-tube with longer upper lobes.
2 Yellow Bartsia (*Parentucellia viscosa*) is stickily hairy and the sepal-tube is not swollen. **3 Common Cow-wheat** (*Melampyrum pratense*), a woodland plant, also has a slender sepal-tube but the leaves are not toothed.

long teeth

sepals not swollen

narrow

sticky

Greater Broomrape *Orobanche rapum-genistae*

This curious plant is a parasite, deriving all sustenance from its host, usually a shrub of Broom or Gorse. It has no need of green pigment, so stems and scale-like leaves are a lurid yellow or purple, and give an impression of unhealthiness.

Status: native; fairly common, from south to southern Scotland.

hairy

pointed bract

no leaves

fruit splits open

not green

yellowish stigma

petals joined

unequal peta[l]

GREATER BROOMRAPE

Type	perennial, parasite
Height	20–80cm
Habitat	heaths, woodland clearings; mainly on Gorse or Broom
Flowering	May–July

STEMS AND LEAVES

Stem	single, unbranched, stout, yellowish or purple-tinged
Root	swollen, scaly; fibrous roots attach to other plants
Hairs	sticky, gland-tipped
Stipules	absent
Leaves	spirally around stem, 15–25mm, scale-like, spear-shaped, yellowish, pointed, edge unbroken
Leaf-stalk	absent

FLOWERS

Position	many in long, crowded spike at stem-tip
Bracts	long, slender, pointed
Type	♂
Size	20–25mm
Colour	pale yellow, tinged purple
Stalk	almost absent
Sepals	4, 8–15mm, bases joined, teeth unequal, slender
Petals	5, 20–25mm, bases form curved tube, lower 3 lobes bent downwards, upper short
Stamens	4, inside petal-tube
Stigma	1, 2-lobed, pale yellow
Ovary	1, 1-celled

FRUIT

Type	capsule, splits lengthwise
Size	10–14mm
Seeds	many, 0.3–0.4mm, dust-like

SIMILAR SPECIES

1 Common Broomrape *(O. minor)*, mainly on Clovers, is usually smaller, with fewer flowers and purple stigmas. **2 Toothwort** *(Lathraea squamaria)*, mainly on Hazel or Elm, has one-sided heads of pinkish flowers, broad bracts and equal sepal-teeth. **3 Yellow Bird's-nest** *(Monotropa hypopitys)* has yellow, nodding flowers and grows on decaying leaves in woodland.

purple stigma

nodding

3

1-sided

1

2

broad bracts

Pinguicula vulgaris **Common Butterwort**

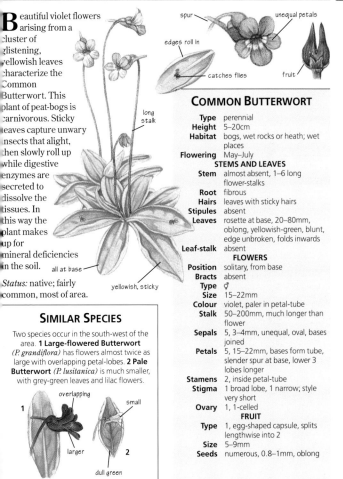

Beautiful violet flowers arising from a cluster of glistening, yellowish leaves characterize the Common Butterwort. This plant of peat-bogs is carnivorous. Sticky leaves capture unwary insects that alight, then slowly roll up while digestive enzymes are secreted to dissolve the tissues. In this way the plant makes up for mineral deficiencies in the soil.

Status: native; fairly common, most of area.

spur — unequal petals

edges roll in

catches flies

fruit

long stalk

all at base

yellowish, sticky

COMMON BUTTERWORT

Type	perennial
Height	5–20cm
Habitat	bogs, wet rocks or heath; wet places
Flowering	May–July
STEMS AND LEAVES	
Stem	almost absent, 1–6 long flower-stalks
Root	fibrous
Hairs	leaves with sticky hairs
Stipules	absent
Leaves	rosette at base, 20–80mm, oblong, yellowish-green, blunt, edge unbroken, folds inwards
Leaf-stalk	absent
FLOWERS	
Position	solitary, from base
Bracts	absent
Type	♂
Size	15–22mm
Colour	violet, paler in petal-tube
Stalk	50–200mm, much longer than flower
Sepals	5, 3–4mm, unequal, oval, bases joined
Petals	5, 15–22mm, bases form tube, slender spur at base, lower 3 lobes longer
Stamens	2, inside petal-tube
Stigma	1 broad lobe, 1 narrow; style very short
Ovary	1, 1-celled
FRUIT	
Type	1, egg-shaped capsule, splits lengthwise into 2
Size	5–9mm
Seeds	numerous, 0.8–1mm, oblong

SIMILAR SPECIES

Two species occur in the south-west of the area. **1 Large-flowered Butterwort** (*P. grandiflora*) has flowers almost twice as large with overlapping petal-lobes. **2 Pale Butterwort** (*P. lusitanica*) is much smaller, with grey-green leaves and lilac flowers.

overlapping

small

1

larger

2

dull green

Greater Bladderwort *Utricularia vulgaris*

Spikes of rich yellow flowers mark where this aquatic plant floats near the surface of the water. Finely-cut leaves bear small bladders, each a trap sprung when a tiny water-animal touches a bristle. A trap-door springs open and shut, sucking in the prey which is gradually digested.

Status: native; scattered, most of area.

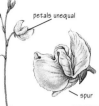

petals unequal

spur

animal-trapping bladders

capsule

long stem

bladders

SIMILAR SPECIES

Flowering is sporadic, making identification difficult. **1 Bladderwort** *(U. australis)* has flowers with a long upper lip and flatter lower lip. Other species have two sorts of leaf. **2 Lesser Bladderwort** *(U. minor)* lacks leaf-bristles and has a broad spur. **3 Intermediate Bladderwort** *(U. intermedia)* has bristle-edged leaves and a slender spur.

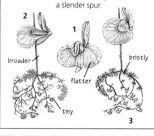

broader

flatter

2

1

bristly

tiny

3

GREATER BLADDERWORT

Type	perennial
Height	15–100cm
Habitat	ponds, lakes, ditches; still, often deep water
Flowering	July–August
STEMS AND LEAVES	
Stem	long, leafy, submerged, floats near surface
Root	absent
Hairs	absent
Stipules	absent
Leaves	spirally placed on stem, 20–25mm, finely cut, edges slightly toothed, bristly, some with tiny bladders
Leaf-stalk	shorter than blade
FLOWERS	
Position	2–8 in spike-like head above water, stalk 100–200mm
Bracts	shorter than flower-stalks
Type	☿
Size	12–18mm
Colour	deep yellow
Stalk	shorter than flower
Sepals	2, oval, slightly toothed
Petals	bases joined, with conical spur, lobes form 2 lips, fold of lower lip about equalling upper lip
Stamens	2, inside petal-tube
Stigma	flattened lobe and much smaller lobe; style short
Ovary	1, 1-celled
FRUIT	
Type	1, capsule, globular
Size	3–5mm
Seeds	many, 0.5–0.7mm, angular

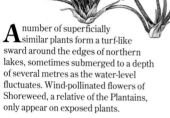

tuft of leaves   long stamens

♂ flower

slender

fruit hard

♀ flower

A number of superficially
similar plants form a turf-like
sward around the edges of northern
lakes, sometimes submerged to a depth
of several metres as the water-level
fluctuates. Wind-pollinated flowers of
Shoreweed, a relative of the Plantains,
only appear on exposed plants.

Status: native; most of area, more
common in north.

SIMILAR SPECIES

1 Mudwort (*Limosella aquatica*) has five
petals and short stamens. **2 Awlwort**
(*Subularia aquatica*), a relative of the
Cabbage, has spike-like heads of four-
petalled flowers and pod-like fruits. The most
attractive of these plants is **3 Water Lobelia**
(*Lobelia dortmanna*), the long-stalked heads
of white or lilac flowers with unequal petals.

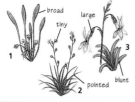

broad   large

tiny

1

2   pointed   blunt

3

SHOREWEED

Type	perennial
Height	15–100mm, rarely 250mm
Habitat	lakes, ponds; in or by lime-free water
Flowering	June–August

STEMS AND LEAVES

Stem	creeping, producing upright tufts of leaves
Root	rather thick
Hairs	absent
Stipules	absent
Leaves	in rosette, 15–100mm, rarely 250mm, slender, almost cylindrical, edge unbroken, base broad, sheaths stem
Leaf-stalk	absent

FLOWERS

Position	single ♂, sometimes several ♀ near base of stalked head
Bracts	oval, papery
Type 1	♂ with stamens
Type 2	♀ stalkless, with ovary
Size	5–6mm
Colour	whitish, translucent
Stalk	longer than flower
Sepals	3–4, edges papery, 3–5mm, oval or slender
Petals	3–4, 4–6mm, bases joined
Stamens	4, protruding, 10–20mm
Stigma	1; style long
Ovary	1, 1-celled

FRUIT

Type	1, dry, hard, oblong, enclosed by petal-tube
Size	1.5–2mm
Seeds	1, not released

Greater Plantain *Plantago major*

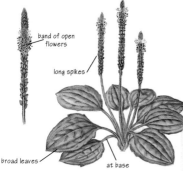

band of open flowers

long spikes

broad leaves

at base

4 petals

papery sepals

fruit opens

seed

A rosette of broad, tough leaves and long spikes of insignificant flowers are characteristic of the Greater Plantain. It is often a weed of lawns. The flowers are pollinated by the wind: anthers dangle from the flowers to shed pollen, and a long, roughened stigma catches airborne pollen. Sparrows and Finches eagerly seek the seeds in the long fruiting-heads.

Status: native; common, throughout area.

SIMILAR SPECIES

Hoary Plantain *(Plantago media)*, a more attractive plant, has leaves of similar shape but with soft, whitish hairs and shorter, creamy-white flower-heads with lilac stamens.

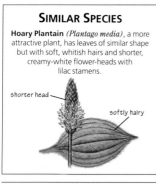

shorter head

softly hairy

GREATER PLANTAIN

Type	perennial
Height	10–15cm, rarely to 50cm
Habitat	cultivated and waste ground, grassy places
Flowering	May–September
STEMS AND LEAVES	
Stem	very short, stout; flower-stalks long
Root	thick, whitish
Hairs	absent or short
Stipules	absent
Leaves	rosette at base, 100–300mm, oval or elliptical, blunt, edge unbroken or slightly toothed, base squarish
Leaf-stalk	about equalling blade
FLOWERS	
Position	numerous, in long, slender, stalked, often curved spike
Bracts	shorter than flower, brown
Type	♂
Size	2–3mm
Colour	yellowish-white
Stalk	absent
Sepals	4, 1.5–2.5mm, oval, almost equal, edges papery
Petals	4, 2–3mm, bases form tube, lobes oval
Stamens	4, protruding
Stigma	1, slender
Ovary	1, 2-celled
FRUIT	
Type	1, capsule, oblong, top splits away
Size	2–4mm
Seeds	6–13, 1–1.5mm, elliptical, flattened

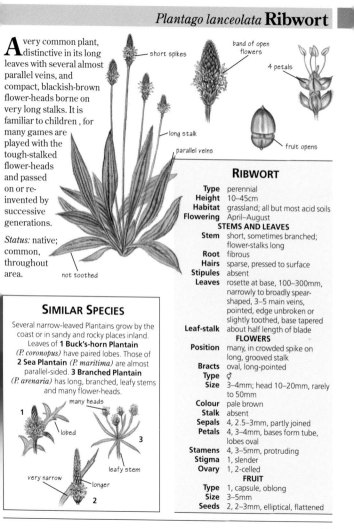

A very common plant, distinctive in its long leaves with several almost parallel veins, and compact, blackish-brown flower-heads borne on very long stalks. It is familiar to children , for many games are played with the tough-stalked flower-heads and passed on or re-invented by successive generations.

Status: native; common, throughout area.

short spikes

band of open flowers

4 petals

long stalk

parallel veins

fruit opens

not toothed

SIMILAR SPECIES

Several narrow-leaved Plantains grow by the coast or in sandy and rocky places inland. Leaves of **1 Buck's-horn Plantain** (*P. coronopus*) have paired lobes. Those of **2 Sea Plantain** (*P. maritima*) are almost parallel-sided. **3 Branched Plantain** (*P. arenaria*) has long, branched, leafy stems and many flower-heads.

many heads

1

lobed

3

leafy stem

very narrow

longer

2

RIBWORT

Type	perennial
Height	10–45cm
Habitat	grassland; all but most acid soils
Flowering	April–August

STEMS AND LEAVES

Stem	short, sometimes branched; flower-stalks long
Root	fibrous
Hairs	sparse, pressed to surface
Stipules	absent
Leaves	rosette at base, 100–300mm, narrowly to broadly spear-shaped, 3–5 main veins, pointed, edge unbroken or slightly toothed, base tapered
Leaf-stalk	about half length of blade

FLOWERS

Position	many, in crowded spike on long, grooved stalk
Bracts	oval, long-pointed
Type	♂
Size	3–4mm; head 10–20mm, rarely to 50mm
Colour	pale brown
Stalk	absent
Sepals	4, 2.5–3mm, partly joined
Petals	4, 3–4mm, bases form tube, lobes oval
Stamens	4, 3–5mm, protruding
Stigma	1, slender
Ovary	1, 2-celled

FRUIT

Type	1, capsule, oblong
Size	3–5mm
Seeds	2, 2–3mm, elliptical, flattened

Honeysuckle *Lonicera periclymenum*

Sweet-scented Honeysuckle is a favourite hedgerow plant, its compact heads of creamy, trumpet-shaped flowers often flushed with red or purple. In Autumn it is also conspicuous, with its clusters of crimson berries. Night-flying moths are attracted by the scent, which is strongest at dusk, and pollinate the flowers as they seek nectar.

Status: native; common, most of area except extreme north.

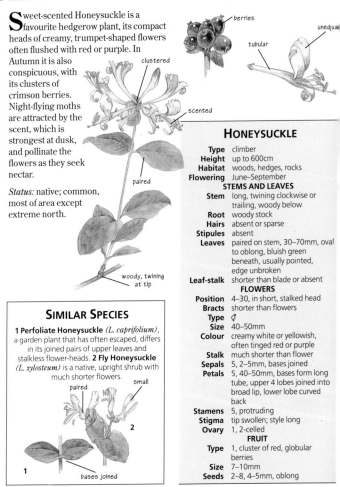

berries

tubular

unequal

clustered

scented

paired

woody, twining at tip

SIMILAR SPECIES

1 Perfoliate Honeysuckle (*L. caprifolium*), a garden plant that has often escaped, differs in its joined pairs of upper leaves and stalkless flower-heads. **2 Fly Honeysuckle** (*L. xylosteum*) is a native, upright shrub with much shorter flowers.

paired

small

2

1

bases joined

HONEYSUCKLE

Type	climber
Height	up to 600cm
Habitat	woods, hedges, rocks
Flowering	June–September
STEMS AND LEAVES	
Stem	long, twining clockwise or trailing, woody below
Root	woody stock
Hairs	absent or sparse
Stipules	absent
Leaves	paired on stem, 30–70mm, oval to oblong, bluish green beneath, usually pointed, edge unbroken
Leaf-stalk	shorter than blade or absent
FLOWERS	
Position	4–30, in short, stalked head
Bracts	shorter than flowers
Type	♂
Size	40–50mm
Colour	creamy white or yellowish, often tinged red or purple
Stalk	much shorter than flower
Sepals	5, 2–5mm, bases joined
Petals	5, 40–50mm, bases form long tube, upper 4 lobes joined into broad lip, lower lobe curved back
Stamens	5, protruding
Stigma	tip swollen; style long
Ovary	1, 2-celled
FRUIT	
Type	1, cluster of red, globular berries
Size	7–10mm
Seeds	2–8, 4–5mm, oblong

Adoxa moschatellina **Moschatel**

4 petals
5 petals
5 flowers

stalk droops

long stalk

berry-like fruits

leaflets in 3s

This curious species often lurks unnoticed at the base of a hedgerow, its greenish-yellow flowers lost against the delicate, rather Fern-like foliage. It is worth searching out the plant because the flower-heads have a unique arrangement: four flowers face outwards and a single flower faces upwards. Such an unusual arrangement has earned this species the picturesque alternative common name of 'Townhall Clock'. The top flower has four petals but the side flowers have five. The flowers have a musk-like scent, particularly in the evening. No native plant resembles Moschatel at all closely, so its relationship to other species is obscure. Some place it with the Fumitories because of a vague similarity in the foliage, but the form of the flowers is closer to that of Honeysuckle.

Status: native; rather scattered, most of area except many islands, mainly in mountains in south.

Similar species: none.

MOSCHATEL

Type	perennial
Height	5–10cm
Habitat	woods, hedges, rocks
Flowering	April–May

STEMS AND LEAVES

Stem	upright, unbranched
Root	creeping, scaly, under-ground stem
Hairs	absent
Stipules	absent
Leaves	basal with 2–3 on stem, 8–30mm, divided into threes, leaflets often 3–lobed, pale green, blunt
Leaf-stalk	basal long, upper short

FLOWERS

Position	5, head 6–9mm, long-stalked, at stem-tip
Bracts	absent
Type	⚥, slightly scented
Size	6–8mm
Colour	yellowish green
Stalk	absent
Sepals	2–3, 1.5–2mm, oval
Petals	4–5, 2–3.5mm, bases joined, lobes oval, spreading widely
Stamens	4–5, divided and appearing as 8 or 10
Stigmas	4–5; styles short
Ovary	1, partly below sepals, 3–5-celled

FRUIT

Type	1, globular, berry-like, green, rarely produced
Size	3–5mm
Seeds	1, 2–3mm, oval, flattened

183

Common Cornsalad *Valerianella locusta*

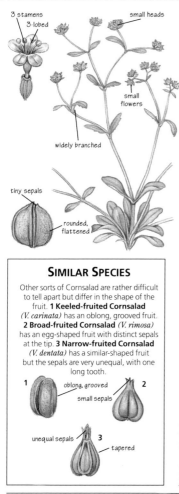

3 stamens
3-lobed
small heads
small flowers
widely branched
tiny sepals
rounded, flattened

An easily overlooked, rather weedy plant that has compact heads of tiny flowers. The plant was formerly used and sometimes cultivated as a salad plant, especially in France.

Status: native; scattered through most of area, rarer in north.

SIMILAR SPECIES

Other sorts of Cornsalad are rather difficult to tell apart but differ in the shape of the fruit. **1 Keeled-fruited Cornsalad** (*V. carinata*) has an oblong, grooved fruit. **2 Broad-fruited Cornsalad** (*V. rimosa*) has an egg-shaped fruit with distinct sepals at the tip. **3 Narrow-fruited Cornsalad** (*V. dentata*) has a similar-shaped fruit but the sepals are very unequal, with one long tooth.

1 oblong, grooved
small sepals
2
unequal sepals
3
tapered

COMMON CORNSALAD

Type	annual
Height	7–40cm
Habitat	cultivated or waste ground, rocks, dunes; dry soils
Flowering	April–June
STEMS AND LEAVES	
Stem	upright, slender, brittle, angular, widely branched
Root	fibrous
Hairs	stem minutely bristly
Stipules	absent
Leaves	basal or paired on stem, 20–70mm, oblong to spoon-shaped, mostly blunt, edge unbroken or some toothed
Leaf-stalk	shorter than blade
FLOWERS	
Position	compact heads at stem-tips, sometimes single flowers in forks of branches
Bracts	smaller than leaves
Type	♂
Size	2–3mm
Colour	pale lilac
Stalk	absent
Sepals	5, 0.1–0.3mm, indistinct
Petals	5, 2–3mm, bases joined, funnel-shaped, lobes spreading widely
Stamens	3, protruding
Stigma	3-lobed; style long
Ovary	1, below petals, 3-celled
FRUIT	
Type	1, dry, nearly circular, flattened, smooth
Size	2–2.5mm
Seeds	1, not released

Valeriana officinalis **Common Valerian**

A tall, conspicuous plant of river banks and damp ditches, its leaves cut into narrow leaflets and broad heads of lilac flowers. This plant still has several medicinal uses. Extracts from the roots have a sedative effect and were used for epilepsy, headaches and insomnia, although the drug can be addictive.

Status: native; throughout area.

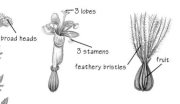

broad heads

3 lobes

3 stamens

feathery bristles

fruit

paired leaflets

toothed

COMMON VALERIAN

Type	perennial
Height	20–150cm, rarely 240cm
Habitat	grassy places, scrub; mostly damp soils
Flowering	June–August

STEMS AND LEAVES

Stem	upright, rarely short, creeping stems at base
Root	short underground stem
Hairs	mostly below, absent above
Stipules	absent
Leaves	paired on stem, 25–200mm, paired, spear-shaped, toothed leaflets, leaflet at tip
Leaf-stalk	shorter than blade, upper almost absent

FLOWERS

Position	many, in compact, branched, rounded heads at stem-tips
Bracts	shorter than flowers
Type	♂
Size	4–5mm
Colour	pinkish lilac
Stalk	more or less absent
Sepals	15 lobes, up to 6mm, rolled inwards, enlarging, becoming feathery in fruit
Petals	5, 4–5mm, bases form tube, side swollen, lobes oblong
Stamens	3, protruding, white
Stigma	1, 3-lobed; style long
Ovary	1, apparently 1-celled

FRUIT

Type	nut-like, oval, flattish, with feathery parachute
Size	2.5–4mm
Seeds	1, not released

SIMILAR SPECIES

1 Marsh Valerian *(V. dioica)* has rounded lower leaves on the separate male and female plants. **2 Red Valerian** *(Centranthus ruber)* is an introduced plant which is very common on cliffs and walls in the west of the area. It has broad, bluish leaves and spurred flowers with one stamen.

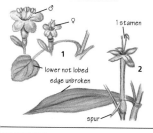

♂   ♀

1 stamen

1

lower not lobed

edge unbroken

2

spur

Teasel *Dipsacus fullonum*

A striking plant, with large, spiny heads that bear rings of rosy-purple flowers. Bases of the stem-leaves are joined and fill with water, often drowning small insects. It has been speculated that the Teasel could benefit from these animals and might be carnivorous, although tropical plants use similar water-traps to protect flowers from insect attack. Spiny heads of Teasels have long been used to raise the nap on fabric.

Status: native; often common, most of area except parts of north.

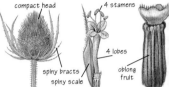

compact head · 4 stamens · 4 lobes · spiny bracts · spiny scale · oblong fruit

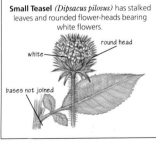

bases joined · paired leaves

SIMILAR SPECIES

Small Teasel *(Dipsacus pilosus)* has stalked leaves and rounded flower-heads bearing white flowers.

white · round head · bases not joined

TEASEL

Type	biennial
Height	up to 200cm
Habitat	grassy places, river banks; often on clay soils
Flowering	July–August
STEMS AND LEAVES	
Stem	short in first year, then upright, with prickly angles, branched above
Root	stout, yellowish tap-root
Hairs	only scattered prickles
Stipules	absent
Leaves	rosette at base or paired on stem, oblong to spear-shaped, edge unbroken or toothed, bases of upper stem-leaves joined
Leaf-stalk	only on basal leaves
FLOWERS	
Position	numerous in conical, blunt, upright, long-stalked heads
Bracts	long, spiny under head; spine-tipped under flower
Type	♂
Size	8–12mm; heads 30–80mm
Colour	rosy purple, rarely white
Stalk	absent
Sepals	1–1.5mm, joined, fringed
Petals	4, 8–12mm, bases form long tube; lobes unequal
Stamens	4, protruding
Stigma	1; style long
Ovary	1, under petals, 1-celled
FRUIT	
Type	1, nut-like, oblong, 4-angled, with sepals at tip
Size	4–5mm
Seeds	1, not released

Knautia arvensis **Field Scabious**

broad head

bristles

hardly domed

fruit

An attractive Summer-flowering meadow plant, its broad, bluish flower-heads are visible from a distance. Species of Scabious were used to treat scabies, hence the common name, and many other afflictions of the skin including sores caused by bubonic plague.

Status: native; most of area except many northern islands, most common in south.

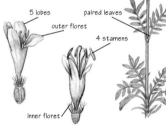

5 lobes

paired leaves

outer floret

4 stamens

inner floret

FIELD SCABIOUS

Type	perennial
Height	25–100cm
Habitat	grassy places; dry soils
Flowering	July–September
STEMS AND LEAVES	
Stem	upright, branched
Root	tap-root
Hairs	long, stiffish, throughout, angled downwards on stem
Stipules	absent
Leaves	basal rosette or paired on stem, lowest to 300mm long, spear-shaped, upper smaller, with paired lobes, pointed, edge unbroken or toothed
Leaf-stalk	shorter than blade
FLOWERS	
Position	numerous, in rounded, flattish, long-stalked heads
Bracts	oval, only under head, shorter than flowers
Type	♂or♀, outer larger
Size	8–14, heads 30–40mm
Colour	bluish lilac
Stalk	absent beneath flowers, long under heads
Sepals	2–4mm, 8 slender teeth
Petals	4, 7–14mm, bases form tube, lobes unequal
Stamens	4, protruding, pink
Stigma	1, notched; style long
Ovary	1, below petals, 1-celled
FRUIT	
Type	1, nut-like, cylindrical, hairy
Size	5–6mm
Seeds	1, not released

SIMILAR SPECIES

Other species have more elongated heads with tiny bracts between the flowers and only five sepal-teeth. **1 Small Scabious** (*Scabiosa columbaria*) has five-lobed flowers and divided leaves; **2 Devil's-bit Scabious** (*Succisa pratensis*) has four-lobed flowers, all of the same size, and most leaves with unbroken edges.

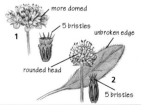

more domed

5 bristles

1

rounded head

unbroken edge

2

5 bristles

Nettle-leaved Bellflower *Campanula trachelium*

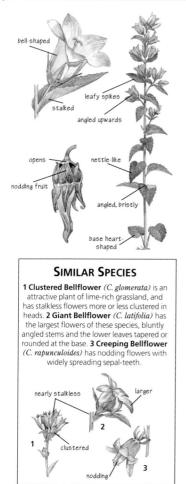

bell-shaped

leafy spikes

stalked

angled upwards

opens

nettle-like

nodding fruit

angled, bristly

base heart-shaped

A tall plant of hedgerows and woodland margins, with toothed, nettle-like leaves and a spike of bluish, bell-shaped flowers. It was widely used for treating throat infections.

Status: native; scattered throughout most of area, except many islands.

NETTLE-LEAVED BELLFLOWER

Type	perennial
Height	50–100cm
Habitat	woods, hedges; usually clay soils
Flowering	July–September
STEMS AND LEAVES	
Stem	upright, sharply angled, sometimes branched, red-tinged, with yellowish sap
Root	tap-root
Hairs	stiff, leaves rough
Stipules	absent
Leaves	spirally placed on stem, up to 100mm, coarsely toothed; lower oval or triangular, base heart-shaped, upper oblong, pointed
Leaf-stalk	shorter than blade
FLOWERS	
Position	long head, 1–4 on branches
Bracts	narrow
Type	⚥, angled upwards
Size	25–50mm
Colour	purplish blue
Stalk	shorter than flower
Sepals	5, 13–15mm, bases joined, teeth triangular, pointed
Petals	5, 25–50mm, equal, joined, bell-shaped, lobes pointed
Stamens	5, long, soon withering
Stigmas	3; style long
Ovary	1, below sepals, 3-celled
FRUIT	
Type	nodding capsule, half spherical, pores at base
Size	6–8mm
Seeds	numerous, 0.6–0.8mm, oblong

SIMILAR SPECIES

1 Clustered Bellflower *(C. glomerata)* is an attractive plant of lime-rich grassland, and has stalkless flowers more or less clustered in heads. **2 Giant Bellflower** *(C. latifolia)* has the largest flowers of these species, bluntly angled stems and the lower leaves tapered or rounded at the base. **3 Creeping Bellflower** *(C. rapunculoides)* has nodding flowers with widely spreading sepal-teeth.

nearly stalkless

larger

clustered

nodding

bell-shaped

fruit opens

Dainty, nodding, pale blue bells of the Harebell are a common sight on dry, grassy banks in Summer. In Scotland the plant is called 'Bluebell', although a different species bears the name in England. Upper and lower leaves of this plant are so different that they appear to belong to different species.

Status: native; usually common, most of area.

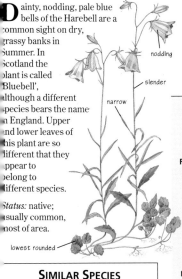

nodding

slender

narrow

lowest rounded

HAREBELL

Type	perennial
Height	15–40cm, rarely 70cm
Habitat	grassy places, dunes; mostly dry soils
Flowering	July–September
STEMS AND LEAVES	
Stem	low-growing, turning upright to flower
Root	creeping underground stems
Hairs	absent above, short below
Stipules	absent
Leaves	on alternate sides of stem; lower 5–15mm, oval to nearly circular, toothed, base heart-shaped; upper narrow, straight-sided
Leaf-stalk	lower much longer than blade; upper absent
FLOWERS	
Position	solitary at stem-tip or few in widely branched head
Bracts	small, straight-sided
Type	♂
Size	10–20mm
Colour	blue, rarely white
Stalk	long, slender, nodding
Sepals	5, 5–8mm, slender, spreading apart
Petals	5, 10–20mm, joined, bell-shaped, lobes broadly oval
Stamens	5, inside tube
Stigmas	3; style long
Ovary	1, below sepals, 3-celled
FRUIT	
Type	capsule, cone-shaped, nodding, pores at base
Size	4–6mm
Seeds	numerous, 0.6–0.8mm, oblong

SIMILAR SPECIES

The smaller relatives of the Bellflowers include **1 Venus's-looking-glass** (*Legousia hybrida*), a cornfield annual with upright, purplish flowers and long, cylindrical capsules. **2 Ivy-leaved Bellflower** (*Wahlenbergia hederacea*) is a creeping plant of boggy places, with small, Ivy-shaped leaves and nodding, pale blue flowers.

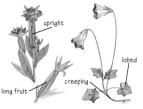

upright

lobed

creeping

long fruit

189

Sheep's-bit *Jasione montana*

On dry, grassy banks and heathland, Sheep's-bit bears its rounded heads of pale blue flowers at the end of almost leafless stems. Although the flower-heads resemble those of Scabious species, this is a relative of the Bellflowers, and has joined stamens and capsules that release seeds.

Status: native; scattered throughout area, often common.

heads of flowers

long stem

narrow

5 petals

fruit opens

thin sepals

small leaves

hairy

not toothed

SIMILAR SPECIES

Rampions have similar flower-heads but with curved buds and almost hairless stems and leaves. **1 Round-headed Rampion** *(Phyteuma orbiculare)* has short heads of violet flowers and occurs in the south of the area. **2 Spiked Rampion** *(P. spicatum)* is more widespread and has longer heads of yellowish flowers.

rounded

longer

1

2 yellow

narrow base

hairless

SHEEP'S-BIT

Type	biennial, sometimes annual
Height	5–50cm
Habitat	grassy places, heaths, cliffs; lime-free soils
Flowering	May–August
STEMS AND LEAVES	
Stem	low-growing, turns upright to flower, some branched
Root	fibrous
Hairs	more or less throughout
Stipules	absent
Leaves	spirally placed on lower part of stem, to 50mm, narrowly oblong or spear-shaped, mostly blunt, edge straight or wavy
Leaf-stalk	lower short, upper absent
FLOWERS	
Position	up to 200 in almost globular head at stem-tip
Bracts	many, oval below head
Type	♂
Size	4–6mm; head 5–35mm
Colour	blue, rarely white
Stalk	absent; head long-stalked
Sepals	5, 1.5–2.5mm, bases joined, teeth thin
Petals	5, 4–6mm, bases joined, narrow lobes spread apart
Stamens	5, elongated, joined
Stigmas	2; style long, protruding
Ovary	1, below petals, 2-celled
FRUIT	
Type	1, capsule, egg-shaped, sepals attached, opens by 2 short teeth
Size	3–4mm
Seeds	numerous, c0.5mm, glossy

This handsome, purple and yellow Daisy is commonly encountered in salt-marshes, where it covers extensive areas. Most plants have strap-shaped outer florets, but some only have the yellow inner florets. Sea Aster was formerly cultivated and used as a wound-herb.

Status: native; common around coasts of region.

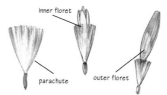

inner floret

parachute

outer floret

mostly have outer florets

slightly succulent

upright

SEA ASTER

Type	perennial
Height	15–100cm
Habitat	salt-marsh, sea-cliffs, rocks; salty soils
Flowering	July–October
STEMS AND LEAVES	
Stem	upright, stout, branched
Root	short underground stem
Hairs	mostly absent
Stipules	absent
Leaves	spirally placed on stem, 70–120mm, fleshy, edge unbroken or hardly toothed, lower spear-shaped, tapered upper oblong, broad-based
Leaf-stalk	long below, absent above
FLOWERS	
Position	daisy-like heads of florets surrounded by bracts
Bracts	papery-edged around head; none between florets
Type 1	inner ⚥, 7–8mm, tubular
Type 2	outer florets ♀ usually 10–30, 9–12mm, strap-shaped
Size	heads 8–20mm
Colour	yellow and purplish blue
Stalk	absent; short under heads
Sepals	a ring of hairs
Petals	5, 8–12mm, joined, tubular, lobes equal or very unequal
Stamens	5, joined into tube
Stigma	1, 2-lobed; style long
Ovary	1, below petals, 1-celled
FRUIT	
Type	nut-like, flattened, hairy, with parachute of hairs
Size	5–6mm
Seeds	1, not released

SIMILAR SPECIES

Several species of **Michaelmas-daisy** are grown in gardens and commonly escape. Perhaps the most common is **1** *Aster novi-belgii*, with broad-based leaves and mostly bluish outer florets. **2** *Aster lanceolatus* has narrower leaves with tapered bases and thin, white or bluish outer florets.

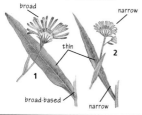

broad

narrow

thin

1

2

broad-based

narrow

Hemp-agrimony *Eupatorium cannabinum*

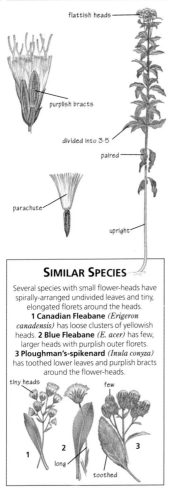

flattish heads

purplish bracts

divided into 3-5

paired

parachute

upright

A tall plant of riverbanks, with broad, fluffy heads of reddish or pink flowers. Hemp-agrimony has its small flower-heads clustered together and in sunny weather the whole top of the plant becomes alive with butterflies.

Status: native; common, most of area except far north.

SIMILAR SPECIES

Several species with small flower-heads have spirally-arranged undivided leaves and tiny, elongated florets around the heads.
1 Canadian Fleabane *(Erigeron canadensis)* has loose clusters of yellowish heads. **2 Blue Fleabane** *(E. acer)* has few, larger heads with purplish outer florets.
3 Ploughman's-spikenard *(Inula conyza)* has toothed lower leaves and purplish bracts around the flower-heads.

tiny heads

few

1

long

2

3

toothed

HEMP-AGRIMONY

Type	perennial
Height	30–120cm, rarely 175cm
Habitat	banks of rivers, streams, marshes, woods; damp places
Flowering	July–September
STEMS AND LEAVES	
Stem	upright, few branches
Root	woody stock
Hairs	short, almost throughout
Stipules	absent
Leaves	paired on stem, to 100mm, divided into 3, rarely 5, elliptical parts, pointed, toothed; lowest undivided
Leaf-stalk	much shorter than blade
FLOWERS	
Position	heads of 5–6 tiny flowers (florets) surrounded by bracts, in broad, flattish clusters
Bracts	purplish around head; none between florets
Type	florets ♂, 4.5–7mm, tubular
Size	heads 5–8mm
Colour	pale reddish purple or pink
Stalk	absent; short under heads
Sepals	a ring of hairs
Petals	5, joined, tubular, lobes equal
Stamens	5, joined into tube
Stigma	1, 2-lobed; style long
Ovary	1, below petals, 1-celled
FRUIT	
Type	1, dry, nut-like, 5-angled, with parachute of hairs
Size	2.5–3mm
Seeds	1, not released

Solidago virgaurea **Goldenrod**

This late-flowering plant is common in hilly places on dry grassland, cliffs and among rocks, but is rarely seen in lowland areas of the south. Long clusters of golden-yellow flower-heads contrast with the dark foliage and often blackish stems. Goldenrod was widely used as a wound-herb and was formerly in great demand.

Status: native; almost throughout area, sometimes common.

few long florets

outer floret

inner floret

small parachute

branched

upright, leafy

fruit ridged

heads of florets

SIMILAR SPECIES

Canadian Goldenrod *(S. canadensis)* has many more, smaller flower-heads, arranged on almost horizontal branches. This garden plant has often escaped and can be abundant around towns on railway embankments and disused sidings.

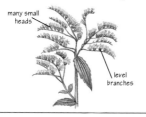

many small heads

level branches

GOLDENROD

Type	perennial
Height	5–75cm, rarely 100cm
Habitat	grassy places, cliffs, rocks, woods; dry soils
Flowering	July–September

STEMS AND LEAVES

Stem	upright, branched above
Root	stout stock
Hairs	absent or short
Leaves	spirally placed on stem, 20–100mm, rarely 300mm, oval to elliptical, pointed, toothed
Leaf-stalk	short or absent

FLOWERS

Position	daisy-like heads of tiny flowers (florets) surrounded by bracts
Bracts	4.5–8mm, narrow, yellowish green around head; none between florets
Type 1	inner florets ♂, 10–30, 4–6mm, tubular
Type 2	outer florets ♀, 6–12, 6–9mm, strap-shaped
Size	heads 8–20mm
Colour	yellow
Stalk	absent; short under heads
Sepals	a ring of hairs
Petals	5, joined, tubular
Stamens	5, joined into tube
Stigma	1, 2-lobed; style long
Ovary	1, below petals, 1-celled

FRUIT

Type	1, dry, nut-like, ribbed, with parachute of hairs
Size	3–4mm
Seeds	1, not released

Daisy *Bellis perennis*

many outer florets

Inner floret

all from base

outer floret

no parachute

from base

Familiar to children as a favourite flower for picking, and the raw material for daisy-chains, this plant is also known to gardeners as a pernicious weed that is almost impossible to eradicate from lawns. The flower-heads, carried singly above a rosette of leaves, close at night or in dull weather and provide the origin of the common name ('day's-eye').

Status: native; very common, throughout area.

SIMILAR SPECIES

Mexican Fleabane (*Erigeron mucronatus*) has flower-heads similar to the Daisy, but longer, branched stems with small leaves. Often escaping from cultivation, this plant forms small, bushy mounds on old walls.

narrow outer florets

branched stem

small

DAISY

Type	perennial
Height	3–20cm
Habitat	short grassland
Flowering	March–October
STEMS AND LEAVES	
Stem	short; flower-heads stalked
Root	stout, fibrous; short stock
Hairs	rather sparse
Stipules	absent
Leaves	rosette at base, 20–40mm, rarely 80mm, oval to spoon-shaped, rounded, toothed
Leaf-stalk	shorter than blade
FLOWERS	
Position	solitary heads of tiny flowers (florets) surrounded by bracts
Bracts	3–5mm, oblong, blunt around head; none between florets
Type 1	inner florets ⚥, 2–3mm, tubular
Type 2	outer florets ♀, 4–8mm, strap-shaped
Size	heads 16–25mm
Colour	inner florets yellow, outer white, often tinged red
Stalk	absent; 3–20mm under heads
Sepals	a ring of hairs
Petals	5, joined, tubular, lobes equal or very unequal
Stamens	5, joined into tube
Stigma	1, 2-lobed; style long
Ovary	1, below petals, 1-celled
FRUIT	
Type	dry, nut-like, flattened, hairy, without parachute
Size	1.5–2mm
Seeds	1, not released

Antennaria dioica **Mountain Everlasting**

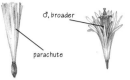

σ. broader

parachute

♀, slender

σ

petal-like bracts

silvery under

A small plant of mountains, or lower altitudes in the north. The flower-heads are enclosed by pink or white papery bracts which keep their form and colour after drying, hence the common name. Male and female flowers are on separate plants.

Status: native; much of area, most common in north, mostly in mountains in south.

SIMILAR SPECIES

Other species do not have male and female plants. **1 Everlasting** (*Helichrysum arenarium*), of dry, sandy places in the south-east, has almost globular, yellow or orange flower-heads. **2 Pearly Everlasting** (*Anaphalis margaritacea*), an escaped garden plant, is more robust and has pearly-white bracts.

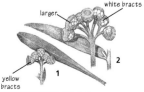

white bracts

larger

2

yellow bracts

1

MOUNTAIN EVERLASTING

Type	perennial
Height	5–20cm
Habitat	grassland, rocky slopes; dry, sandy or stony places
Flowering	June–July
STEMS AND LEAVES	
Stem	creeping, mat-forming; flowering stems upright
Root	woody stock, stems root
Hairs	woolly except above leaves
Stipules	absent
Leaves	basal or spiral on stem, 5–40mm, lower oval, broad-tipped, upper narrow, upright, edge unbroken
Leaf-stalk	short or absent
FLOWERS	
Position	σ and ♀ on different plants; 2–8 daisy-like heads of florets
Bracts	many under head, woolly-based, papery, σ broad, petal-like; ♀ narrow; none between florets
Type 1	σ, 4–5mm, funnel-shaped
Type 2	♀, 6–7mm, very slender
Size	σ heads 8–12mm; ♀ 5–7mm
Colour	white or pink
Stalk	absent; short under heads
Sepals	hair-like; σ thick-tipped
Petals	5, tubular, lobes equal
Stamens	5, joined into tube
Stigma	1, 2-lobed; style long
Ovary	1, below petals, 1-celled
FRUIT	
Type	nut-like, with parachute
Size	1–1.5mm
Seeds	1, not released

195

Common Fleabane *Pulicaria dysenterica*

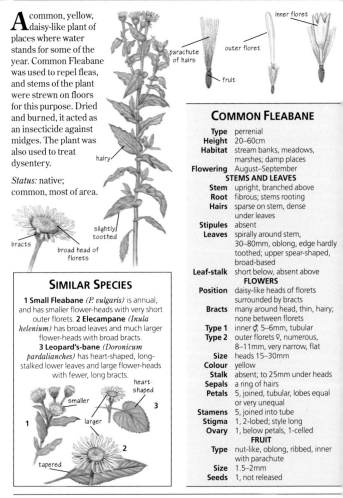

A common, yellow, daisy-like plant of places where water stands for some of the year. Common Fleabane was used to repel fleas, and stems of the plant were strewn on floors for this purpose. Dried and burned, it acted as an insecticide against midges. The plant was also used to treat dysentery.

Status: native; common, most of area.

parachute of hairs

fruit

inner floret

outer floret

hairy

slightly toothed

bracts

broad head of florets

SIMILAR SPECIES

1 Small Fleabane (*P. vulgaris*) is annual, and has smaller flower-heads with very short outer florets. **2 Elecampane** (*Inula helenium*) has broad leaves and much larger flower-heads with broad bracts.
3 Leopard's-bane (*Doronicum pardalianches*) has heart-shaped, long-stalked lower leaves and large flower-heads with fewer, long bracts.

smaller

larger

heart-shaped

tapered

1   2   3

COMMON FLEABANE

Type	perennial
Height	20–60cm
Habitat	stream banks, meadows, marshes; damp places
Flowering	August–September

STEMS AND LEAVES

Stem	upright, branched above
Root	fibrous; stems rooting
Hairs	sparse on stem, dense under leaves
Stipules	absent
Leaves	spirally around stem, 30–80mm, oblong, edge hardly toothed; upper spear-shaped, broad-based
Leaf-stalk	short below, absent above

FLOWERS

Position	daisy-like heads of florets surrounded by bracts
Bracts	many around head, thin, hairy; none between florets
Type 1	inner ♂, 5–6mm, tubular
Type 2	outer florets ♀, numerous, 8–11mm, very narrow, flat
Size	heads 15–30mm
Colour	yellow
Stalk	absent; to 25mm under heads
Sepals	a ring of hairs
Petals	5, joined, tubular, lobes equal or very unequal
Stamens	5, joined into tube
Stigma	1, 2-lobed; style long
Ovary	1, below petals, 1-celled

FRUIT

Type	nut-like, oblong, ribbed, inner with parachute
Size	1.5–2mm
Seeds	1, not released

A waterside plant, often disregarded because the flower-heads lack the usual outer florets of daisy-relatives, and soon fade to brown. A variant with outer florets is much more attractive, and has flower-heads almost twice as large. Small, barbed bristles on the fruits stick to passing animals and are spread to new localities.

Status: native; most of area, rarer in north.

nodding

outer bracts leafy

paired

inner bracts

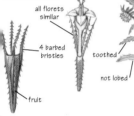

all florets similar

4 barbed bristles

toothed

not lobed

fruit

NODDING BUR-MARIGOLD

Type	annual
Height	8–60cm
Habitat	ponds, streams; wet places
Flowering	July–September
STEMS AND LEAVES	
Stem	upright, branched above
Root	fibrous
Hairs	absent or sparse
Stipules	absent
Leaves	paired on stem, 40–150mm, spear-shaped, pointed, toothed
Leaf-stalk	absent
FLOWERS	
Position	daisy-like heads of florets enclosed by bracts, nodding
Bracts	2 rows around head, outer leaf-like, inner oval, papery, dark-streaked; scale-like between florets
Type 1	inner florets ☿, many, 6–7mm, tubular
Type 2	outer rarely present, sterile, 10–12mm, flattened
Size	heads 15–25mm, rarely 45mm
Colour	yellow
Stalk	absent; long under heads
Sepals	4, bristle-like
Petals	5, joined, tubular, lobes equal, rarely very unequal
Stamens	5, joined into tube
Stigma	1, 2-lobed; style long
Ovary	1, below petals, 1-celled
FRUIT	
Type	nut-like, 4-angled, tip with 4 barbed bristles
Size	5–6mm
Seeds	1, not released

SIMILAR SPECIES

Two other species have divided leaves, upright flowers and fruits with two bristles. **1 Trifid Bur-marigold** *(B. tripartita)* has mostly three-lobed leaves and barbed angles on the fruits. **2 Beggarticks** *(B. frondosa)* has mostly five-lobed leaves and almost smooth-angled fruits.

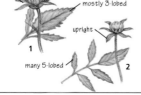

upright

mostly 3-lobed

upright

1

many 5-lobed

2

Yarrow *Achillea millefolium*

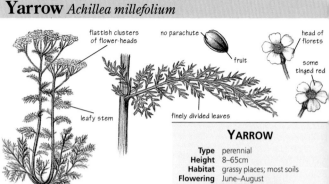

flattish clusters of flower-heads

no parachute

fruit

head of florets

some tinged red

leafy stem

finely divided leaves

A common plant of road-verges, easily identified by the broad, flat clusters of small daisy-like flower-heads and feathery foliage. The cluster of heads functions as a single, large flower and attracts many insects, including beetles, butterflies and hover-flies. It has had many medicinal uses. Related species are grown in gardens for use as 'everlasting' flowers.

Status: native; common, throughout area.

SIMILAR SPECIES

Sneezewort *(Achillea ptarmica)* is readily distinguished by its undivided leaves and less numerous, much larger flower-heads. Acrid leaves were used as a form of snuff and to relieve toothache.

fewer flower-heads

larger

undivided

YARROW

Type	perennial
Height	8–65cm
Habitat	grassy places; most soils
Flowering	June–August

STEMS AND LEAVES

Stem	upright, grooved, branched above, strongly scented
Root	tap-root; stems root
Hairs	more or less woolly
Stipules	absent
Leaves	spirally arranged on stem, 50–160mm, oblong in outline, finely divided 2–3 times
Leaf-stalk	shorter than blade or absent above

FLOWERS

Position	flat-topped clusters, many daisy-like heads of florets enclosed by bracts
Bracts	dark-edged around heads; scale-like between florets
Type 1	inner ☿, 2–3mm, tubular
Type 2	outer florets ♀, 4–5mm, broad, 3-toothed
Size	heads 4–6mm wide
Colour	white or tinged red
Stalk	absent; short under heads
Sepals	absent
Petals	5, joined, tubular, lobes equal or very unequal
Stamens	5, joined into tube
Stigma	1, 2-lobed; style long
Ovary	1, below petals, 1-celled

FRUIT

Type	nut-like, flattened, shiny, blunt, without parachute
Size	1.5–2mm
Seeds	1, not released

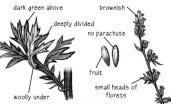

dark green above

deeply divided

woolly under

brownish

no parachute

fruit

small heads of florets

A tall plant with deeply divided dark-green leaves, silvery beneath, and branched clusters of insignificant reddish-brown flower-heads. Common along roadsides, it often has a dusty, neglected look. In ancient times it was believed to have powerful magical properties. Mugwort had many uses, as a herbalist medicine, to repel insects, to flavour ale, or as a herb for stuffing ducks and geese.

Status: native; common, throughout area.

grooved

SIMILAR SPECIES

1 Wormwood (*A. absinthium*) has silky hairs on both sides of the leaves and wider flower-heads. **2 Sea Wormwood** (*A. maritima*) has strongly scented woolly leaves, cut into very narrow segments.

narrow lobes

woolly above

wider

1

2

silky hairs

MUGWORT

Type	perennial
Height	60–120cm, rarely 210cm
Habitat	waste ground, hedgerows
Flowering	July–September
STEMS AND LEAVES	
Stem	upright, grooved, reddish
Root	branched stock
Hairs	white; woolly under leaves
Stipules	absent
Leaves	spirally arranged on stem, 50–80mm, deeply lobed and toothed, lower broad, upper smaller, broad-based
Leaf-stalk	short or absent
FLOWERS	
Position	large, branched clusters of daisy-like heads with florets enclosed by bracts
Bracts	2.5–3mm around head, papery-edged; none between florets
Type 1	inner florets ☿, 2–3mm, tubular, broader above
Type 2	outer florets ♀, 2–3mm, very narrowly tubular
Size	heads 3–4mm
Colour	reddish brown
Stalk	absent; short under heads
Sepals	absent
Petals	5, tubular, lobes equal
Stamens	5, joined into tube
Stigma	1, 2-lobed; style long
Ovary	1, below petals, 1-celled
FRUIT	
Type	nut-like, cylindrical, smooth, without parachute
Size	1–1.5mm
Seeds	1, not released

199

Scentless Mayweed *Tripleurospermum inodorum*

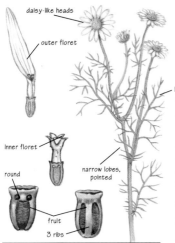

daisy-like heads

outer floret

hairless

inner floret

round

narrow lobes, pointed

fruit

3 ribs

One of the Daisies of cornfields, that has large white and yellow flowers above finely divided leaves. Common on waste ground, it also colonizes new road-verges.

Status: native; common, most of area.

SCENTLESS MAYWEED

Type	annual
Height	15–80cm
Habitat	cultivated and waste ground; most soils
Flowering	July–September
STEMS AND LEAVES	
Stem	upright, often branched
Root	fibrous
Hairs	absent
Stipules	absent
Leaves	spirally placed on stem, 20–100mm, finely divided 2–3 times into thin segments
Leaf-stalk	short or absent
FLOWERS	
Position	daisy-like heads of florets surrounded by bracts
Bracts	2 rows around head, oblong, papery-edged; none between florets
Type 1	inner florets ⚥, 3–4mm, tubular
Type 2	outer florets ♀, 12–22, 10–18mm, strap-shaped
Size	heads 15–45mm
Colour	yellow and white
Stalk	absent; long under heads
Sepals	an inconspicuous rim
Petals	5, joined, tubular, lobes equal or very unequal
Stamens	5, joined into tube
Stigma	1, 2-lobed; style long
Ovary	1, below petals, 1-celled
FRUIT	
Type	nut-like, oblong, 3-ribbed, without parachute
Size	2–3mm
Seeds	1, not released

SIMILAR SPECIES

1 Sea Mayweed *(T. maritimum)* is a low-growing coastal plant with shorter, fleshier leaf-segments. Both species have two brown oil-bearing glands on each fruit, but in this plant they are elongated, not round. Two species have flower-heads with a dome-shaped, hollow base and five-ribbed fruits.
2 Scented Mayweed *(Matricaria recutita)* has pleasantly scented leaves.
3 Pineappleweed *(M. matricarioides)* has strong-smelling leaves and no outer florets.

elongated

no long florets

1

3

fleshy, blunt

conical

bend back

2

5 ribs

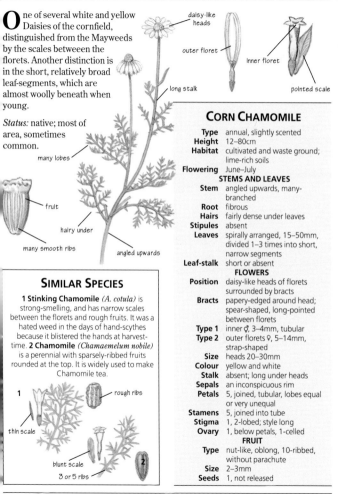

One of several white and yellow Daisies of the cornfield, distinguished from the Mayweeds by the scales betweeen the florets. Another distinction is in the short, relatively broad leaf-segments, which are almost woolly beneath when young.

Status: native; most of area, sometimes common.

daisy-like heads

outer floret

inner floret

long stalk

pointed scale

many lobes

fruit

hairy under

many smooth ribs

angled upwards

CORN CHAMOMILE

Type	annual, slightly scented
Height	12–80cm
Habitat	cultivated and waste ground; lime-rich soils
Flowering	June–July
STEMS AND LEAVES	
Stem	angled upwards, many-branched
Root	fibrous
Hairs	fairly dense under leaves
Stipules	absent
Leaves	spirally arranged, 15–50mm, divided 1–3 times into short, narrow segments
Leaf-stalk	short or absent
FLOWERS	
Position	daisy-like heads of florets surrounded by bracts
Bracts	papery-edged around head; spear-shaped, long-pointed between florets
Type 1	inner ♂, 3–4mm, tubular
Type 2	outer florets ♀, 5–14mm, strap-shaped
Size	heads 20–30mm
Colour	yellow and white
Stalk	absent; long under heads
Sepals	an inconspicuous rim
Petals	5, joined, tubular, lobes equal or very unequal
Stamens	5, joined into tube
Stigma	1, 2-lobed; style long
Ovary	1, below petals, 1-celled
FRUIT	
Type	nut-like, oblong, 10-ribbed, without parachute
Size	2–3mm
Seeds	1, not released

SIMILAR SPECIES

1 Stinking Chamomile (*A. cotula*) is strong-smelling, and has narrow scales between the florets and rough fruits. It was a hated weed in the days of hand-scythes because it blistered the hands at harvest-time. **2 Chamomile** (*Chamaemelum nobile*) is a perennial with sparsely-ribbed fruits rounded at the top. It is widely used to make Chamomile tea.

rough ribs

thin scale

blunt scale

3 or 5 ribs

Tansy *Tanacetum vulgare*

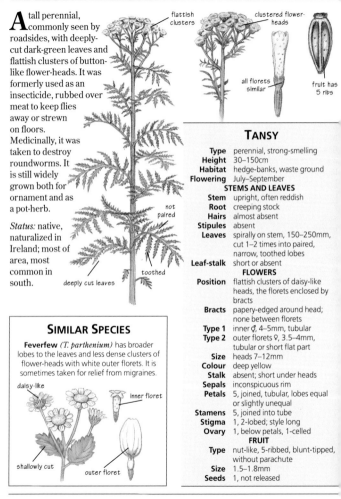

A tall perennial, commonly seen by roadsides, with deeply-cut dark-green leaves and flattish clusters of button-like flower-heads. It was formerly used as an insecticide, rubbed over meat to keep flies away or strewn on floors. Medicinally, it was taken to destroy roundworms. It is still widely grown both for ornament and as a pot-herb.

Status: native, naturalized in Ireland; most of area, most common in south.

flattish clusters

clustered flower-heads

all florets similar

fruit has 5 ribs

not paired

toothed

deeply cut leaves

SIMILAR SPECIES

Feverfew (*T. parthenium*) has broader lobes to the leaves and less dense clusters of flower-heads with white outer florets. It is sometimes taken for relief from migraines.

daisy-like

inner floret

shallowly cut

outer floret

TANSY

Type	perennial, strong-smelling
Height	30–150cm
Habitat	hedge-banks, waste ground
Flowering	July–September
STEMS AND LEAVES	
Stem	upright, often reddish
Root	creeping stock
Hairs	almost absent
Stipules	absent
Leaves	spirally on stem, 150–250mm, cut 1–2 times into paired, narrow, toothed lobes
Leaf-stalk	short or absent
FLOWERS	
Position	flattish clusters of daisy-like heads, the florets enclosed by bracts
Bracts	papery-edged around head; none between florets
Type 1	inner ☿, 4–5mm, tubular
Type 2	outer florets ♀, 3.5–4mm, tubular or short flat part
Size	heads 7–12mm
Colour	deep yellow
Stalk	absent; short under heads
Sepals	inconspicuous rim
Petals	5, joined, tubular, lobes equal or slightly unequal
Stamens	5, joined into tube
Stigma	1, 2-lobed; style long
Ovary	1, below petals, 1-celled
FRUIT	
Type	nut-like, 5-ribbed, blunt-tipped, without parachute
Size	1.5–1.8mm
Seeds	1, not released

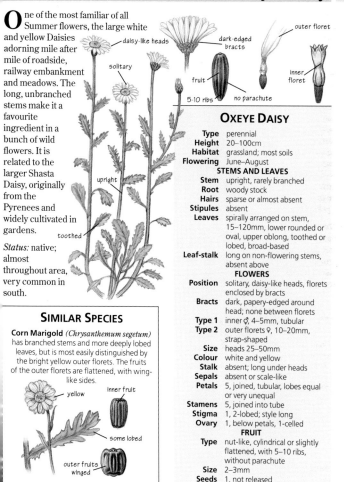

One of the most familiar of all Summer flowers, the large white and yellow Daisies adorning mile after mile of roadside, railway embankment and meadows. The long, unbranched stems make it a favourite ingredient in a bunch of wild flowers. It is related to the larger Shasta Daisy, originally from the Pyrenees and widely cultivated in gardens.

Status: native; almost throughout area, very common in south.

Labels on illustration: daisy-like heads; solitary; upright; toothed; dark-edged bracts; fruit; 5–10 ribs; no parachute; outer floret; inner floret

SIMILAR SPECIES

Corn Marigold *(Chrysanthemum segetum)* has branched stems and more deeply lobed leaves, but is most easily distinguished by the bright yellow outer florets. The fruits of the outer florets are flattened, with wing-like sides.

Labels: yellow; inner fruit; some lobed; outer fruits winged

OXEYE DAISY

Type	perennial
Height	20–100cm
Habitat	grassland; most soils
Flowering	June–August

STEMS AND LEAVES

Stem	upright, rarely branched
Root	woody stock
Hairs	sparse or almost absent
Stipules	absent
Leaves	spirally arranged on stem, 15–120mm, lower rounded or oval, upper oblong, toothed or lobed, broad-based
Leaf-stalk	long on non-flowering stems, absent above

FLOWERS

Position	solitary, daisy-like heads, florets enclosed by bracts
Bracts	dark, papery-edged around head; none between florets
Type 1	inner ♂, 4–5mm, tubular
Type 2	outer florets ♀, 10–20mm, strap-shaped
Size	heads 25–50mm
Colour	white and yellow
Stalk	absent; long under heads
Sepals	absent or scale-like
Petals	5, joined, tubular, lobes equal or very unequal
Stamens	5, joined into tube
Stigma	1, 2-lobed; style long
Ovary	1, below petals, 1-celled

FRUIT

Type	nut-like, cylindrical or slightly flattened, with 5–10 ribs, without parachute
Size	2–3mm
Seeds	1, not released

Colt's-foot *Tussilago farfara*

fruit has parachute

2 sorts of floret

One of the earliest Spring flowers with clumps of scaly, purplish stems, each ending in a yellow flower-head. It rivals bulbous plants for early flowering because it has thick underground stems that store food. Large leaves arise direct from the ground after the flowers, each initially covered with thick, felt-like hairs and opening to make a dense, shady canopy beneath which few other plants survive.

large

from ground

single head

scaly

Status: native; very common, most of area.

flowers without leaves

SIMILAR SPECIES

1 Butterbur *(Petasites hybridus)* has thick flowering stems with many pink flower-heads and even larger, Rhubarb-like leaves.
2 Winter Heliotrope *(P. fragrans)* has few, larger, vanilla-scented flower-heads.

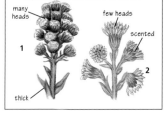

many heads

few heads

scented

1

2

thick

COLT'S-FOOT

Type	perennial
Height	5–15cm
Habitat	cultivated or waste ground, shingle; often clay soils
Flowering	March–April

STEMS AND LEAVES

Stem	flowering stem upright, scaly, leafless, purplish
Root	creeping, underground stem
Hairs	stems woolly; felt-like hairs mainly under leaves
Stipules	absent
Leaves	from ground after flowers, 100–300mm, rounded or 5–12 angles, base heart-shaped
Leaf-stalk	about equals blade, grooved

FLOWERS

Position	solitary daisy-like head of florets enclosed by bracts
Bracts	mostly 1 row around head, blunt; none between florets
Type 1	few inner ♂, 7–8mm, tubular
Type 2	outer florets ♀, up to 300, 6–15mm, flattened, narrow
Size	heads 15–35mm
Colour	bright yellow
Stalk	absent; short under head
Sepals	a ring of hairs
Petals	5, joined, tubular, lobes equal or very unequal
Stamens	5, joined into tube
Stigma	1, 2-lobed; style long
Ovary	1, below petals, 1-celled

FRUIT

Type	nut-like, cylindrical, with parachute of long hairs
Size	5–10mm
Seeds	1, not released

Arctium minus **Lesser Burdock**

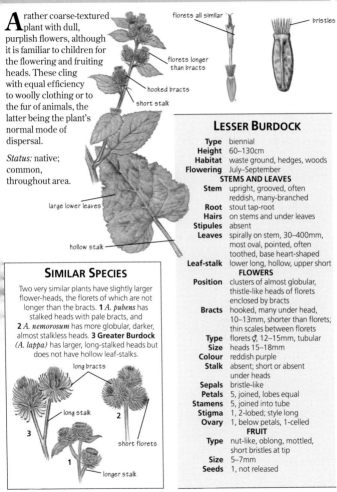

A rather coarse-textured plant with dull, purplish flowers, although it is familiar to children for the flowering and fruiting heads. These cling with equal efficiency to woolly clothing or to the fur of animals, the latter being the plant's normal mode of dispersal.

Status: native; common, throughout area.

florets all similar

bristles

florets longer than bracts

hooked bracts

short stalk

large lower leaves

hollow stalk

SIMILAR SPECIES

Two very similar plants have slightly larger flower-heads, the florets of which are not longer than the bracts. **1** *A. pubens* has stalked heads with pale bracts, and **2** *A. nemorosum* has more globular, darker, almost stalkless heads. **3 Greater Burdock** (*A. lappa*) has larger, long-stalked heads but does not have hollow leaf-stalks.

long bracts

long stalk

3

2

short florets

1

longer stalk

LESSER BURDOCK

Type	biennial
Height	60–130cm
Habitat	waste ground, hedges, woods
Flowering	July–September
STEMS AND LEAVES	
Stem	upright, grooved, often reddish, many-branched
Root	stout tap-root
Hairs	on stems and under leaves
Stipules	absent
Leaves	spirally on stem, 30–400mm, most oval, pointed, often toothed, base heart-shaped
Leaf-stalk	lower long, hollow, upper short
FLOWERS	
Position	clusters of almost globular, thistle-like heads of florets enclosed by bracts
Bracts	hooked, many under head, 10–13mm, shorter than florets; thin scales between florets
Type	florets ⚥, 12–15mm, tubular
Size	heads 15–18mm
Colour	reddish purple
Stalk	absent; short or absent under heads
Sepals	bristle-like
Petals	5, joined, lobes equal
Stamens	5, joined into tube
Stigma	1, 2-lobed; style long
Ovary	1, below petals, 1-celled
FRUIT	
Type	nut-like, oblong, mottled, short bristles at tip
Size	5–7mm
Seeds	1, not released

Common Ragwort *Senecio jacobaea*

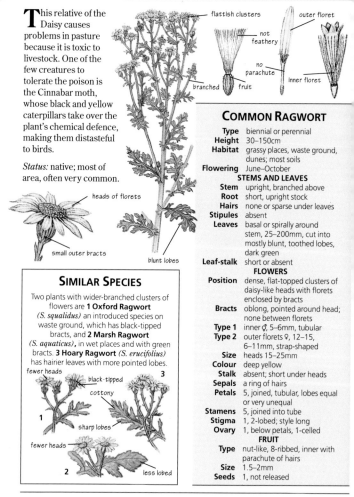

This relative of the Daisy causes problems in pasture because it is toxic to livestock. One of the few creatures to tolerate the poison is the Cinnabar moth, whose black and yellow caterpillars take over the plant's chemical defence, making them distasteful to birds.

Status: native; most of area, often very common.

flattish clusters

not feathery

no parachute

branched fruit

outer floret

inner floret

heads of florets

small outer bracts

blunt lobes

COMMON RAGWORT

Type	biennial or perennial
Height	30–150cm
Habitat	grassy places, waste ground, dunes; most soils
Flowering	June–October
STEMS AND LEAVES	
Stem	upright, branched above
Root	short, upright stock
Hairs	none or sparse under leaves
Stipules	absent
Leaves	basal or spirally around stem, 25–200mm, cut into mostly blunt, toothed lobes, dark green
Leaf-stalk	short or absent
FLOWERS	
Position	dense, flat-topped clusters of daisy-like heads with florets enclosed by bracts
Bracts	oblong, pointed around head; none between florets
Type 1	inner ♂, 5–6mm, tubular
Type 2	outer florets ♀, 12–15, 6–11mm, strap-shaped
Size	heads 15–25mm
Colour	deep yellow
Stalk	absent; short under heads
Sepals	a ring of hairs
Petals	5, joined, tubular, lobes equal or very unequal
Stamens	5, joined into tube
Stigma	1, 2-lobed; style long
Ovary	1, below petals, 1-celled
FRUIT	
Type	nut-like, 8-ribbed, inner with parachute of hairs
Size	1.5–2mm
Seeds	1, not released

SIMILAR SPECIES

Two plants with wider-branched clusters of flowers are **1 Oxford Ragwort** (*S. squalidus*) an introduced species on waste ground, which has black-tipped bracts, and **2 Marsh Ragwort** (*S. aquaticus*), in wet places and with green bracts. **3 Hoary Ragwort** (*S. erucifolius*) has hairier leaves with more pointed lobes.

fewer heads

3

black-tipped

cottony

1

sharp lobes

fewer heads

2

less lobed

One of the most familiar of garden weeds, multiplying rapidly by fruits which form even in the absence of pollinating insects and then survive many years in the soil. Silky parachutes carry tiny fruits aloft to colonize any piece of cleared ground. Some plants have a few strap-shaped florets at the edges of the flower-heads.

Status: native; very common, throughout region, often a problematic weed.

heads of florets

broad base

sometimes outer florets

hairy fruit

florets usually similar

lobed leaves

often hairless

GROUNDSEL

Type	annual
Height	8–45cm
Habitat	cultivated and waste ground
Flowering	January–December
STEMS AND LEAVES	
Stem	usually upright, rather succulent, few branches
Root	fibrous
Hairs	absent or slightly cottony
Stipules	absent
Leaves	spirally on stem, oblong, irregular, toothed lobes, blunt; upper broad-based
Leaf-stalk	absent or short
FLOWERS	
Position	cylindrical heads of florets, enclosed by bracts
Bracts	black-tipped around head; none between florets
Type 1	florets usually ♂, 5–7mm, tubular
Type 2	outer florets sometimes present, ♀, up to 12, 8–10mm, strap-shaped
Size	heads 8–10mm, rarely 14mm
Colour	yellow
Stalk	absent; short under heads
Sepals	a ring of hairs
Petals	5, tubular, lobes usually equal
Stamens	5, joined, tube-like
Stigma	1, 2-lobed; style long
Ovary	1, below petals, 1-celled
FRUIT	
Type	dry, cylindrical, with hairy ribs, parachute of hairs
Size	1.5–2mm
Seeds	1, not released

SIMILAR SPECIES

1 Sticky Groundsel *(S. viscosus)* has sticky, strong-smelling foliage and fruit with hairless ribs. **2 Heath Groundsel** *(S. sylvaticus)* has outer bracts about half as long as the inner, and the fruit has stiffly hairy ribs.

sticky

outer florets

smooth

1

hairy

2

hairy

Spear Thistle *Cirsium vulgare*

A handsome plant with large, reddish-purple flower-heads above sharply spiny leaves. This is probably the plant adopted as a national emblem by Scottish kings. Thistle-down is light because the parachute usually detaches from the heavy nut-like base and floats away without effecting dispersal.

Status: native; common, throughout area.

single floret

feathery hairs

spiny wings

spiny

spiny

short stalk

spiny

SIMILAR SPECIES

Two other species have long, smooth stems below the flower-heads and softly prickly leaves with whitish hairs beneath.
1 Musk Thistle *(Carduus nutans)* has nodding flower-heads. **2 Melancholy Thistle** *(Carduus helenioides)* has broad, rather blunt bracts; **3 Meadow Thistle** *(Carduus dissectum)* has smaller heads with spiny outer bracts.

nodding

1

3

spiny bracts

bluntish

2

whitish under

smooth stalk

SPEAR THISTLE

Type	biennial
Height	30–150cm, rarely 300cm
Habitat	grassland, hedges, waste ground
Flowering	July–October
STEMS AND LEAVES	
Stem	upright, with spiny wings
Root	long tap-root
Hairs	sparse under leaves, prickly hairs above
Stipules	absent
Leaves	basal or spirally on stem, 150–300mm, lobed, wavy, strongly spiny, end lobe spear-shaped; blade of upper joins stem-wings
Leaf-stalk	lower short, upper absent
FLOWERS	
Position	upright heads of florets surrounded by bracts
Bracts	many around head, spiny, slightly hairy; bristle-like between florets
Type	florets ♂ or ♀, 26–36mm
Size	heads 30–50mm
Colour	reddish purple
Stalk	absent; short under heads
Sepals	a ring of hairs
Petals	5, joined, tubular, lobes slightly unequal
Stamens	5, joined into tube
Stigma	1, 2-lobed; style long
Ovary	1, below petals, 1-celled
FRUIT	
Type	nut-like, oblong, parachute of hairs 20–30mm, feathery
Size	3.5–5mm
Seeds	1, not released

all florets similar

petal-like bracts

feathery hairs

An unusual Thistle, the flower-heads have a ring of long, yellowish bracts, resembling the strap-shaped outer florets of Daisies. A more or less stemless species with larger flower-heads is grown for use in dried flower displays.

Status: native; most of area, sometimes common.

spiny

CARLINE THISTLE

Type	biennial
Height	10–30cm, rarely 60cm
Habitat	grassland; lime-rich soils
Flowering	July–October
STEMS AND LEAVES	
Stem	upright, branched, purplish
Root	tap-root
Hairs	sparse, cotton-like
Stipules	absent
Leaves	basal or spirally arranged on stem, 70–130mm, oblong or spear-shaped, pointed, edge wavy, spiny, slightly lobed; upper broad-based
Leaf-stalk	absent
FLOWERS	
Position	2–5 heads of florets enclosed by bracts
Bracts	many around head, outer spiny, inner long, narrow, yellowish; bristle-like between florets
Type	florets ⚥, 10–12mm, tubular
Size	heads 20–40mm
Colour	reddish purple
Stalk	absent; short under heads
Sepals	ring of branched hairs
Petals	5, joined, tubular, lobes equal
Stamens	5, joined into tube
Stigma	1, 2-lobed; style long
Ovary	1, below petals, 1-celled
FRUIT	
Type	nut-like, cylindrical, with reddish hairs, parachute of feathery hairs 7–8mm
Size	2–4mm
Seeds	1, not released

SIMILAR SPECIES

Another small Thistle is the native perennial **Dwarf Thistle** *(Cirsium acaule)*. This has a rosette of leaves and one to three reddish-purple flower-heads on short stems. The plant is familiar to people who take picnics in the country as the tufts of spiny leaves that abound in closely-grazed turf.

short bracts   on ground

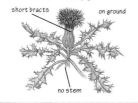

no stem

Saw-wort *Serratula tinctoria*

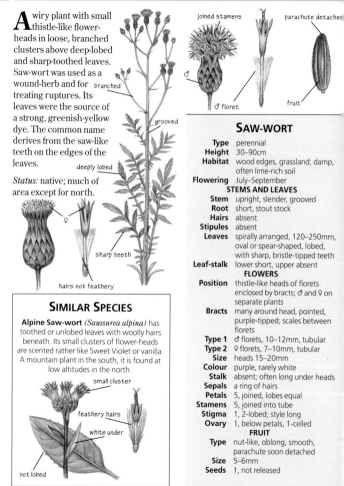

A wiry plant with small thistle-like flower-heads in loose, branched clusters above deep-lobed and sharp-toothed leaves. Saw-wort was used as a wound-herb and for treating ruptures. Its leaves were the source of a strong, greenish-yellow dye. The common name derives from the saw-like teeth on the edges of the leaves.

Status: native; much of area except for north.

branched

grooved

deeply lobed

♀

sharp teeth

hairs not feathery

joined stamens

parachute detaches

♂

♂ floret

fruit

SIMILAR SPECIES

Alpine Saw-wort *(Saussurea alpina)* has toothed or unlobed leaves with woolly hairs beneath. Its small clusters of flower-heads are scented rather like Sweet Violet or vanilla. A mountain plant in the south, it is found at low altitudes in the north.

small cluster

feathery hairs

white under

not lobed

SAW-WORT

Type	perennial
Height	30–90cm
Habitat	wood edges, grassland; damp, often lime-rich soil
Flowering	July–September
STEMS AND LEAVES	
Stem	upright, slender, grooved
Root	short, stout stock
Hairs	absent
Stipules	absent
Leaves	spirally arranged, 120–250mm, oval or spear-shaped, lobed, with sharp, bristle-tipped teeth
Leaf-stalk	lower short, upper absent
FLOWERS	
Position	thistle-like heads of florets enclosed by bracts; ♂ and ♀ on separate plants
Bracts	many around head, pointed, purple-tipped; scales between florets
Type 1	♂ florets, 10–12mm, tubular
Type 2	♀ florets, 7–10mm, tubular
Size	heads 15–20mm
Colour	purple, rarely white
Stalk	absent; often long under heads
Sepals	a ring of hairs
Petals	5, joined, lobes equal
Stamens	5, joined into tube
Stigma	1, 2-lobed; style long
Ovary	1, below petals, 1-celled
FRUIT	
Type	nut-like, oblong, smooth, parachute soon detached
Size	5–6mm
Seeds	1, not released

Centaurea scabiosa **Greater Knapweed**

An attractive flower of Summer meadows, with large reddish-purple flowers that are thistle-like in construction but often confused with species of Scabious. Around the base of each flower-head are bracts which have a papery, blackish, horseshoe-shaped margin divided into feathery lobes. The flowers are much visited by butterflies.

Status: native; most of area, more common in south.

outer florets largest

fringed bracts

floret

bristles

long tube

not paired

deeply lobed

fruit

GREATER KNAPWEED

Type	perennial
Height	30–150cm, rarely 200cm
Habitat	grassland, hedges, cliffs; dry, often lime-rich soils
Flowering	July–September
STEMS AND LEAVES	
Stem	upright, branched above
Root	stout, woody stock
Hairs	short, rough on leaves
Stipules	absent
Leaves	basal or spirally on stem, 50–250mm, mostly divided into paired lobes, toothed
Leaf-stalk	lower shorter than blade, upper absent
FLOWERS	
Position	thistle-like heads of florets enclosed by bracts
Bracts	broad around head, each with feathery, blackish tip; bristle-like between florets
Type	florets ⚥, 12–23mm, tubular, outer often larger, sterile
Size	heads 30–50mm
Colour	reddish purple
Stalk	absent; long under heads
Sepals	a ring of hairs
Petals	5, joined, tubular, lobes slightly unequal
Stamens	5, joined into tube
Stigma	1, 2-lobed; style long
Ovary	1, below petals, 1-celled
FRUIT	
Type	nut-like, oblong, slightly flattened, parachute 4–5mm
Size	4–5mm
Seeds	1, not released

SIMILAR SPECIES

1 Common Knapweed *(C. nigra)* has a similar but smaller flower-head with narrower bracts tipped by a feathery, blackish lobe. The leaves are mostly undivided. **2 Cornflower** *(C. cyanus)*, a cornfield species that has become rare, has bright blue flowers and is grown in gardens.

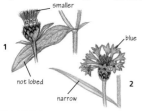

smaller

blue

1

not lobed

2

narrow

Chicory *Cichorium intybus*

The bright blue flowers of Chicory are a beautiful sight along roadsides in late Summer. Opening early in the day, the flowers close soon after midday. Chicory has been cultivated for medicinal purposes, as a vegetable or as a coffee substitute, the roots being dried, roasted and ground.

Status: native or often introduced; most of area, rare in extreme north and Ireland.

heads of florets

bright blue

2 sorts of bract

nearly stalkless head

all long florets

no parachute

fruit

hairy

mostly lobed

CHICORY

Type	perennial
Height	30–120cm
Habitat	roadsides, grassland, waste ground; often lime-rich soil
Flowering	July–October
STEMS AND LEAVES	
Stem	upright, grooved, sap milky
Root	long, stout tap-root
Hairs	stiff on stems, gland-tipped among flowers
Stipules	absent
Leaves	basal or spirally on stem, 70–300mm, spear-shaped, most lobed or toothed, upper clasp stem
Leaf-stalk	lower short, upper absent
FLOWERS	
Position	dandelion-like heads of florets enclosed by bracts
Bracts	2 rows under head, inner long; none between florets
Type	florets ⚥, 12–18mm
Size	heads 25–40mm
Colour	bright blue
Stalk	absent; very short under heads
Sepals	a scaly rim
Petals	5, joined, flattened above, 5-toothed
Stamens	5, joined into tube
Stigma	1, 2-lobed; style long
Ovary	1, below petals, 1-celled
FRUIT	
Type	nut-like, almost egg-shaped, mottled, without parachute
Size	2–3mm
Seeds	1, not released

SIMILAR SPECIES

Two Dandelion-relatives have stalked, deep-blue flower-heads. **1 Alpine Blue-sow-thistle** (*Cicerbita alpina*), an uncommon mountain plant, has reddish hairs above; **2 Blue Lettuce** (*Lactuca perennis*), found only in the south-east of the area, is hairless.

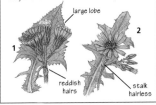

large lobe

2

1

reddish hairs

stalk hairless

A familiar roadside plant, not for the pale yellow flowers, but for the fruiting heads which look like enormous dandelion-clocks. The greyish parachutes have feathery bristles, the fine hairs distinctly interwoven. The common name derives from these conspicuous fruits. Unlike the Dandelion, Goat's-beard has narrow, almost grass-like leaves, without lobes. Its long tap-roots were formerly used as a vegetable.

Status: native; most of area, often common.

heads of florets

long bracts

narrow

straight-sided

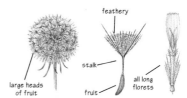

feathery

stalk

large heads of fruit

fruit

all long florets

SIMILAR SPECIES

Viper's-grass *(Scorzonera humilis)* has broader basal leaves and the oval bracts are much shorter than the florets.

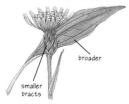

broader

smaller bracts

GOAT'S-BEARD

Type	annual to perennial
Height	30–70cm
Habitat	grassland, roadsides, waste ground, dunes; dry soils
Flowering	June–July

STEMS AND LEAVES

Stem	upright, scarcely branched; sap milky
Root	long tap-root
Hairs	more or less absent
Stipules	absent
Leaves	basal or spirally arranged on stem, narrow, veins whitish, long-pointed, edge unbroken, base sheaths stem
Leaf-stalk	absent

FLOWERS

Position	solitary, dandelion-like head of florets surrounded by bracts
Bracts	1 row around head, 25–30mm, thin; none between florets
Type	florets ⚥, 20–25mm
Size	heads 15–22mm
Colour	yellow
Stalk	absent; long under heads
Sepals	a ring of hairs
Petals	5, joined, flattened above, 5-toothed
Stamens	5, joined into tube
Stigma	1, 2-lobed; style long
Ovary	1, below petals, 1-celled

FRUIT

Type	nut-like, ribbed, long, thin tip, parachute 12–23mm, hairs feathery, interwoven
Size	10–22mm
Seeds	1, not released

Bristly Oxtongue *Picris echioides*

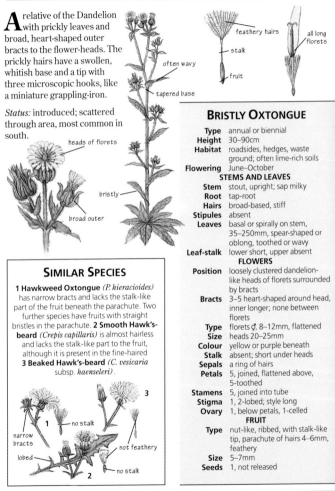

A relative of the Dandelion with prickly leaves and broad, heart-shaped outer bracts to the flower-heads. The prickly hairs have a swollen, whitish base and a tip with three microscopic hooks, like a miniature grappling-iron.

Status: introduced; scattered through area, most common in south.

feathery hairs

stalk

fruit

all long florets

often wavy

tapered base

heads of florets

bristly

broad outer

BRISTLY OXTONGUE

Type	annual or biennial
Height	30–90cm
Habitat	roadsides, hedges, waste ground; often lime-rich soils
Flowering	June–October
STEMS AND LEAVES	
Stem	stout, upright; sap milky
Root	tap-root
Hairs	broad-based, stiff
Stipules	absent
Leaves	basal or spirally on stem, 35–250mm, spear-shaped or oblong, toothed or wavy
Leaf-stalk	lower short, upper absent
FLOWERS	
Position	loosely clustered dandelion-like heads of florets surrounded by bracts
Bracts	3–5 heart-shaped around head, inner longer; none between florets
Type	florets ⚥, 8–12mm, flattened
Size	heads 20–25mm
Colour	yellow or purple beneath
Stalk	absent; short under heads
Sepals	a ring of hairs
Petals	5, joined, flattened above, 5-toothed
Stamens	5, joined into tube
Stigma	1, 2-lobed; style long
Ovary	1, below petals, 1-celled
FRUIT	
Type	nut-like, ribbed, with stalk-like tip, parachute of hairs 4–6mm, feathery
Size	5–7mm
Seeds	1, not released

SIMILAR SPECIES

1 Hawkweed Oxtongue (*P. hieracioides*) has narrow bracts and lacks the stalk-like part of the fruit beneath the parachute. Two further species have fruits with straight bristles in the parachute. **2 Smooth Hawk's-beard** (*Crepis capillaris*) is almost hairless and lacks the stalk-like part to the fruit, although it is present in the fine-haired **3 Beaked Hawk's-beard** (*C. vesicaria* subsp. *haenseleri*).

3

1

narrow bracts

not feathery

lobed

no stalk

no stalk

An abundant plant on waste land around towns or along roadsides, it has fleshy, hollow stems bearing weakly spiny leaves and dandelion-like flowers. At each leaf-base are two ear-like lobes, the shape being used to distinguish the species. Rather crisp leaves of Sow-thistles are edible, like the related Dandelion and Lettuce, or were fed to livestock.

Status: native; common, throughout area.

heads of florets

all long florets

hairless

stalkless

hairs not feathery

fleshy

weak spines

upright, hollow

rounded lobes

PRICKLY SOW-THISTLE

Type	annual, some overwintering
Height	2–150cm, rarely 200cm
Habitat	cultivated and waste ground
Flowering	June–August
STEMS AND LEAVES	
Stem	stout, upright, 5-angled, hollow; sap milky
Root	slender tap-root
Hairs	absent
Stipules	absent
Leaves	basal or spirally around stem, often lobed, wavy, weakly spiny, base of upper leaves with ear-like lobes clasping stem
Leaf-stalk	mostly absent
FLOWERS	
Position	dandelion-like heads of florets enclosed by bracts
Bracts	long, smooth around head; none between florets
Type	florets ⚥, 10–15mm, flattened
Size	heads 20–25mm
Colour	yellow, some purple beneath
Stalk	absent; longish under heads
Sepals	a ring of hairs
Petals	5, joined, flattened above, 5-toothed
Stamens	5, joined into tube
Stigma	1, 2-lobed; style long
Ovary	1, below petals, 1-celled
FRUIT	
Type	nut-like, flattened, smooth ribs, parachute 6–9mm
Size	2–3mm
Seeds	1, not released

SIMILAR SPECIES

1 Smooth Sow-thistle *(S. oleraceus)* has pointed lobes at the leaf-base and wrinkled fruits. **2 Perennial Sow-thistle** *(S. arvensis)* has rounded lobes at the leaf-base and flower-heads about twice as large, the bracts usually covered with gland-tipped hairs.

larger

hairy

pointed lobes

rounded

Cat's-ear *Hypochaeris radicata*

One of the most common of many yellow-flowered, dandelion-like plants, brightening the Summer meadow and roadside alike with its large, golden flower-heads. Often a problem on lawns, it is one of the best plants to try and establish if a lawn is being turned deliberately into an informal wild-flower meadow. The common name refers to small bracts on the stems, which in shape resemble cat's ears.

Status: native; most of area except north-east.

all long florets

feathery hairs

scales between florets

stalk

scales

bract

longer than bracts

hairy

leaves at base

SIMILAR SPECIES

Smooth Cat's-ear *(H. glabra)* is an annual that has almost hairless leaves and flower-heads which only open in sunny weather. The florets are little longer than the bracts.

shorter

nearly hairless

outer fruit stalkless

CAT'S-EAR

Type	perennial
Height	20–60cm, rarely 100cm
Habitat	grassland, roadsides, dunes
Flowering	June–September
STEMS AND LEAVES	
Stem	upright, usually no leaves, few branches; sap milky
Root	tap-root
Hairs	rather stiff, on leaves
Stipules	absent
Leaves	basal rosette, 70–250mm, oblong or spear-shaped with wavy lobes or teeth
Leaf-stalk	shorter than blade
FLOWERS	
Position	few dandelion-like heads of florets enclosed by bracts
Bracts	many around head, spear-shaped, bristly; long scales between florets
Type	florets ☿, 12–18mm, flattened
Size	heads 25–40mm
Colour	bright yellow, outer florets greenish beneath
Stalk	absent; under heads
Sepals	a ring of hairs
Petals	5, joined, flattened above, 5-toothed
Stamens	5, joined into tube
Stigma	1, 2-lobed; style long
Ovary	1, below petals, 1-celled
FRUIT	
Type	nut-like, ribbed, rough, top stalk-like, parachute of feathery hairs 9–12mm
Size	4–8mm
Seeds	1, not released

Taraxacum officinale **Common Dandelion**

long stalk · smooth · lobed leaves · milky sap · all from base

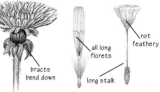

all long florets · not feathery · bracts bend down · long stalk

A weed, flavouring for a wine, food for pets or a salad vegetable; the lobed leaves and hollow-stalked flowers of Dandelions are familiar to most people. But their biology is complex and more than a thousand species have been described from Europe alone.

Status: native; throughout area, very common.

SIMILAR SPECIES

1 Narrow-leaved Marsh-dandelion (*T. palustre*) has upright pale-edged bracts and narrow sparsely-lobed leaves. Two related plants have small bracts on the stems and feathery hairs making up the parachute. **2 Autumn Hawkbit** (*Leontodon autumnalis*) is nearly hairless, often with branched stems, and **3 Rough Hawkbit** (*L. hispidus*) is hairy.

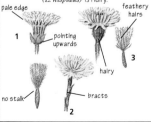

pale edge · pointing upwards · feathery hairs · hairy · no stalk · bracts

COMMON DANDELION

Type	perennial
Height	5–40cm
Habitat	grassland, roadsides, lawns, waste ground
Flowering	March–October
STEMS AND LEAVES	
Stem	upright, unbranched, hollow, leafless; sap milky
Root	tap-root
Hairs	near top of flower-stalks
Stipules	absent
Leaves	basal, 50–400mm, oblong or spear-shaped, variably lobed and toothed
Leaf-stalk	short, edges often wing-like
FLOWERS	
Position	head of florets enclosed by bracts, solitary
Bracts	2 rows around head, inner upright, outer curved back; none between florets
Type	florets ⚥, 15–20mm, flattened
Size	heads 30–60mm
Colour	yellow, outer brownish under
Stalk	absent; long under heads
Sepals	a ring of hairs
Petals	5, joined, flattened above, 5-toothed
Stamens	5, joined into tube
Stigma	1, 2-lobed; style long
Ovary	1, below petals, 1-celled
FRUIT	
Type	dry, cylindrical, rough above, top stalk-like, parachute of hairs 5–6mm
Size	3.5–4mm
Seeds	1, not released

Nipplewort *Lapsana communis*

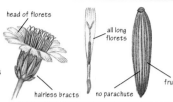

small heads

One of the dandelion relatives with small flowers, common by roadsides or as a garden weed. Lemon-yellow flowers open only in bright weather. Like the related Lettuce, the leaves are edible. The common name derives from a vague similarity in the shape of the buds and milky sap.

branched

Status: native; common, throughout area.

divided

milky sap

head of florets

all long florets

hairless bracts

no parachute

fruit

NIPPLEWORT

Type	annual
Height	20–125cm
Habitat	woods, hedges, roadsides, waste ground
Flowering	July–September
STEMS AND LEAVES	
Stem	upright, leafy, widely branched above; sap milky
Root	tap-root
Hairs	absent except at base
Stipules	absent
Leaves	basal or spirally arranged on stem, 10–150mm, with wavy teeth, lower lobed
Leaf-stalk	lower shorter than blade, upper absent
FLOWERS	
Position	dandelion-like heads of florets enclosed by bracts
Bracts	8–10 around head, narrow, upright; none between florets
Type	florets ⚥, 8–15, 7–11mm, all strap-shaped
Size	heads 15–20mm
Colour	pale yellow
Stalk	absent; slender under heads
Sepals	a ring of hairs
Petals	5, joined, flattened above, 5-toothed
Stamens	5, joined into tube
Stigma	1, 2-lobed; style long
Ovary	1, below petals, 1-celled
FRUIT	
Type	1, nut-like, flattened, smoothly ribbed, without parachute, outer curved
Size	2.5–9mm
Seeds	1, not released

SIMILAR SPECIES

Two other small-flowered species have fruits with a parachute. **1 Great Lettuce** *(Lactuca virosa)* has prickly stem-leaves with rounded ear-like lobes at the base, and fruits with a stalk beneath the parachute. **2 Wall Lettuce** *(Mycelis muralis)* has smaller flower-heads, usually with five florets, and fruits without a stalk beneath the parachute.

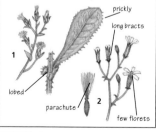

prickly

long bracts

lobed

parachute

few florets

A tall plant with branched heads of dandelion-like flowers. Also like the Dandelion, its unusual reproductive biology has resulted in hundreds of very similar species.

Status: native; most of area, most common in south.

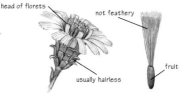

head of florets

not feathery

fruit

usually hairless

branched

all long florets

leafy stem

narrow

SIMILAR SPECIES

Probably the most common species in the northern half of the area, **1 Common Hawkweed** (*H. vulgatum*) has nearly all of its broader leaves in a basal rosette and has hairy bracts. **2 Fox-and-cubs** (*H. aurantiacum*) is often grown in gardens for its orange or red flowers. **3 Mouse-ear Hawkweed** (*H. pilosella*) has creeping stems that produce rosettes of leaves, whitish with dense hairs beneath, and short stems ending with a single, lemon-yellow flower-head.

solitary

hairy

1

3

at base

orange or red

at base

2

HAWKWEED

Type	perennial
Height	30–100cm, rarely 150cm
Habitat	grassland, hedges, waste ground
Flowering	June–October
STEMS AND LEAVES	
Stem	upright, slender; sap milky
Root	fibrous with slender stock
Hairs	rather sparse
Stipules	absent
Leaves	many, spirally arranged on stem, 15–150mm, narrow, with few teeth, pointed
Leaf-stalk	lower short, upper absent
FLOWERS	
Position	dandelion-like heads of florets surrounded by bracts, in branched clusters
Bracts	many around head, 9–11mm, usually hairless, blackish-green; none between florets
Type	florets ⚥, 10–15mm
Size	heads 20–30mm
Colour	bright yellow
Stalk	absent; long under heads, with small bracts
Sepals	a ring of hairs
Petals	5, joined, flattened above, 5-toothed
Stamens	5, joined into tube
Stigma	1, 2-lobed; style long
Ovary	1, below petals, 1-celled
FRUIT	
Type	nut-like, smoothly ridged, parachute 5–6mm, hairs unequal
Size	3–4mm
Seeds	1, not released

Arrowhead *Sagittaria sagittifolia*

3 petals

in spike

arrow shaped

narrow in water

flattened fruit

clusters of fruits

A water-plant with attractive white, blackish-centred flowers. Its leaves are remarkably variable. The plant lasts the Winter as a bright blue and yellow bud, sunken in the mud. Submerged leaves are at first ribbon-like, the tips expanded when later leaves reach the surface and float. Only leaves above water have arrow-shaped blades that give the plant its name.

Status: native; most of area, rarer in north.

SIMILAR SPECIES

1 Water-plantain *(Alisma plantago-aquatica)* has small, pinkish flowers in branched heads, and the leaf-blades are broadly oval. **2 Lesser Water-plantain** *(Baldellia ranunculoides)* has much narrower blades, and all flower-stalks usually arise at the same point.

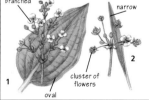

branched

narrow

cluster of flowers

oval

1

2

ARROWHEAD

Type	perennial
Height	30–90cm
Habitat	ponds, slow rivers, canals; in shallow water on mud
Flowering	July–August
STEMS AND LEAVES	
Stem	flowering stems upright; creeping stems at base
Root	thick, white
Hairs	absent
Stipules	absent
Leaves	submerged ribbon-like, translucent; floating with broad tip; above water with blade 50–200mm, arrow-shaped
Leaf-stalk	much longer than blade
FLOWERS	
Position	rings of 3–5 around stem, ♂ and ♀ on same plant
Bracts	triangular, short
Type 1	♂, in upper part of head
Type 2	♀, at base of head, short-stalked
Size	18–25mm
Colour	white, centre dark violet
Stalk	about equalling flower
Sepals	3, 6–8mm, oval, edge whitish
Petals	3, 9–11mm, nearly circular
Stamens	many, shorter than petals
Stigmas	1 per ovary
Ovaries	numerous, 1-celled
FRUIT	
Type	many, in globular clusters, dry, flattened edges
Size	4–5mm
Seeds	1 per fruit, not released

Hydrocharis morsus-ranae **Frogbit**

floating · 3 petals · kidney-shaped

bud forms
new plant

3 sepals

A water-plant with floating leaves like small Water-lilies, but white, three-petalled flowers carried above the water. It spends the Winter as a bud with scale-like leaves, protected from frost and ice in the mud at the bottom of the pond. Although rooted when growth commences, bubbles produced within the tissues soon cause it to float.

Status: native; scattered through area, sometimes common, rarer in north.

SIMILAR SPECIES

Water-soldier *(Stratiotes aloides)* is a floating aquatic plant that has similar flowers but very different foliage. Its tuft of long, pointed, spiny leaves floats in the Summer but sinks in the Winter.

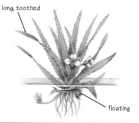

long, toothed

floating

FROGBIT

Type	perennial
Height	floating
Habitat	ponds, ditches; usually lime-rich water
Flowering	July–August
STEMS AND LEAVES	
Stem	long, rooting; over-wintering as bud
Root	fibrous
Hairs	absent
Stipules	large, translucent
Leaves	tufts along stem, blade 25–40mm, kidney-shaped to nearly circular, floating
Leaf-stalk	longer than blade
FLOWERS	
Position	♂ and ♀ flowers usually on different plants, above water
Bracts	broad, translucent
Type 1	2–3 ♂ from pairs of bracts
Type 2	♀ solitary from bract
Size	18–25mm
Colour	white, base yellow
Stalk	longer than flower
Sepals	3, 4–5mm, oval
Petals	3, 9–12mm, nearly circular, crumpled
Stamens	12, shorter than petals
Stigma	1, 2-lobed on each of 6 styles
Ovary	1, below petals, 6-celled
FRUIT	
Type	1, berry-like, not opening, almost globular, rarely produced
Size	c12mm
Seeds	many, c2mm, sticky-coated

Flowering-rush *Butomus umbellatus*

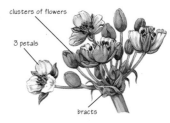

clusters of flowers

3 petals

bracts

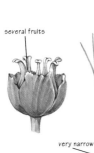

several fruits

long stem

very narrow

swollen base

A beautiful plant, brightening banks of ponds and rivers with its heads of pink and purple. The attractive, three-petalled flowers seem quite out of context with the sedge-like (rather than rush-like) foliage that is usually associated with inconspicuous, blackish or brown flowers. Flowering-rush is often cultivated in ornamental ponds and is readily available commercially. The swollen stems at the base of the leaves are edible, but it would be a criminal act to take them from the scarce wild plants. However, if surplus garden plants are thinned out then culinary experiments could be attempted. Introduced as a garden plant to North America, Flowering-rush has escaped into the wild and has conquered the Great Lakes.

Status: native; scattered through area, most common in south.

Similar species: none.

FLOWERING-RUSH	
Type	perennial
Height	50–150cm
Habitat	ditches, ponds, rivers, canals; edges of fresh-water
Flowering	July–September
STEMS AND LEAVES	
Stem	upright, leafless flowering stem
Root	thick, fleshy, underground stem
Hairs	absent
Stipules	absent
Leaves	all from base, 50–150mm, long and narrow, 3-angled, upright, pointed, edge unbroken, base sheaths stem
Leaf-stalk	absent
FLOWERS	
Position	many, in head at stem-tip
Bracts	narrowly triangular, papery
Type	♂
Size	25–30mm
Colour	pink with darker veins
Stalk	longer than flower, unequal, to 100mm
Sepals	3, 8–10mm, oblong, purplish
Petals	3, 10–15mm, oval
Stamens	6–9
Stigmas	1 per ovary
Ovaries	6–9, 2-celled
FRUIT	
Type	6–9, capsule, almost egg-shaped, tip beak-like
Size	9–12mm
Seeds	many, 1.5–2mm, narrowly oblong

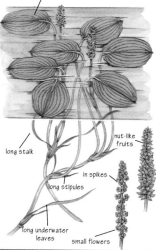

broad floating leaves

long stalk

nut-like fruits

in spikes

long stipules

long underwater leaves

small flowers

An aquatic plant with broad, floating leaves and spikes of tiny flowers above the water. In slow rivers and canals the leaves align with the gentle current, and fish (especially young Pike) lie alongside, beautifully camouflaged until they move.

Status: native; throughout area, common.

BROAD-LEAVED PONDWEED

Type	perennial
Height	up to 100cm, rarely 500cm
Habitat	rivers, lakes, ponds; mostly on mud in fresh-water
Flowering	May–September
STEMS AND LEAVES	
Stem	long, submerged, rarely branched
Root	creeping, underground stem
Hairs	absent
Stipules	50–120mm, conspicuous
Leaves	on alternate sides of stem, blade 25–125mm, floating, elliptical to broadly spear-shaped; submerged leaves ribbon-like, grooved
Leaf-stalk	up to 500mm, jointed and wing-like near top
FLOWERS	
Position	many in crowded, stalked spike, from leaf-base or stem-tip, above water
Bracts	absent
Type	♂
Size	3–4mm
Colour	green
Stalk	absent
Perianth	4 lobes, 1.5–2mm, rounded with stalk-like base
Stamens	4, very short
Stigmas	1 per ovary; style absent
Ovaries	4, 1-celled
FRUIT	
Type	in cylindrical spike, almost egg-shaped, pointed, olive-green, not opening
Size	4–5mm
Seeds	1, not released

SIMILAR SPECIES

Of many other species, most have only submerged leaves. **1 Curled Pondweed** (*P. crispus*) has attractively curled and twisted, fine-toothed, translucent leaves. **2 Fennel Pondweed** (*P. pectinatus*) has grass-like leaves and stipules joined into a sheath. **3 Perfoliate Pondweed** (*P. perfoliatus*) has broad leaves with the base clasping the stem.

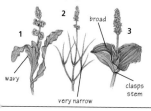

1

wavy

2

broad

3

clasps stem

very narrow

Bog Asphodel *Narthecium ossifragum*

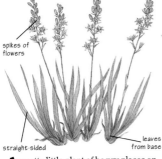

spikes of flowers

straight-sided

leaves from base

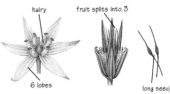

hairy

fruit splits into 3

6 lobes

long seed

A pretty little plant of boggy places on moor and heath, flowering among the Sphagnum mosses and the Sundews. The leaves resemble a diminutive Iris and the yellow, six-petalled flowers deepen in hue to a reddish orange. The base of each of the six stamens has a fuzzy mass of hairs and the pollen-bearing anthers are usually a bright crimson. The flower-spikes were used to make a yellow dye.

Status: native; throughout area, most common in north.

SIMILAR SPECIES

Scottish Asphodel *(Tofieldia pusilla)* differs in the small, white flowers and narrower leaves.

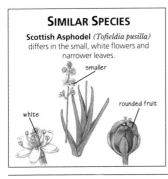

smaller

white

rounded fruit

BOG ASPHODEL

Type	perennial
Height	5–40cm
Habitat	bogs, heaths, moors; wet places, acid soil
Flowering	July–September
STEMS AND LEAVES	
Stem	flowering stems upright
Root	creeping, fleshy stem; roots thick, fibrous
Hairs	absent
Stipules	absent
Leaves	mostly basal, 50–300mm, slender, usually curved, with 5 parallel veins, pointed, edge unbroken
Leaf-stalk	absent
FLOWERS	
Position	many in stalked spike, 20–100mm long, at stem-tip, stalk with sheath-like leaves at base
Bracts	spear-shaped, equal to flower-stalk
Type	♂
Size	12–16mm
Colour	yellow, turning orange
Stalk	about equal to flower
Perianth	6 lobes, 6–8mm, narrowly spear-shaped, spread apart
Stamens	6, anthers red, base woolly
Stigma	1, tip swollen; style short
Ovary	1, 3-celled
FRUIT	
Type	1, capsule, tapered, grooved, splits into 3
Size	10–14mm
Seeds	many, 8–10mm, middle swollen, ends thin, tail-like

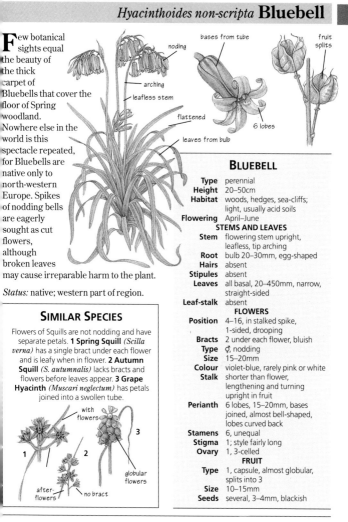

bases from tube

fruit splits

noding

arching

leafless stem

flattened

6 lobes

leaves from bulb

Few botanical sights equal the beauty of the thick carpet of Bluebells that cover the floor of Spring woodland. Nowhere else in the world is this spectacle repeated, for Bluebells are native only to north-western Europe. Spikes of nodding bells are eagerly sought as cut flowers, although broken leaves may cause irreparable harm to the plant.

Status: native; western part of region.

SIMILAR SPECIES

Flowers of Squills are not nodding and have separate petals. **1 Spring Squill** *(Scilla verna)* has a single bract under each flower and is leafy when in flower. **2 Autumn Squill** *(S. autumnalis)* lacks bracts and flowers before leaves appear. **3 Grape Hyacinth** *(Muscari neglectum)* has petals joined into a swollen tube.

with flowers

3

1

2

globular flowers

after-flowers

no bract

BLUEBELL

Type	perennial
Height	20–50cm
Habitat	woods, hedges, sea-cliffs; light, usually acid soils
Flowering	April–June
STEMS AND LEAVES	
Stem	flowering stem upright, leafless, tip arching
Root	bulb 20–30mm, egg-shaped
Hairs	absent
Stipules	absent
Leaves	all basal, 20–450mm, narrow, straight-sided
Leaf-stalk	absent
FLOWERS	
Position	4–16, in stalked spike, 1-sided, drooping
Bracts	2 under each flower, bluish
Type	⚥, nodding
Size	15–20mm
Colour	violet-blue, rarely pink or white
Stalk	shorter than flower, lengthening and turning upright in fruit
Perianth	6 lobes, 15–20mm, bases joined, almost bell-shaped, lobes curved back
Stamens	6, unequal
Stigma	1; style fairly long
Ovary	1, 3-celled
FRUIT	
Type	1, capsule, almost globular, splits into 3
Size	10–15mm
Seeds	several, 3–4mm, blackish

Meadow Saffron *Colchicum autumnale*

Pinkish-purple crocus-like flowers of Meadow Saffron appear in Autumn, long before any foliage. Leaves and fruits follow in the Spring and are hard to reconcile with the flower of the previous year. Although potentially lethal, this plant yields a drug used to treat gout and arthritis.

Status: native or sometimes introduced; scattered through area, mainly in south.

6 petals

leaves with fruit

6 stamens

long petal-tube

no leaves with flowers

fruit splits open

MEADOW SAFFRON

Type	perennial
Height	80–300cm
Habitat	meadows, woods; damp, often lime-rich soils
Flowering	August–October
STEMS AND LEAVES	
Stem	absent in flower, short in fruit, sheathed by leaf-bases
Root	corm 30–50mm, with brown scales
Hairs	absent
Stipules	absent
Leaves	absent in flower, all basal, 120–300mm, oblong, straight-sided, glossy, blunt
Leaf-stalk	absent
FLOWERS	
Position	1–3, from corm
Bracts	absent
Type	⚥, crocus-like
Size	lobes 30–45mm
Colour	pale purple
Stalk	only stalk-like base of petals visible
Perianth	6 petal-like lobes, 30–45mm, bases joined forming apparent stalk, 50–200mm long
Stamens	6, anthers orange
Stigmas	3; styles long
Ovary	1, underground, 3-celled
FRUIT	
Type	1, capsule, oblong to egg-shaped, splits into 3
Size	30–50mm
Seeds	numerous, 3–4mm, almost globular

SIMILAR SPECIES

1 Spring Crocus (*Crocus vernus*) has only three stamens and the grass-like leaves are present when the flowers open. **2 Sand Crocus** (*Romulea columnae*) has a distinct stalk bearing the small flower, its petals joined only at the base and spreading widely apart.

3 stamens

1

2

leaves with flowers

short petal-tube

Fritillaria meleagris **Fritillary**

Attractive and unique in form, Fritillaries are found in wet meadows almost only where they are protected from flower-pickers and farmers seeking to 'improve' the land. The curious pattern of squarish markings is also visible within the translucent petals.

Status: native or escaped from gardens; scattered through area, common in some southern localities.

splits open

nodding

usually chequered

oblong

leafy stem

sometimes white

SIMILAR SPECIES

Two Lilies with nodding, spotted flowers are found in the south of the area. **1 Martagon Lily** (*Lilium martagon*) has rings of leaves and purplish flowers; **2 Pyrenean Lily** (*L. pyrenaicum*) has spirally-arranged leaves and yellow flowers. Also native in the south, **3 Wild Tulip** (*Tulipa sylvestris*) has yellow, upright flowers.

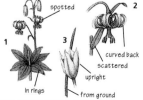

spotted

1

2

3

curved back

scattered

upright

in rings

from ground

FRITILLARY

Type	perennial
Height	20–50cm
Habitat	grassy places; damp soil
Flowering	April–May
STEMS AND LEAVES	
Stem	upright
Root	small bulb with white scales
Hairs	absent
Stipules	absent
Leaves	on alternate sides of stem, 3–6, 80–200mm, narrow, straight-sided, tip pointed
Leaf-stalk	absent
FLOWERS	
Position	solitary, rarely paired, at stem-tip
Bracts	absent
Type	☿, nodding
Size	30–50mm
Colour	purplish, usually chequered with light and dark markings, rarely white
Stalk	almost equal to flower
Perianth	6 lobes, 30–50mm, all petal-like, equal, oblong, thickened at tip
Stamens	3, shorter than petals
Stigma	1, 3-lobed; style long
Ovary	1, 3-celled
FRUIT	
Type	1, capsule, oblong, upright, splits into 3
Size	15–20mm
Seeds	many, 5–7mm, almost circular, flattened, brown

Star-of-Bethlehem *Ornithogalum umbellatum*

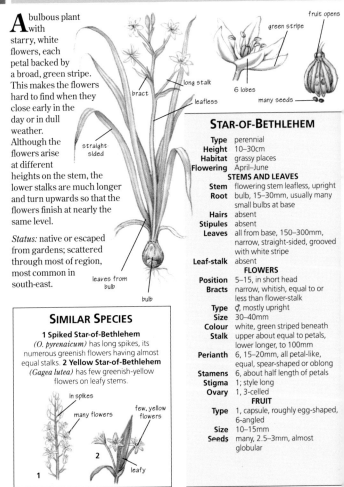

A bulbous plant with starry, white flowers, each petal backed by a broad, green stripe. This makes the flowers hard to find when they close early in the day or in dull weather. Although the flowers arise at different heights on the stem, the lower stalks are much longer and turn upwards so that the flowers finish at nearly the same level.

Status: native or escaped from gardens; scattered through most of region, most common in south-east.

Labels on main illustration: fruit opens; green stripe; long stalk; bract; 6 lobes; leafless; many seeds; straight-sided; leaves from bulb; bulb

SIMILAR SPECIES

1 Spiked Star-of-Bethlehem (*O. pyrenaicum*) has long spikes, its numerous greenish flowers having almost equal stalks. **2 Yellow Star-of-Bethlehem** (*Gagea lutea*) has few greenish-yellow flowers on leafy stems.

in spikes; many flowers; few, yellow flowers; leafy

STAR-OF-BETHLEHEM

Type	perennial
Height	10–30cm
Habitat	grassy places
Flowering	April–June
STEMS AND LEAVES	
Stem	flowering stem leafless, upright
Root	bulb, 15–30mm, usually many small bulbs at base
Hairs	absent
Stipules	absent
Leaves	all from base, 150–300mm, narrow, straight-sided, grooved with white stripe
Leaf-stalk	absent
FLOWERS	
Position	5–15, in short head
Bracts	narrow, whitish, equal to or less than flower-stalk
Type	☿, mostly upright
Size	30–40mm
Colour	white, green striped beneath
Stalk	upper about equal to petals, lower longer, to 100mm
Perianth	6, 15–20mm, all petal-like, equal, spear-shaped or oblong
Stamens	6, about half length of petals
Stigma	1; style long
Ovary	1, 3-celled
FRUIT	
Type	1, capsule, roughly egg-shaped, 6-angled
Size	10–15mm
Seeds	many, 2.5–3mm, almost globular

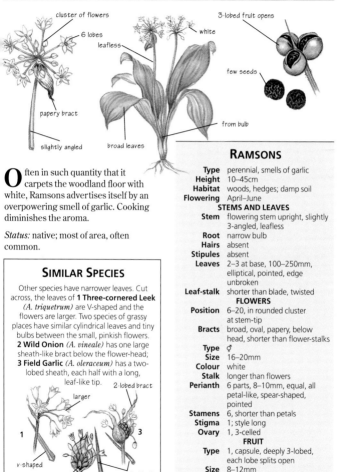

cluster of flowers
6 lobes
leafless
white
3-lobed fruit opens
few seeds
papery bract
slightly angled
broad leaves
from bulb

Often in such quantity that it carpets the woodland floor with white, Ramsons advertises itself by an overpowering smell of garlic. Cooking diminishes the aroma.

Status: native; most of area, often common.

SIMILAR SPECIES

Other species have narrower leaves. Cut across, the leaves of **1 Three-cornered Leek** (*A. triquetrum*) are V-shaped and the flowers are larger. Two species of grassy places have similar cylindrical leaves and tiny bulbs between the small, pinkish flowers. **2 Wild Onion** (*A. vineale*) has one large sheath-like bract below the flower-head; **3 Field Garlic** (*A. oleraceum*) has a two-lobed sheath, each half with a long, leaf-like tip.

larger
2-lobed bract
v-shaped
tiny bulbs
cylindrical

RAMSONS

Type	perennial, smells of garlic
Height	10–45cm
Habitat	woods, hedges; damp soil
Flowering	April–June
STEMS AND LEAVES	
Stem	flowering stem upright, slightly 3-angled, leafless
Root	narrow bulb
Hairs	absent
Stipules	absent
Leaves	2–3 at base, 100–250mm, elliptical, pointed, edge unbroken
Leaf-stalk	shorter than blade, twisted
FLOWERS	
Position	6–20, in rounded cluster at stem-tip
Bracts	broad, oval, papery, below head, shorter than flower-stalks
Type	♂
Size	16–20mm
Colour	white
Stalk	longer than flowers
Perianth	6 parts, 8–10mm, equal, all petal-like, spear-shaped, pointed
Stamens	6, shorter than petals
Stigma	1; style long
Ovary	1, 3-celled
FRUIT	
Type	1, capsule, deeply 3-lobed, each lobe splits open
Size	8–12mm
Seeds	few, 3–4mm, angular, black

Herb-Paris *Paris quadrifolia*

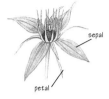

solitary

usually 4

fleshy fruit

sepal

petal

upright, unbranched

A curious plant with a collar of broad leaves beneath the solitary green flower. Four green sepals spread sideways making a cross, separating the very slender, insignificant petals. Although fairly uncommon in the region as a whole, the plants abound in some deciduous woodlands on chalk or limestone. Herb-Paris was believed to have powerful magical properties and was associated with witchcraft. Despite being used medicinally to treat a variety of ailments, the plant is toxic and should be treated with caution.

Status: native; scattered through area, more common in east. Although no native species are similar, Herb-Paris is related to the Wake-Robin of North America, and several related species are grown in gardens. Most have larger, white or red flowers and some were used in folk-medicine by the North American Indians.

Similar species: none.

HERB-PARIS

Type	perennial
Height	15–40cm
Habitat	woods; damp, lime-rich soils
Flowering	May–August

STEMS AND LEAVES

Stem	upright, unbranched, leafy
Root	creeping underground stem
Hairs	absent
Stipules	absent
Leaves	usually 4, in ring around stem, 60–120mm, oval, broadest towards tip, 3–5 main veins, pointed, edge unbroken, base wedge-shaped
Leaf-stalk	almost absent

FLOWERS

Position	solitary, at stem-tip
Bracts	absent
Type	♂, upright
Size	40–70mm
Colour	green
Stalk	20–80mm, usually longer than flower
Sepals	4, rarely to 6, 25–35mm, spear-shaped, spread apart
Petals	4, rarely to 6, 20–30mm, very slender
Stamens	4–6, elongated
Stigmas	4–5 on separate styles
Ovary	1, 4–5-celled

FRUIT

Type	1, berry-like, globular, black, eventually opens
Size	14–18mm
Seeds	many, 2.5–3mm, angular, flattened

230

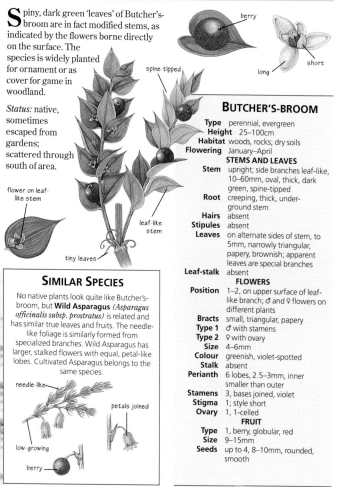

S piny, dark green 'leaves' of Butcher's-broom are in fact modified stems, as indicated by the flowers borne directly on the surface. The species is widely planted for ornament or as cover for game in woodland.

Status: native, sometimes escaped from gardens; scattered through south of area.

berry

long

short

spine-tipped

flower on leaf-like stem

leaf-like stem

tiny leaves

BUTCHER'S-BROOM

Type	perennial, evergreen
Height	25–100cm
Habitat	woods, rocks; dry soils
Flowering	January–April

STEMS AND LEAVES

Stem	upright; side branches leaf-like, 10–60mm, oval, thick, dark green, spine-tipped
Root	creeping, thick, underground stem
Hairs	absent
Stipules	absent
Leaves	on alternate sides of stem, to 5mm, narrowly triangular, papery, brownish; apparent leaves are special branches
Leaf-stalk	absent

FLOWERS

Position	1–2, on upper surface of leaf-like branch; ♂ and ♀ flowers on different plants
Bracts	small, triangular, papery
Type 1	♂ with stamens
Type 2	♀ with ovary
Size	4–6mm
Colour	greenish, violet-spotted
Stalk	absent
Perianth	6 lobes, 2.5–3mm, inner smaller than outer
Stamens	3, bases joined, violet
Stigma	1; style short
Ovary	1, 1-celled

FRUIT

Type	1, berry, globular, red
Size	9–15mm
Seeds	up to 4, 8–10mm, rounded, smooth

SIMILAR SPECIES

No native plants look quite like Butcher's-broom, but **Wild Asparagus** (*Asparagus officinalis subsp. prostratus*) is related and has similar true leaves and fruits. The needle-like foliage is similarly formed from specialized branches. Wild Asparagus has larger, stalked flowers with equal, petal-like lobes. Cultivated Asparagus belongs to the same species.

needle-like

petals joined

low-growing

berry

Solomon's-seal *Polygonatum multiflorum*

Graceful, arching stems of Solomon's-seal bear small clusters of nodding flowers at the base of broad, parallel-veined leaves. The plant propagates itself by thick, white stems, which run underground along the woodland floor. Round blackish berries contain several seeds.

Status: native; scattered through most of area except Ireland.

broad leaves

clusters

leaves on stem

blackish berries

rounded

SOLOMON'S-SEAL

Type	perennial
Height	30–80cm
Habitat	woods
Flowering	May–June
STEMS AND LEAVES	
Stem	upright, arching above, smoothly rounded sides
Root	thick, creeping, under-ground stem
Hairs	more or less absent
Stipules	absent
Leaves	on alternate side of stem, 50–150mm, oval or broadly elliptical, tip pointed, edge unbroken
Leaf-stalk	absent
FLOWERS	
Position	2–5, in branched cluster at leaf-base
Bracts	absent
Type	♂, nodding
Size	9–15mm
Colour	greenish white
Stalk	shorter than flower
Perianth	6, equal, petal-like parts, bases form tube, narrowed in middle; lobes oval
Stamens	6, inside petal-tube
Stigma	1, 3-lobed; style long
Ovary	1, 3-celled
FRUIT	
Type	1, berry, globular, bluish black
Size	8–10mm
Seeds	up to 6, nearly globular

SIMILAR SPECIES

1 Angular Solomon's-seal *(P. odoratum)* has angled stems and the scented, usually solitary flowers are broader at the middle.
2 Lily-of-the-valley *(Convallaria majalis)*, a familiar garden plant, usually has two leaves at the base. The flowering stem bears short, nodding, sweetly-scented flowers, and the berries are red.

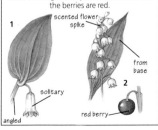

scented flower spike

from base

1

2

solitary

angled

red berry

nodding

long outer

narrow leaves

short inner

fruit

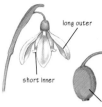

One of the first heralds of Spring, pushing its clean, white flowers up through the snow, Snowdrop can flower so early because it stores food in a bulb, enabling it to grow without the need to extract materials from the still-frozen ground. It is often grown in gardens, and has many named variants; most populations in the countryside originate from cultivated plants.

Status: introduced or native in extreme south; most of area.

SNOWDROP

Type	perennial
Height	15–25cm
Habitat	woods, grassy places; damp soil, often by streams
Flowering	January–March

STEMS AND LEAVES

Stem	flowering stem upright, curved at tip, base with tubular, papery sheath
Root	egg-shaped bulb, 10–20mm
Hairs	absent
Stipules	absent
Leaves	all at base, 50–250mm, narrow, straight-sided, tip blunt
Leaf-stalk	absent

FLOWERS

Position	solitary, at stem-tip
Bracts	leaf-like, papery-edged, tip forked
Type	♂, nodding
Size	22–30mm
Colour	pure white; inner lobes with green mark near tip
Stalk	about equal to flower
Perianth	6 parts, petal-like, unequal; outer 3 14–17mm, elliptical, blunt; inner 3 6–11mm, oblong or oval, tip notched
Stamens	6, inside flower
Stigma	1; style long
Ovary	1, below petals, 3-celled

FRUIT

Type	1, capsule, egg-shaped
Size	12–15mm
Seeds	many, 5–6mm, elongated, swollen in middle

SIMILAR SPECIES

1 Summer Snowflake (*Leucojum aestivum*) is a much larger plant of wet meadows and has broader, equal petals.
2 Spring Snowflake (*L. vernum*) differs in the shorter stems, usually bearing a solitary flower.

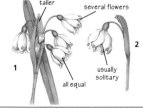

taller

several flowers

all equal

usually solitary

1

2

Wild Daffodil *Narcissus pseudonarcissus*

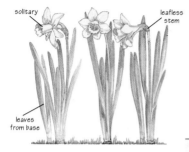

solitary

leafless stem

leaves from base

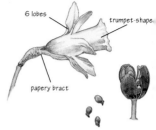

6 lobes

trumpet-shape

papery bract

Familiar as a garden plant, the Daffodil was formerly much more common in the wild although its numbers were greatly depleted as people uprooted the bulbs. There are still a few places where great drifts of the nodding, yellow flowers flourish in deciduous woodland.

Status: native or often introduced; southern half of area, fairly abundant in some localities.

SIMILAR SPECIES

Primrose-peerless *(N.* x *medioluteus)* is one of the long-established garden hybrids and is often naturalized. The central trumpet is much shorter than the whitish petal-lobes and the flowers are usually carried in pairs.

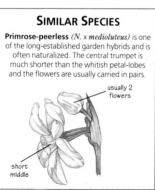

usually 2 flowers

short middle

WILD DAFFODIL

Type	perennial
Height	20–50cm
Habitat	woods, grassland; damp soils
Flowering	February–April
STEMS AND LEAVES	
Stem	flowering stem upright, slightly flattened, with 2 angles
Root	bulb, 20–50mm
Hairs	absent
Stipules	absent
Leaves	all at base, 120–500mm, narrow, straight-sided, bluish green, tip blunt
Leaf-stalk	absent
FLOWERS	
Position	solitary, at stem-tip
Bracts	20–60mm, broad, papery
Type	♂, often nodding
Size	35–60mm
Colour	pale yellow, centre darker
Stalk	short beneath flower; long stem bears bract and flower
Perianth	6, 35–60mm, equal, petal-like, bases form tube with trumpet-like extra tube on inner face; lobes oval, spread apart
Stamens	6, inside petal-tube
Stigma	1, tip swollen; style long
Ovary	1, below petals, 3-celled
FRUIT	
Type	capsule, oval or globular
Size	12–25mm
Seeds	many, 4–5mm, egg-shaped, slightly roughened

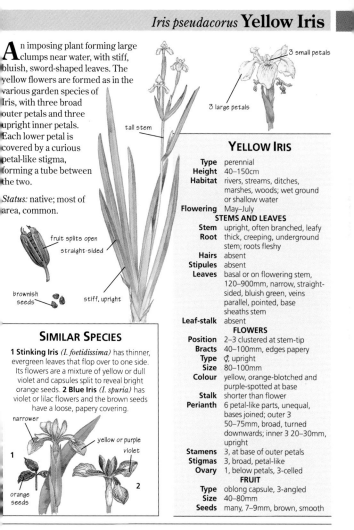

Iris pseudacorus **Yellow Iris**

An imposing plant forming large clumps near water, with stiff, bluish, sword-shaped leaves. The yellow flowers are formed as in the various garden species of Iris, with three broad outer petals and three upright inner petals. Each lower petal is covered by a curious petal-like stigma, forming a tube between the two.

Status: native; most of area, common.

3 small petals

3 large petals

tall stem

fruit splits open

straight-sided

brownish seeds

stiff, upright

YELLOW IRIS

Type	perennial
Height	40–150cm
Habitat	rivers, streams, ditches, marshes, woods; wet ground or shallow water
Flowering	May–July

STEMS AND LEAVES

Stem	upright, often branched, leafy
Root	thick, creeping, underground stem; roots fleshy
Hairs	absent
Stipules	absent
Leaves	basal or on flowering stem, 120–900mm, narrow, straight-sided, bluish green, veins parallel, pointed, base sheaths stem
Leaf-stalk	absent

FLOWERS

Position	2–3 clustered at stem-tip
Bracts	40–100mm, edges papery
Type	♂, upright
Size	80–100mm
Colour	yellow, orange-blotched and purple-spotted at base
Stalk	shorter than flower
Perianth	6 petal-like parts, unequal, bases joined; outer 3 50–75mm, broad, turned downwards; inner 3 20–30mm, upright
Stamens	3, at base of outer petals
Stigmas	3, broad, petal-like
Ovary	1, below petals, 3-celled

FRUIT

Type	oblong capsule, 3-angled
Size	40–80mm
Seeds	many, 7–9mm, brown, smooth

SIMILAR SPECIES

1 Stinking Iris (*I. foetidissima*) has thinner, evergreen leaves that flop over to one side. Its flowers are a mixture of yellow or dull violet and capsules split to reveal bright orange seeds. **2 Blue Iris** (*I. spuria*) has violet or lilac flowers and the brown seeds have a loose, papery covering.

narrower

1

orange seeds

yellow or purple

violet

2

Lords-and-Ladies *Arum maculatum*

These peculiar flowers are actually complex flower-heads. A central spike-like part gives off a smell and heat which attracts small flies. The hood-like upper part funnels the flies into the base, to be trapped by backward-pointing hairs until they have pollinated the tiny flowers.

Status: native; most of area except north, often common.

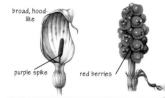

broad, hood-like

purple spike

red berries

spotted

SIMILAR SPECIES

1 Italian Lords-and-Ladies *(A. italicum)* produces its pale-veined leaves earlier and has a yellow spike-like part to the flower-head. **2 Bog Arum** *(Calla palustris)* has a smaller, white flower-head; **3 Sweet-flag** *(Acorus calamus)* has iris-like foliage and a leaf-like upper part to the flower-head.

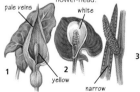

pale veins

white

yellow

narrow

1

2

3

LORDS-AND-LADIES

Type	perennial
Height	30–50cm
Habitat	woods, hedges; often lime-rich soils
Flowering	April–May
STEMS AND LEAVES	
Stem	upright
Root	fleshy underground stem
Hairs	absent
Stipules	absent
Leaves	basal, blade 70–200mm, with backward-pointing lobes, usually spotted
Leaf-stalk	15–25mm, base sheaths stem
FLOWERS	
Position	at stem-tip, petal-like bract encloses flower-head with purplish, spike-like upper part, ♂ and ♀ flowers on same plant
Bracts	150–250mm, upright, hooded
Type 1	♂ above ♀ flowers on spike
Type 2	♀ at base of spike
Size	1–2.5mm
Colour	yellowish green, sometimes marked with purple
Stalk	absent; head long-stalked
Sepals	absent
Petals	absent
Stamens	3–4
Stigma	1; style absent
Ovary	1, 1-celled
FRUIT	
Type	berries, in cluster 30–50mm long at stem-tip, scarlet
Size	4–6mm
Seeds	1–3, 3–5mm, globular, pitted

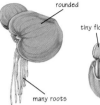
rounded

tiny flowers

many roots

floating, leaf-like

More like an alga than a flowering plant, the diminutive Duckweed forms a floating carpet of green on still water. Although tiny, Duckweeds are distantly related to Lords-and-Ladies.

Status: native; most of area, fairly common.

SIMILAR SPECIES

Two species have only a single root beneath. **1 Fat Duckweed** *(Lemna gibba)* is swollen below, whereas **2 Common Duckweed** *(L. minor)* is smaller and flat below. **3 Ivy-leaved Duckweed** *(L. trisulca)* forms interconnected masses, usually floating just beneath the surface. The smallest native flowering plant, **4 Rootless Duckweed** *(Wolffia arrhiza)* makes a round blob up to one millimetre across.

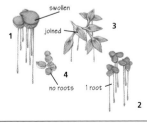
swollen
joined
3
1
4
no roots   1 root
2

GREATER DUCKWEED

Type	perennial, floating
Height	0.1–0.2cm, width 0.5–1cm
Habitat	ponds, ditches; fresh-water
Flowering	June–July
STEMS AND LEAVES	
Stem	solitary or 2–5 connected, flattened, oval or circular, leaf-like, often purple below, floating; smaller purplish buds sink and over-winter
Root	5–15 per plant, up to 30mm, straight
Hairs	absent
Stipules	absent
Leaves	absent; stems leaf-like
FLOWERS	
Position	♂ and ♀ flowers on same plant, few, rarely produced, 1 ♀ with 2 ♂ flowers in pocket
Bracts	tiny, cup-like, papery
Type 1	♂ with stamen
Type 2	♀ with ovary
Size	1–1.5mm
Colour	green
Stalk	absent
Sepals	absent
Petals	absent
Stamens	1 per flower
Stigma	1; style short
Ovary	1, 1-celled
FRUIT	
Type	1, more or less globular, not opening
Size	c1mm
Seeds	1–4, ridged or smooth

Broad-leaved Helleborine *Epipactis helleborine*

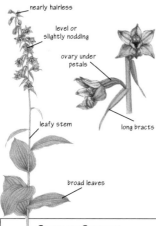

nearly hairless

level or slightly nodding

ovary under petals

leafy stem

long bracts

broad leaves

A tall, rather uncommon Orchid, usually found in the shade of deciduous trees or beneath hedges. Slightly nodding, green and purple flowers are borne towards the same side of the stem.

Status: native; scattered through area.

BROAD-LEAVED HELLEBORINE

Type	perennial
Height	25–80cm
Habitat	woods, hedges
Flowering	July–October
STEMS AND LEAVES	
Stem	1–3, upright, often purple-tinged, leafy
Root	short underground stem, many roots
Hairs	few, short, near top of stem
Stipules	absent
Leaves	spirally arranged, to 170mm, lowest scale-like, middle broadly oval or elliptical
Leaf-stalk	absent
FLOWERS	
Position	15–50, in one-sided, spike-like head, 70–300mm long
Bracts	spear-shaped, lower equal flower, upper shorter
Type	☿, nodding
Size	10–16mm wide
Colour	yellowish green and purple
Stalk	very short
Sepals	3, 9–11mm, petal-like, oval
Petals	3; 2 side petals oval; lower petal 6–8mm, hollow, end lobe bent back; spur absent
Stamen	1, stalkless
Stigmas	2; style absent
Ovary	1, below petals, 1-celled
FRUIT	
Type	1, capsule, oblong, angular, points downwards, splits lengthwise
Size	minute
Seeds	numerous, dust-like

SIMILAR SPECIES

1 Marsh Helleborine *(E. palustris)* has short hairs on the base of the flowers and the frilled lower lip turns up at the edges. Two white-flowered species have the ovary and centre of the flower angled upwards, rather than horizontal or nodding. **2 Narrow-leaved Helleborine** *(Cephalanthera longifolia)* has slender leaves, short bracts and pointed sepals. **3 White Helleborine** *(C. damasonium)* has oval leaves, bracts mostly longer than the flower, and blunt sepals.

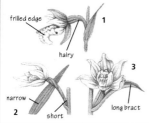

frilled edge

hairy

1

narrow

short

2

3

long bract

Relatives of Bee Orchid have a remarkable method of pollination. The lower petal resembles an insect and the flower is pollinated as the male insect tries to mate with it. Plants of the Bee Orchid in northern Europe have largely abandoned the method and are self-pollinated.

Status: native; scattered, southern half of area.

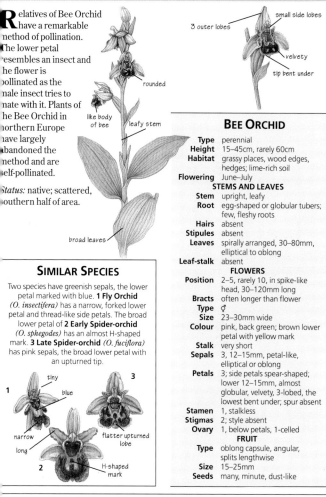

3 outer lobes

small side lobes

velvety

tip bent under

rounded

like body of bee

leafy stem

broad leaves

SIMILAR SPECIES

Two species have greenish sepals, the lower petal marked with blue. **1 Fly Orchid** (*O. insectifera*) has a narrow, forked lower petal and thread-like side petals. The broad lower petal of **2 Early Spider-orchid** (*O. sphegodes*) has an almost H-shaped mark. **3 Late Spider-orchid** (*O. fuciflora*) has pink sepals, the broad lower petal with an upturned tip.

1

tiny

blue

narrow

long

2

H-shaped mark

3

flatter upturned lobe

BEE ORCHID

Type	perennial
Height	15–45cm, rarely 60cm
Habitat	grassy places, wood edges, hedges; lime-rich soil
Flowering	June–July
STEMS AND LEAVES	
Stem	upright, leafy
Root	egg-shaped or globular tubers; few, fleshy roots
Hairs	absent
Stipules	absent
Leaves	spirally arranged, 30–80mm, elliptical to oblong
Leaf-stalk	absent
FLOWERS	
Position	2–5, rarely 10, in spike-like head, 30–120mm long
Bracts	often longer than flower
Type	♂
Size	23–30mm wide
Colour	pink, back green; brown lower petal with yellow mark
Stalk	very short
Sepals	3, 12–15mm, petal-like, elliptical or oblong
Petals	3; side petals spear-shaped; lower 12–15mm, almost globular, velvety, 3-lobed, the lowest bent under; spur absent
Stamen	1, stalkless
Stigmas	2; style absent
Ovary	1, below petals, 1-celled
FRUIT	
Type	oblong capsule, angular, splits lengthwise
Size	15–25mm
Seeds	many, minute, dust-like

Pyramidal Orchid *Anacamptis pyramidalis*

One of the most common Orchids on chalk grassland, often forming large colonies marked by their conical heads of magenta-pink flowers. The long, very slender, curved spur at the base of the flower is an adaptation to pollination by butterflies.

Status: native; scattered through area, common in some localities.

narrow

not branched

3-lobed petal

long spur

leafy stem

PYRAMIDAL ORCHID

Type	perennial
Height	20–75cm
Habitat	grassy places, dunes; lime-rich soils
Flowering	June–August

STEMS AND LEAVES

Stem	upright, slightly angled
Root	egg-shaped or globular tubers; few, fleshy roots
Hairs	absent
Stipules	absent
Leaves	spirally arranged, to 150mm, lower scale-like, upper narrowly spear-shaped, pointed, base sheaths stem
Leaf-stalk	absent

FLOWERS

Position	many, in crowded, conical head, 20–50mm long
Bracts	narrowly spear-shaped, about equalling flower
Type	☿, strong-smelling
Size	12–15mm
Colour	purplish pink
Stalk	very short
Sepals	3, 5–6mm, petal-like, spear-shaped
Petals	3; side petals form hood with upper sepal; lower 6–7mm, wedge-shaped, 3-lobed; spur 9–12mm, thin, curved
Stamen	1, stalkless
Stigmas	2; style absent
Ovary	1, below petals, 1-celled

FRUIT

Type	1, capsule, oblong, angular, splits lengthwise
Size	10–15mm
Seeds	numerous, minute, dust-like

SIMILAR SPECIES

1 Fragrant Orchid (*Gymnadenia conopsea*) has more cylindrical heads of sweetly scented flowers. Another Orchid with a short, dense head of flowers, though short-spurred, is **2 Burnt Orchid** (*Orchis ustulata*). The upper buds are purplish brown, as though burnt, and fade as the flowers age.

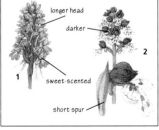

longer head

darker

1

2

sweet-scented

short spur

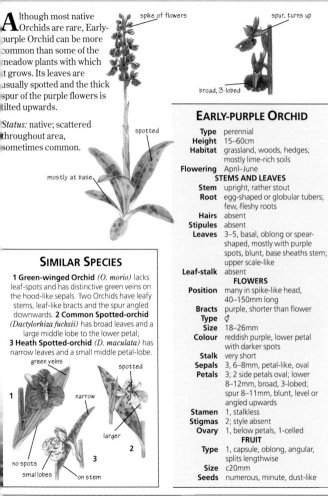

spike of flowers

spur, turns up

broad, 3-lobed

Although most native Orchids are rare, Early-purple Orchid can be more common than some of the meadow plants with which it grows. Its leaves are usually spotted and the thick spur of the purple flowers is tilted upwards.

Status: native; scattered throughout area, sometimes common.

spotted

mostly at base

SIMILAR SPECIES

1 Green-winged Orchid *(O. morio)* lacks leaf-spots and has distinctive green veins on the hood-like sepals. Two Orchids have leafy stems, leaf-like bracts and the spur angled downwards. **2 Common Spotted-orchid** *(Dactylorhiza fuchsii)* has broad leaves and a large middle lobe to the lower petal; **3 Heath Spotted-orchid** *(D. maculata)* has narrow leaves and a small middle petal-lobe.

green veins

spotted

1

narrow

larger

no spots

small lobes

2

3

on stem

EARLY-PURPLE ORCHID

Type	perennial
Height	15–60cm
Habitat	grassland, woods, hedges; mostly lime-rich soils
Flowering	April–June
STEMS AND LEAVES	
Stem	upright, rather stout
Root	egg-shaped or globular tubers; few, fleshy roots
Hairs	absent
Stipules	absent
Leaves	3–5, basal, oblong or spear-shaped, mostly with purple spots, blunt, base sheaths stem; upper scale-like
Leaf-stalk	absent
FLOWERS	
Position	many in spike-like head, 40–150mm long
Bracts	purple, shorter than flower
Type	♂
Size	18–26mm
Colour	reddish purple, lower petal with darker spots
Stalk	very short
Sepals	3, 6–8mm, petal-like, oval
Petals	3; 2 side petals oval; lower 8–12mm, broad, 3-lobed; spur 8–11mm, blunt, level or angled upwards
Stamen	1, stalkless
Stigmas	2; style absent
Ovary	1, below petals, 1-celled
FRUIT	
Type	1, capsule, oblong, angular, splits lengthwise
Size	c20mm
Seeds	numerous, minute, dust-like

241

Greater Butterfly-orchid *Platanthera chlorantha*

A delicate woodland Orchid, with greenish-white flowers. At the base of each flower is a slender, curved spur which holds the nectar. Few insects other than butterflies and moths have tongues that are long enough to reach the nectar, the latter being drawn by a scent which is strongest at night. The long lower petal acts as a landing platform where the insect can alight.

Status: native; scattered throughout area, most common in south.

flowers in spike

fragrant

usually 2 leaves, mostly at base

long spur

long bract

narrow petal

GREATER BUTTERFLY ORCHID

Type	perennial
Height	20–40cm, rarely 60cm
Habitat	woods, grassy places; mostly lime-rich soils
Flowering	May–July
STEMS AND LEAVES	
Stem	upright, leafy
Root	swollen, tapering tubers; few, fleshy roots
Hairs	absent
Stipules	absent
Leaves	spirally arranged, to 200mm, usually 2, elliptical, blunt, 1–5 small leaves above
Leaf-stalk	absent
FLOWERS	
Position	many, in spike-like head, 50–200mm long
Bracts	nearly equal to flower
Type	☿, strongly scented
Size	23–35mm
Colour	greenish white
Stalk	very short
Sepals	3, 10–11mm, petal-like, oval to nearly triangular
Petals	3; side petals spear-shaped; lower 10–16mm, narrow, tapered, blunt; spur 19–28mm, slender, usually curved
Stamen	1, stalkless
Stigmas	2; style absent
Ovary	1, below petals, 1-celled
FRUIT	
Type	cylindrical capsule, angular, splits lengthwise
Size	c25mm
Seeds	numerous, minute, dust-like

SIMILAR SPECIES

1 Lesser Butterfly-orchid *(P. bifolia)* is smaller in all its parts and is more common in the north. Also more common in the north, **2 Small-white Orchid** *(Pseudorchis albida)* has tiny flowers lacking a spur.

1

tiny flowers

smaller

2

no spur

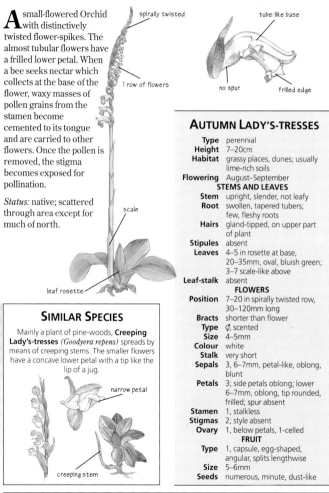

spirally twisted

1 row of flowers

tube-like base

no spur

frilled edge

scale

leaf rosette

A small-flowered Orchid with distinctively twisted flower-spikes. The almost tubular flowers have a frilled lower petal. When a bee seeks nectar which collects at the base of the flower, waxy masses of pollen grains from the stamen become cemented to its tongue and are carried to other flowers. Once the pollen is removed, the stigma becomes exposed for pollination.

Status: native; scattered through area except for much of north.

AUTUMN LADY'S-TRESSES

Type	perennial
Height	7–20cm
Habitat	grassy places, dunes; usually lime-rich soils
Flowering	August–September
STEMS AND LEAVES	
Stem	upright, slender, not leafy
Root	swollen, tapered tubers; few, fleshy roots
Hairs	gland-tipped, on upper part of plant
Stipules	absent
Leaves	4–5 in rosette at base, 20–35mm, oval, bluish green; 3–7 scale-like above
Leaf-stalk	absent
FLOWERS	
Position	7–20 in spirally twisted row, 30–120mm long
Bracts	shorter than flower
Type	⚥, scented
Size	4–5mm
Colour	white
Stalk	very short
Sepals	3, 6–7mm, petal-like, oblong, blunt
Petals	3; side petals oblong; lower 6–7mm, oblong, tip rounded, frilled; spur absent
Stamen	1, stalkless
Stigmas	2; style absent
Ovary	1, below petals, 1-celled
FRUIT	
Type	1, capsule, egg-shaped, angular, splits lengthwise
Size	5–6mm
Seeds	numerous, minute, dust-like

SIMILAR SPECIES

Mainly a plant of pine-woods, **Creeping Lady's-tresses** *(Goodyera repens)* spreads by means of creeping stems. The smaller flowers have a concave lower petal with a tip like the lip of a jug.

narrow petal

creeping stem

Common Twayblade *Listera ovata*

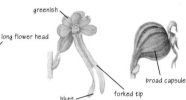

greenish

long flower head

broad capsule

blunt

forked tip

Contrary to the popular image, many Orchids have greenish, insignificant flowers. Common Twayblade's most obvious feature, giving rise to its common name, is a pair of broad stem-leaves. Nectar secreted on to the lower petal attracts beetles and flies. As the insect's head touches the centre of the flower, a drop of cement squirts out and sets rapidly, anchoring the masses of pollen.

2 broad leaves

Status: native; throughout area, sometimes common.

leaves on stem

COMMON TWAYBLADE

Type	perennial
Height	20–60cm
Habitat	woods, hedges, pastures; damp, usually lime-rich soil
Flowering	June–July
STEMS AND LEAVES	
Stem	upright, leafy, scale-like below
Root	horizontal underground stem; many roots
Hairs	gland-tipped on upper part of stem
Stipules	absent
Leaves	2 almost paired on stem, 50–200mm, broadly elliptical, 3–5 main veins, blunt
Leaf-stalk	absent
FLOWERS	
Position	many, in spike-like head, 70–250mm long
Bracts	much shorter than flowers
Type	♂, scented
Size	14–20mm
Colour	yellowish green, with reddish edges
Stalk	much shorter than flower
Sepals	3, 4–5mm, oval
Petals	3; side petals oblong; lower 10–15mm, oblong, bent down, tip forked; spur absent
Stamen	1, stalkless
Stigmas	2; style absent
Ovary	1, below petals, 1-celled
FRUIT	
Type	1, capsule, globular, splits lengthwise
Size	c10mm
Seeds	numerous, minute, dust-like

SIMILAR SPECIES

1 Lesser Twayblade *(L. cordata)* is smaller, the lower petal with pointed lobes. Two species have basal leaves. The large petal of **2 Musk Orchid** *(Herminium monorchis)* is three-lobed; that of **3 Fen Orchid** *(Liparis loeselii)* is frilled and points upwards.

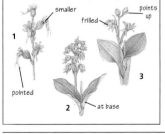

smaller

points up

frilled

1

3

pointed

2

at base

244

An unusual Orchid, its long, twisted, ribbon-like lower petal has two slender lobes near the base. Although generally very rare in the region, it is fairly abundant on stabilized sand-dunes in the extreme south-west. Here, its tall, pale flower-heads rise above surrounding plants and are easily visible at a distance.

Status: native; south of area, scattered, mostly rare.

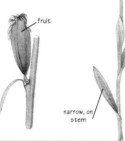

fruit

narrow, on stem

large flower-head

greenish

side lobes

long lobe

LIZARD ORCHID

Type	perennial
Height	20–40cm, rarely 90cm
Habitat	woods, grassy places, dunes; lime-rich soils
Flowering	May–July
STEMS AND LEAVES	
Stem	upright, stout, leafy
Root	egg-shaped or globular tubers; few, fleshy roots
Hairs	absent
Stipules	absent
Leaves	4–6 spirally arranged, to 150mm, narrowly elliptical or oblong, base sheaths stem; lowest scale-like
Leaf-stalk	absent
FLOWERS	
Position	many in spike-like head, 100–250mm, rarely 500mm long
Bracts	narrow, shorter than flower
Type	☿, strong-smelling
Size	35–55mm
Colour	greenish, purple markings
Stalk	very short
Sepals	3, 7–10mm, oval, blunt
Petals	3; side petals narrow; lower 30–50mm, ribbon-like, twisted, furry at base, 2 long side lobes, tip forked; spur 3–4mm, conical
Stamen	1, stalkless
Stigmas	2; style absent
Ovary	1, below petals, 1-celled
FRUIT	
Type	cylindrical capsule, angular, splits lengthwise
Size	c30mm
Seeds	numerous, minute, dust-like

SIMILAR SPECIES

Although no other native species is quite like the Lizard Orchid, several others have slender, greenish flowers. **Frog Orchid** (*Coeloglossum viride*) has an elongated, much shorter, lower petal with a pair of narrow lobes near the tip. It is fairly common on chalk grassland.

smaller

broad

2-lobed

Bird's-nest Orchid *Neottia nidus-avis*

This curious, pallid Orchid with parchment-coloured flowers is usually found growing in the thick layers of leaf-litter of deciduous woodland, especially beneath Beech trees. Lacking green pigment, it looks like a parasite but is a saprophyte, for the plant obtains its nourishment from dead and decaying plant material. The short, fleshy roots form a thick, tangled mass, which give rise to the common name.

Status: native; scattered through area.

no green pigment

forked

brownish flowers

no leaves

BIRD'S-NEST ORCHID

Type	perennial, saprophyte
Height	20–45cm
Habitat	shady woods; lime-rich soils, often on leaf mould
Flowering	June–July
STEMS AND LEAVES	
Stem	upright, with dense scales
Root	short underground stem, hidden by many short, fleshy roots
Hairs	gland-tipped, in flower-head
Stipules	absent
Leaves	spirally arranged, scale-like, papery, brownish
Leaf-stalk	absent
FLOWERS	
Position	many, in spike-like head, 50–200mm long
Bracts	shorter than flower
Type	⚥, scented
Size	12–16mm
Colour	pale brown, darker on lower petal
Stalk	much shorter than flower
Sepals	3, 4–6mm, petal-like, oval
Petals	3; side petals oval; lower 9–12mm, 2-lobed, angled downwards; spur absent
Stamen	1, stalkless
Stigmas	2; style absent
Ovary	1, below petals, 1-celled
FRUIT	
Type	swollen, angular capsule, splits lengthwise
Size	10–12mm
Seeds	numerous, minute, dust-like

SIMILAR SPECIES

1 Coralroot Orchid *(Corallorhiza trifida)* has few smaller, greenish-yellow and white flowers. The very rare **2 Ghost Orchid** *(Epipogium aphyllum)* has the large petal and blunt spur pointing upwards.

3-lobed

spur upwards

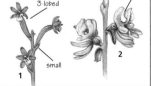

small

1

2

usually solitary

large flower

twisted

pouch-like

A large, pouch-like petal, of lemon-yellow spotted with crimson, surrounded by slender, chocolate-brown side petals and sepals, could not be identified as any native flower other than the Lady's-slipper Orchid. The beauty of this exotic-looking flower is matched by its scarcity. Its numbers have been greatly reduced by people picking flowers and uprooting plants for cultivation. In most of its former range, it is extremely rare or extinct. It survives today only through strict laws preventing removal of material from the wild, and international controls on import and export. Although it is possible to obtain legitimate material for your garden, cultivation is extremely difficult for, like other Orchids, the Lady's-slipper needs a fungus present in its roots to survive. Unless conditions are exactly right for both Orchid and fungus, the Orchid soon perishes.

broad leaves

Status: native; very rare, scattered through area.

Similar native species: none.

LADY'S-SLIPPER

Type	perennial
Height	15–45cm
Habitat	woods; lime-rich soils
Flowering	May–June

STEMS AND LEAVES

Stem	upright, leafy
Root	creeping underground stem
Hairs	short, denser above
Stipules	absent
Leaves	3–4, spirally arranged, 70–170mm, lower scale-like, upper broadly elliptical to oval, base sheaths stem
Leaf-stalk	absent

FLOWERS

Position	1–2, at stem-tip
Bracts	large, leaf-like
Type	☿
Size	60–90mm
Colour	reddish brown, lower petal yellow, red-spotted within
Stalk	very short
Sepals	3, 35–50mm, petal-like, spear-shaped, lower 2 often joined except at tips, pointing downwards
Petals	3; side petals 40–60mm, slender, twisted; lower 25–35mm, rounded, hollow, pouch-like; spur absent
Stamens	2, stalkless
Stigmas	3; style absent
Ovary	1, below petals, 1-celled

FRUIT

Type	oblong capsule, angular, splits lengthwise
Size	c40mm
Seeds	numerous, minute, dust-like

Index

248

Index

Index

Index

Index

Societies and useful addresses

Botanical Society of the British Isles
c/o British Museum (Natural History),
Cromwell Road,
London, SW7 5BD.

Fauna and Flora Preservation Society
79/83 North Street,
Brighton,
West Sussex, BN1 12A.

English Nature
Northminster House,
Peterborough, PE1 1UA.

Scottish Natural Heritage
12 Hope Terrace,
Edinburgh, EH9 2AS.

Countryside Council for Wales
Plas Penrhos, Penrhos Road,
Bangor,
Gwynedd, LL57 2LQ.

Royal Society for Nature Conservation
The Green, Nettleham,
Lincolnshire, LN2 2NR.

Wild Flower Society
Rams Hill House,
Horsmonden, Tonbridge,
Kent, TN12 8DD.